1971

A SHORT HISTORY OF THE MAIL SERVICE

A SHORT HISTORY OF THE MAIL SERVICE

CARL H. SCHEELE
Associate Curator in Charge
Division of Philately and Postal History
Smithsonian Institution

Smithsonian Institution Press
City of Washington
1970

CONTENTS

INTRODUCTION

1

ACKNOWLEDGMENTS

3

PART ONE

OLD WORLD BACKGROUNDS

5

PART TWO

**COLONIAL POSTAL SERVICE
IN NORTH AMERICA**

43

PART THREE

**POSTAL SERVICE IN
THE UNITED STATES**

61

REFERENCES

213

INDEX

230

TABLES

1. Growth of United States Postal Service, 1845-1860.................................. 78
2. Mail Service in Western United States and Territories, 1859.................... 81
3. United States Post Office Statistics, 1860-1867... 90
4. United States Domestic Mail Transportation, 1862-1874........................ 97
5. United States Post Office Statistics, 1875-1895....................................... 112
6. Streetcar Railway Post Offices in the United States................................ 130
7. Pneumatic Tube Postal Mileage in United States Cities, 1910 and 1915.. 133
8. Government-owned Motor Vehicles in Postal Service............................. 139
9. United States Domestic Airmail Rates, 1918-1949................................. 158
10. United States Post Office Revenues and Expenditures, 1920-1930.......... 167
11. United States Post Office Revenues and Expenditures, 1931-1936.......... 169
12. United States Post Office Mail Volume, 1900-1946................................ 175
13. Growth of United States Postal Service, 1945-1965............................... 176

INTRODUCTION

The need for postal systems results from rather complex forms of cultural organization requiring dependable communication. For the most part, this survey is limited to the study of systems which were organized to carry and exchange written communications.

The earliest postal systems, as one would expect, were uncomplicated in nature. Often there was little or at least a very slow progression from simple to more complex organizations. The postal system of the ancient Persians —serving a vast empire which was ruled with a firm hand—was the wonder of the times to the highly civilized and literate Greeks who, despite their colonies and periodic political or military alliances, had not organized a postal system which could begin to compare with the sophisticated messenger services of their opponents. Highly developed postal systems were generally maintained by the most powerful of the ancient states. Postal service in the ancient world reached its highest level of development under the Romans, and when their empire collapsed so did the posts.

Until recent times, government postal systems generally served the needs of the state only. Yet, the exchange of business correspondence has always been of great importance and, while merchants were often left to their own devices for exchanging letters, the flow of commercial mail generally benefited from the protection of a strong state and international tranquility. During the Renaissance, the transportation of mail itself became a profitable enterprise.

With the spread of literacy, the growth of population, the increase of cheap and efficient transportation, the thirst for speed in all human affairs, and a desire of the rulers of states to share in the profits from carrying the mails, the postal services once again became state monopolies. Postal service was one of the earliest enterprises to become "socialized."

Under the modern state-operated systems, postal organization rapidly grew from a simple structure to a very complex agency. Today's state-operated systems may no longer be profitable enterprises, but government control enables them to regulate not only the frequency of information exchange but also the nature of the information exchanged. Therefore, monopoly of the posts is still jealously guarded by governments.

Although there have been many books written about the postal service, there is no single up-to-date volume in the United States which provides an Old World background and which presents a continuous survey of American posts from Colonial times to the present. During the past fifty years, philatelists have examined certain phases of postal history in great detail. Their work, however, tends to be centered around physical evidence in the nature of postage stamps, markings, and covers. Therefore, certain aspects of the postal service—the use of automobiles, for example—are generally neglected. This, then, is an attempt to at least touch upon all important material aspects of postal history in one outline.

ACKNOWLEDGMENTS

Even a short history of the postal service involves many people. The subject is vast and individual areas of study within the general field require knowledge of a special nature which cannot be mastered by any single person. A study of the postal service also reveals that there are many unexplored aspects and, in touching upon these uncharted byways, there are always the uncertainties which attend such ventures, e.g., emphasis, treatment, and completeness. The author has been fortunate, however, in discussing with various scholars certain topics which were not clarified by the available resources. As a result, unsettled matters crystallized and misinterpretations were corrected. The shortcomings which remain are, of course, the author's responsibility entirely.

Mrs. Rita Lloyd Moroney, author, researcher, and editor with the U.S. Post Office Department, devoted a great deal of thought and effort in suggesting many improvements for the original manuscript. Her observations were invaluable in many areas of U.S. postal history, and the author gives special thanks to her for the many comments which she so generously gave.

Mr. Maurice Blake also reviewed certain portions dealing with Colonial postage rates and offered some important suggestions.

Much original knowledge was generously contributed by Mr. Roy J. Joroleman, a retired engineer who had spent many years with the Post Office Department. Mr. Joroleman's files and verbal accounts of early mechanical equipment developed by the Department were very helpful.

In the section dealing with the first transcontiental airmail service, Mr. William Nimberger of Cleveland, Ohio, particularly helped with materials and information gained through his original research of the DeHavilland mail planes, equipment, and field facilities.

Mr. Alfred P. H. Overment's comments concerning postage meter machine development and Mr. Walter Swan's assistance with postage meter corporate history are most gratefully acknowledged.

Mr. Ernst Cohn, a respected philatelic scholar, gave freely of his time on several occasions and reviewed portions of the airmail story treating the Paris balloon mail flights of 1870-1871. Since available accounts of this service often conflict, Mr. Cohn's expert advice was most important.

Mr. Harold Barnes of the U.S. Post Office Department made available materials relating to the Railway Mail Service and Highway Post Offices. Other material was also made available by Mr. Fred Glotzer of the Chicago Post Office, Mr. Leo Dunphy of the Boston Post Office, and Messrs. Ernest Appel and James Catoggio of the Philadelphia Post Office.

Mr. Arthur Hecht of the National Archives, and Dr. William Reiner-Deutsch have also been generous in contributing a considerable amount of time and assistance. Librarians Geneva Chancey and Gertrude Enders of the U.S. Post Office Department, and Jack Goodwin and Charles Berger of the Smithsonian's National Museum of History and Technology have been most helpful.

By no means least in importance, with respect to lending endless hours of assistance and offering sound and often pithy comments, Mr. Leo Gordon of the Smithsonian's Division of Postal History has remained steadfast and extremely patient.

PART ONE

OLD
WORLD
BACKGROUNDS

MESOPOTAMIA,
ASSYRIA, AND
PERSIA

The emergence of civilized society in ancient Mesopotamia is characterized by the domestication of certain animals and the appearance of crop agriculture; the gradual growth of villages into towns and cities; the growing importance of the market place, the temple, and the palace; the dependence of the individual upon specialists such as farmers, merchants, and artisans; and the development of writing.[1] The earliest written symbols—developed by the Sumerians some five thousand years ago—were at first crude pictographs impressed with a stylus in soft clay tablets. The writing, termed cuneiform, was also inscribed in stone, but the baked clay tablet was the most general form employed for the exchange of correspondence. The writing itself was gradually modified and a phonetic alphabet was developed between 2500 and 2000 B.C. which, by the latter date, could be used for expressing the most complex thoughts. Other Mesopotamian peoples—conquerors and neighbors of the Sumerians—adopted this method of writing on clay tablets.[2]

The increasing power of the rulers of city-states and small empires gave rise to the need for retaining runners for carrying messages. In early ancient times, these runners or heralds probably carried memorized messages as often as they carried clay tablets.[3] There seems, however, to have been a gradual increase in reliance on the written word, infinitely more dependable for accuracy and unquestionably more valuable for its reference uses long after the message had been delivered. Whole caches of cuneiform tablets have been found by modern archeologists.[4]

Clay tablets found at the ancient site of Kanesh in Cappadocia reveal a remarkably advanced system of postal communication which predates the better known posts of the late Assyrian and Persian empires. The tablets from Kanesh are commercial letters and documents dating from the nineteenth century B.C., written in old Assyrian cuneiform and exchanged between Assyrian members of a business community, fellow merchants in Assur, the old Assyrian capital, and other towns along the trade routes. The tablets—cushion-shaped pads, nearly 3 inches square—were enclosed in clay envelopes bearing addresses. The merchant colony at Kanesh was apparently regarded as a component of the Assyrian state, for government messengers carried the business correspondence. The contents of the letters reveal that postal service was safe and regular—no failure of service is noted. The reliability of the service is reflected by such phrases as "by earliest messenger" or "by return of post."[5] The security of the system is indicated in a letter received by a Kanesh merchant from his business associate in Assur: "I have received your instructions and the day the import of your tablet was made known to me, I provided your agents with three minas of silver for the purchase of lead. Now, if you are still my brother, let me have my money by courier."[6]

The Assyrians, noted for their efficient organization of empire, enjoyed political and military ascendancy from the twelfth to early seventh centuries B.C. At the height of Assyrian expansion (746-612 B.C.), the royal postal service enabled the king to maintain direct contact with his administrators in the conquered territories. Official reports and letters were received at Nineveh, then the capital of Assyria, from such far-flung cities as Memphis in Egypt, Tarsus and Sidon on the Mediterranean, and Susa to the east.[7] After the fall of Nineveh in 612 B.C., the final collapse of Assyrian rule in 606 B.C., and the temporary rise of the Babylonians under Nebuchadnezzar (604-561 B.C.), the Persians under Cyrus the Great (d. 529 B.C.), Cambyses (529-521 B.C.), and Darius (521-486 B.C.) created an even greater empire than the Assyrians.

Within a short time, Persian control extended from the Indus River in the east to Thrace and Macedonia in the west; from the Caucasus Mountains and the Aral Sea in the north to Libya and Egypt in the south. The Persians, learning many arts of administration from their Assyrian predecessors, reestablished and perfected postal communications along the old trade routes. So efficient was their postal system that it became the model of the ancient world, inspiring the Romans to imitate its essential features.[8]

Under Darius, the empire was organized into 20 satrapies or vice-royalties, and in each of these the administration of military and civil affairs was entrusted to two officials. These administrators were directly responsible to a high official, called "The King's Eye," at Susa. The roads, maintained to permit the armies and postal couriers to rapidly move about the empire, enabled the Persians to centralize control of their sprawling territories to an extraordinary degree.[9] Herodotus (c.484-c.424 B.C.), the Greek historian, described part of the main Persian road system and its relay stations (brackets are author's):

> Now the true account of the road in question is the following: Royal stations [where the king's couriers and horses were located] exist along its whole length, and excellent caravansaries; and throughout, it traverses an inhabited tract, and is free from danger. In Lydia and Phrygia there are twenty stations within a distance of ninety-four and one-half parasangs. [The original parasang was reckoned as one hour's journey, but calculated by Herodotus as equal to thirty furlongs.] On leaving Phrygia the Halys has to be crossed, and here are gates through which you must pass before you can traverse the stream. A strong force guards this post. When you have made the passage, and are come into Cappadocia, twenty-eight stations and 104 parasangs bring you to the borders of Cilicia, where the road passes through two sets of gates, at each of which there is a guard posted. Leaving these behind, you go on through Cilicia, where you find three stations in a distance of fifteen and one-half parasangs. The boundary between Cilicia and Armenia is the river Euphrates, which it is necessary to cross in boats.[10]

And so on, until the 328 parasangs and 81 courier stations between Sardis and Susa are accounted for. Herodotus states that, for the ordinary traveler, the route represented a journey of three months. Express riders, however, could cover the distance in less time. Herodotus, in telling of how Xerxes (486-464 B.C.) used the posts in sending news of his defeat at Salamis (480 B.C.), described the Persian system in considerable detail:

> Nothing mortal travels so fast as these Persian messengers. The entire plan is a Persian invention; and this is the method of it. Along the whole line of road there are men (they say) stationed with horse, in number equal to the number of days which the journey takes, allowing a man and horse to each day; and these men will not be hindered from accomplishing at their best speed the distance which they have to go, either by snow, or rain, or heat, or by darkness of night. The first rider delivers his dispatch to the second, and the second passes it to the third; and so it is borne from hand to hand along the whole

line, like the light in the torch-race, which the Greeks celebrate to Hephaestus. The Persians give the riding post in this manner, the name of angareion.[11]

The system, also in the time of Xerxes, is further described in the Book of Esther and is of particular interest insofar as the account mentions other animals in addition to the horse:

And he [Mordecai] wrote in the king Ahasuerus' [Xerxes'] name, and sealed it with the king's ring [an official signet, possibly a cylinder seal], and sent letters by posts on horseback, and riders on mules, camels, and young dromedaries . . . .
The copy of the writing for a commandment to be given in every province was published unto all people [in the empire] . . . .
So the posts that rode upon mules and camels went out, being hastened and pressed on by the king's commandment, . . given at Shushan [Susa] the palace.[12]

The act of sealing the letters above was, in this instance, done to establish the authority for the orders. Seals had been used for impressing signatures into the clay tablets and were normally made in the form of cylinders. The incised cylinder left the imprint of the signature in the wet clay as it was rolled across the surface, much the same as a tire leaves its imprint of the tread in a mud road today. Cylinder seals—generally carved from stone—were occasionally carved with elaborate and detailed scenes.[13]

The Persian empire fell to Alexander the Great (336-323 B.C.) after a series of military campaigns culminating in 331 B.C. Upon his death, the vast empire was divided among his generals into three major territories. Ptolemy established a new kingdom in Egypt, Seleucis established an Asiatic Kingdom with Antioch as its capital; and Antigonus finally succeeded in establishing control in Greece. Pergamum, later to lend its name to parchment, constituted yet a fourth independent state. The Hellenistic world, with splendid cities, increased sea trade, and the rise of commerce and banking, flourished despite the lack of a central system of communications. The ease of corresponding in one language—Greek had become the official language of the Balkan Peninsula, Asia Minor, Syria, Mesopotamia, and Egypt—more than offset the absence of a single state post.

EGYPTIAN
POSTS

When the Persians under Cambyses conquered Egypt in 525 B.C., they extended their lines of postal communication into a land which had for many centuries enjoyed the benefits of a highly organized and civilized society. The development of a written language is as closely linked with the Egyptians as it is with the Sumerians. The earliest Egyptian written characters can be traced to about 3400-3000 B.C.[14]

The first form of Egyptian writing, hieroglyphics, was used until 2400 B.C., when a more cursive script was developed with the introduction of papyrus and the reed pen. The use of the pictographic hieroglyphics was thereafter reserved for religious writings and architectural inscriptions. The script form, known as hieratics, was used for everyday business matters and communications until it also underwent a modification about the seventh century B.C. The newer simplified form of writing was known as demotic, and is comparable to our shorthand. Demotic, however, was more generally employed for the conduct of daily business instead of the comparatively limited use shorthand enjoys at the present time.[15]

Papyrus was made from a plant found along the Nile River. The pith was cut into strips, soaked, pressed together, and dried, forming a material with an even surface. When used for letters, the papyrus sheet was rolled and secured with a lump of wax. Gradually, the use of papyrus spread to other lands and, with Egypt retaining a virtual monopoly of its production, remained the most common writing material for some 3,000 years.[16]

The Pharoahs of Egypt had established a courier service by 2,000 B.C. Although the Nile carried much of the commerce, there is evidence that relay stations for overland messengers had been established by 1900 B.C. The horse, introduced by the Hyksos invaders about 1700 B.C., greatly speeded communications. After overthrowing the Hyksos, Egypt entered a period of expansion and extended its territory northward to Cilicia and western Mesopotamia. From about 1550 to 1250 B.C., Egypt's efficient courier service linked local princes and military outposts with the central government, contributing greatly to the control of the empire. About 350 clay tablets, unearthed at Amarna in Middle Egypt in 1888, reveal much about the empire under Amenhotep III (1412-1375 B.C.). Although Egypt had conquered Palestine and Syria, tradition to the north was so strong that Egyptian officials had to correspond in Babylonian cuneiform to govern the subjected peoples. Letters from the dependent king at Babylon, the king of the Mitanni, and other minor kings or kinglets requesting gifts of gold were written in cuneiform. Other correspondence concerning foreign relations such as treaties, alliances, state marriages, and warfare were also written in cuneiform.

While the government's postal system was used for official business, wealthy individuals and merchants relied on slaves or privately employed messengers for carrying correspondence.[17]

The scribes—clerks or secretaries whose main skill was writing—occupied an enviable position in Egyptian society. The ability to write became the key to an official career and, as early as Old Kingdom times (2740-2270 B.C.), meant the difference between a life of menial labor or the infinitely more enviable career as a civil servant. Scribes were educated in state schools which taught writing, the arts of correspondence and practical composition, and morality. By the 14th and 13th centuries B.C., scribes had become vital members of the highly organized bureaucracy which conducted the affairs of the empire.[18]

After a long period of decline, Egypt was successively conquered by the Ethiopians (730 B.C.), the Assyrians (672 B.C.), and the Persians (525 B.C.). Finally, in 332 B.C., the Persian satrap surrendered Egypt to Alexander the Great and the subsequent rule of Egypt by the Ptolomies ended with Cleopatra in 31 B.C. The traditional postal system was substantially unaltered with the exception of the establishment of a camel post, with police guard, for the transportation of goods.[19]

GRECIAN
POSTS

Throughout early ancient times, messengers carried memorized messages which were delivered orally. The most famous legendary account of a runner bearing oral tidings is the report of Greek success in defeating the Persians at Marathon in 490 B.C. The messenger, according to the story, ran non-stop from the scene of battle to the agora of Athens and shouted 'Nike!" (Victory!) with his last breath before falling dead of exhaustion. Although the incident of the runner dramatically dying remains unsubstantiated, there are numerous reliable references to official runners in ancient Greek writings. While the early Greeks did not control vast territories, they did maintain a system of unpaved but well-leveled roads. The postal systems of the Hellenistic states which followed the conquests of Alexander the Great were based on the Persian model.[20]

ROMAN
POSTS

Herodotus referred to wax-coated tablets on which messages were incised with an ivory or metal stylus.[21] The wax surface was smoothed or erased with the flattened end of the writing instrument. Wax-coated tablets remained common throughout Greco-Roman times. Pairs of these tablets were generally hinged together to form a *diptych* which could be sealed, face to face, with a cord that was passed through holes in the tablets. The Romans most commonly used papyrus for correspondence, however, since this material was easily obtainable from Egypt. Another material, parchment—which is prepared from animal skin—came into relatively wide usage after 100 B.C., when improved methods of preparation were developed at Pergamum, the city of Asia Minor which gave its name to the material. The Pergamum process treated the more delicate skins—particularly calf and kid—so that both sides could be used for writing, a definite advantage over papyrus. Parchment, however, was by far less common than papyrus until about the fourth century A.D.[22]

Emperors, senators, and the great host of lesser Roman officials who are discussed by their contemporaries, are frequently depicted carrying their writing materials about. Julius Caesar (c. 100-44 B.C.), in struggling with his murderers, reportedly stabbed Casca with his writing stylus. Caligula (A.D. 12-41) is said to have induced a group of senators to kill one of their number with their "writing-irons," and an indignant knight, on trial before the Emperor Claudius (10 B.C.-A.D. 54) and enraged by the proceedings, hurled his stylus and tablets into the Emperor's face.[23]

Public figures and wealthy citizens also are represented as retainers of personal messengers, frequently slaves. In discussing a phase of Tiberius' life before he became emperor (A.D. 14), Suetonius thinks that it was most unusual that Tiberius would care to stroll about the countryside without a messenger at his side. Although the value of a good messenger was thoroughly appreciated, the courier's social rank was quite lowly, as the same author suggests in stating that Claudius Pulcher, "on being bidden by the Senate to appoint a Dictator, . . . appointed his messenger Glycias, as if again making jest of his country's peril."[24]

The Romans, concerned with efficient communication since the construction of the *Via Appia* (c. 312 B.C.)—the paved road connecting Rome and Capua, and later Brundisium—borrowed and improved upon many elements of postal communication established elsewhere in the ancient world. The first Roman emperor, Augustus (27 B.C.-A.D. 14), is generally credited with the establishment of the imperial postal service in the form described by later writers. The biographer Suetonius (c. A.D. 70-140) stated that Augustus,

> To enable what was going on in each of the provinces to be reported and known more speedily and promptly, . . . at first stationed young men at short intervals along the military roads, and afterwards post-chaises. The latter has seemed the more convenient arrangement, since the same men who bring the dispatches from any place can, if occasion demands, be questioned as well.
>
> In passports, dispatches, and private letters he used as his seal at first a sphinx, later an image of Alexander the Great, and finally his own, carved by the hand of Dioscurides; and this his successors continued to use as their seal. He always attached to all letters the exact hour, not only of the day, but even the night, to indicate precisely when they were written.[25]

The excellent system of military roads gave the central government at Rome great advantages in receiving intelligence and dispatching orders necessary to maintain control of the vast empire. The emperor Hadrian (A.D. 117-138) concerned himself with the improvement of the postal service, and, as late as the reign of the emperor Theodosius (A.D. 379-395), the state posts were still, in some parts of the empire, operating at top efficiency.[26]

While the paved highways were used by everybody, the imperial postal system (the *cursus publicus*) was restricted to the carriage of government letters and the transportation of officials and their baggage. This restriction apparently, was quite rigidly observed. Public officials or private citizens infrequently were granted advance permission—in the form of a *diplomata*—to use the official facilities for private business only under extraordinary conditions. Pliny's wife, Calpurnia, traveled by state post from Bithynia to Italy when her father died, but Pliny (A.D. 62-113), who had given the order without having time to secure Trajan's permission, was careful to write an explanation and secure the emperor's approval as soon as he was able.[27]

Ordinary citizens used the facilities of private companies. These business establishments were generally located at the gates of towns, where carriages could be hired and where changes of horses or mules could be secured. At this time travel and the exchange of correspondence reached their peak in ancient Rome.[28] Pliny requested his wife to write to him twice a day while she was residing in Campania.[29] The Apostle Paul, unable to use the government's postal system, sent his letter to the Romans from Corinth by the hand of "Phebe our sister, . . . a servant of the church."[30] Such private messengers occasionally traveled great distances. It is recalled that the Apostle Peter's First Letter was circulated by this means to churches "throughout Pontus, Galatia, Cappadocia, Asia, and Bithynia." The roads were thronged with merchants, messengers, and travelers. Some of the carriages were large and comfortable enough to permit the traveler to read or to dictate letters to his amanuensis.[31]

The roads were locally maintained. Each canton in Roman Britain, for example, provided labor gangs for the building and maintenance of highways laid out by the central government. The cost of maintaining the imperial posting houses was also borne locally, although emperors occasionally provided funds for draught animals and carriages, as during the reigns of Hadrian and Septimius Severus, when the emperors attempted to gain popularity.[32] During the reign of Tiberius, Tacitus reports that Domitus Corbulo, an ex-praetor, "after raising a cry that most of the roads in Italy were obstructed or impassable through the dishonesty of contractors and the negligence of officials, himself willingly undertook the complete management of the business. This proved not so beneficial to the State as ruinous to many persons, whose property and credit he so mercilessly attacked by convictions and confiscations."[33]

The government courier stations were quite numerous, located from five to twelve miles apart. In addition to providing the necessary animals and carriages, which could be requisitioned for government use when needed, the local communities provided feed for the animals and food and fuel for the couriers. Messengers who rested at the stations in the larger towns enjoyed the luxury of baths.[34]

Maintaining equipment for the system was quite costly. At times, couriers used two horses between each station—one horse for riding and the other for carrying the letter bags. Government passenger carriages were pulled by either mules or horses; vans for the transportation of goods were pulled by oxen. In addition, vessels carrying letters, goods, and passengers over the sea-lanes also maintained postal communication which radiated principally from Rome's port, Ostia, to the islands and the chief Mediterranean ports.[35]

On the average, overland travel in the postal service was 5 miles per hour. From 30 to 50 miles was considered the average day's travel, but 100 miles per day could be accomplished at express speed if necessary. A journey by post from Rheims to Rome—about 1400 Roman miles—in nine days had been recorded. During the reign of Theodosius (A.D. 379-395), Caesarius, a magistrate, traveled by post from Antioch to Constantinople, starting at night and arriving at his destination about noon of the sixth day. The news of Nero's death (A.D. 68) was carried by Icelus, the freedman, from the city of Tarraco to Governor Galba in Clunia—a distance of about 330 miles— in seven days.[36]

The rate of travel by ship on the Mediterranean in Roman times is more difficult to estimate. It is generally conceded that, in good weather, 130 miles per day was possible. Five days were generally required to travel from Putoli to Corinth and from Ostia to Tarraco. Three weeks were required for the trip from Ostia to Alexandria. The nine-day voyage of Valerius Marianus, reported by Pliny, from Alexandria to Puteoli, together with the other voyages described by that author, are considered exceptionally rapid. Occasional references imply that a type of ship (*actuaria*) with a bank of oars was used for postal service. The Romans considered the winter months unsafe for sailing and, even in good weather, could rarely complete the return trip from east to west over the original direct route against headwinds prevailing from the Straits of Messina to Alexandria.[37]

The overland routes, therefore, formed the certain, dependable network over which most written communications were transported. This constant communication and mobility of many travelers contributed largely to welding the empire into one community. Tacitus noted that "the daily records of the Roman people are read attentively in the provinces and the armies" on the frontiers.[38] The unity of the Roman empire achieved through its communications systems, became a vision to Western rulers for many centuries after the magnificent roads had fallen into disuse.

POSTAL SERVICE
IN CHINA

The origins of Chinese writing are obscure, and recorded information which deals with the period before the first millennium B.C. is generally considered unreliable. Nevertheless, it is known that the first imperial posts were established relatively early in the Chou Dynasty (1027-256 B.C.), and that mounted couriers were employed. Confucius (551-479 B.C.) refers to "post" [*Yu*] in drawing the analogy that, "The influence of righteousness travels faster than royal orders by stages and couriers."[39] Later, references to the postal service become more frequent, and the *Historical Records* indicate that a "*feather* attached to a letter mobilizing the army indicated '*urgency.*' " Early writings also note that homing pigeons were used for carrying imperial dispatches. During the Han Dynasty (206 B.C.-A.D. 23), the postal service was officially referred to as *I Chan*.[40]

Until the Sui Dynasty (A.D. 589-618), the postal stations were administered by the Board of War. The Postmaster General was subordinate to the fourth of six Imperial Chancellors, i.e., to the Chancellor of War. During the T'ang Dynasty (A.D. 618-906), there was an administrative reorganization, and control was then centered in the office known as the *Chia Pu*. It is recorded that during this period there were 1,297 land stages, with courier stations located at ten-mile intervals along the routes; 360 stages by water routes; and 86 stages connecting both land and water routes.[41]

The Venetian merchant and traveler, Marco Polo (A.D. 1254?-?1324), while in the employ of Kublai Khan (A.D. 1216-1294), described, in graphic terms, what must have been the best-organized and most extensive system of posts in the world at that time:

> Now you must know that from this city of Cambaluc [Peking] proceed many roads and highways leading to a variety of provinces, one to one province, another to another; and each road receives the name of the province to which it leads; and it is a very sensible plan. And the messengers of the Emperor in travelling from Cambaluc, be the road whichsoever they will, find at every twenty-five miles of the journey a station which they call *Yamb* [a Tartar word], or, as we should say, the "Horse-Post-House." And at each of those stations used by the messengers, there is a large and handsome building for them to put up at, in which they find all the rooms furnished with fine beds and all other necessary articles in rich silk, and where they are provided with everything they can want . . . .
>
> At some of these stations, moreover, there shall be posted some four hundred horses standing ready for the use of the messengers; at others there shall be two hundred, according to requirements . . . At every twenty-five miles, as I have said, or anyhow at every thirty miles, you find one of these stations, on all the principal highways leading to the different provincial

governments; and the same is the case throughout all the chief provinces subject to the Great Kaan. Even when the messengers have to pass through a roadless tract where neither house nor hostel exists, still there the station-houses have been established just the same, excepting that the intervals are somewhat greater, and the day's journey is fixed at thirty-five to forty-five miles, instead of twenty-five to thirty.[42]

Marco Polo stated that 300,000 horses were used for this service and that 10,000 stations were maintained throughout the empire. He also described the supplementary foot courier service:

You must know that by the Great Kaan's orders there has been established between those post-houses, at every interval of three miles, a little fort with some forty houses round about it, in which dwell the people who act as the Emperor's foot-runners. Every one of those runners wears a great wide belt, set all over with bells, so that as they run the three miles from post to post their bells are heard jingling a long way off. And thus on reaching the post the runner finds another man similarly equipt . . . .[43]

Clerks were located at each station and recorded the arrival and departure times of each courier. Each station was visited monthly by imperial inspectors. The couriers were exempted from taxation and were paid from the imperial treasury. Foot-couriers could reduce the usual ten-day journey of the casual traveler to one day and one night. The horse service, apparently reserved for more urgent matters, reportedly carried messages from 200 to 250 miles per day. Marco Polo noted that the speed attained by horsemen was "marvellous," except during the night, when "they cannot go so fast as by day, because they have to be accompanied by footmen with torches." Horsemen carried "a gerfalcon tablet," or badge of office, which empowered them to requisition the first horse encountered in the event their own mount was disabled. The system was locally supported, as in Rome, and only in uninhabited areas did the expense of supplying horses fall to the imperial treasury. The cities or villages at the river crossings also bore the expense of ferry service for the imperial couriers.[44]

Only imperial correspondence was carried by this system until, the Ming emperor Yung Lo (A.D. 1402) opened the imperial service to the reception and delivery of private letters.[45]

During the Ming Dynasty (A.D. 1368-1644), private postal companies (min-chii) sprang up in Ningpo. Although not under official control, these private posting companies were extremely reliable and reimbursed the sender if valuable contents were lost in the mails. These companies were originally connected with banks or merchants' establishments but gradually made their services available to anyone willing to pay the low letter rates of from two to twenty cents. The private posts, which soon connected the important cities of the empire, utilized every available means of transportation, including canal boats and trading vessels. Express delivery was offered for higher fees and was indicated by burning one corner of the cover or allowing the tip of a feather to protrude from the envelope.[46]

The *I Chan* and *min-chii* systems endured until the mid-nineteenth century. The Tientsin Treaty (1858), between the European powers and China required the Manchu government to transport official correspond ence between the various foreign legations. Subsequently, a reformed postal service was organized and, after a series of improvements and reorganizations culminating between 1896 and 1912, resulted in the founding of China's "modern" postal service. China's formal entry into the Universal Postal Union in 1914 dates the complete "Westernization" of that nation's ancient postal system.[47]

POSTAL SERVICE
IN JAPAN

A system of relay stations and a horse-courier service uniting the important centers of the country was officially established in A.D. 645. By A.D. 701 stages were established at 75-mile intervals along the highways radiating from the various capitals. During the seventeenth century, or the "Edo Era," the courier system was enlarged and modified to provide for express service. While these lines of communication were available only to government and military officials, private courier systems were established about 1650 to carry letters and money of the general public.

As in China, Japanese government and private posts continued to render service until recent times. In 1871, as part of the general reform program promulgated during the reign of the Emperor Meiji (1852-1912), Hisoka Maejima carried out a sweeping reorganization of the imperial posts and created a modern system modeled after European prototypes. Japan became a member of the Universal Postal Union in 1877.[48]

MEDIEVAL EUROPEAN
POSTAL SERVICES

Marco Polo's admiration of Kublai Khan's postal system was quite understandable. Even the enterprising and commercially astute Venetians of the thirteenth century had not organized a system of communications which could even compare with the state posts of Rome. The extensive ancient postal systems had ended with the collapse of the western Roman Empire and the ensuing decline of trade, travel, and literary enterprise. Clovis (c. A.D. 465-511), king of the Franks, however, utilized the remnants of the old Roman posts in his kingdom. By the eighth century A.D., the Mediterranean, still the focal point of the surviving international commerce with lines of communications radiating northward from such points as Marseilles to the interior, utilized the old Roman roads, where serviceable, and rivers such as the Rhône and Saône. Nevertheless, Charlemagne's attempt to reestablish in his kingdom postal service on the grand scale of Rome ended in failure with his death in A.D. 814.[49]

With the breakdown of central political authority and a drop in the level of literacy, postal service as a state function became virtually nonexistent. Literacy was confined to churchmen, clerks, and a small number of accomplished women. The noblemen who administered affairs of state were, for the most part, illiterate.[50]

The revival of efficient postal services in the west followed the gradual revitalization of European culture in such areas as ecclesiastical affairs, learning, commerce, and politics.

The volume of correspondence began to increase with the founding of large monastic establishments, cathedrals, and universities during and after the eleventh century. Many institutions maintained their own courier services. Unlike the Roman couriers who had sped along on horseback, the new couriers traveled by foot. (These were the *Parvi Nuncii,* or "petty messengers;" not the *Magni Nuncii* which was an honorary title.) Messengers of the University of Paris are mentioned as early as 1297. This service, which survived until the eighteenth century, was established to carry correspondence and money under royal protection between the students and their parents.[51]

The twelfth century witnessed a rapid expansion of commerce, and by the thirteenth century, mounted "Clerks of the fairs" were carrying commercial correspondence between Champagne and Flanders. Communication was extensive between the trade centers of the Hanseatic League during the same period.[52]

The Teutonic Order, or Teutonic Knights of St. Mary's Hospital at Jerusalem, had its origin in the last decade of the twelfth century during the Third Crusade. Concerned with charitable work throughout its history, the Order also took on a military character and served as the conquering organization which eventually subdued the non-Christian Prussian regions. Conquered territories, after 1229, were surrendered to the Holy See and returned to the Order as a fief. Before establishing headquarters at Marienburg, East Prussia (now Poland), in 1309, the Grandmaster ruled the Order from Venice. These far-flung enterprises required fast lines of communication and, in 1276, a mail system linking Marienburg, Vienna, Venice, and Rome was established. Each stronghold of the Order had a postmaster (called a *Wything*) who supervised the carriage of dispatches between his castle and those in either direction on the route. Mounted couriers (called *Jonges*) were employed by each postmaster. Messengers carried the mail one stage, turned over the packets to the next rider, and returned to their original office. Only official mail of the Order was carried. Every letter handled by the postmasters was logged in and out of the offices. Mail was carried in linen bags, waxed for waterproofing, with leather straps which served as shoulder loops for the riders.[53]

During the Middle Ages, present-day Germany was a collection of many principalities. Under such circumstances, a centralized system of posts was slow to develop. Nevertheless, messenger systems (*Boten-Anstalten*) were formed by political administrations, monastic and scholastic institutions, merchant organizations, and individuals. Temporary or "occasional posts" (*Metzger*) and traveling merchants and monks also carried letters. Messenger services established for conveying dispatches for the Reichstag, meetings of the Electors, and congresses called to deliberate on matters of peace or war were also temporary. The *Boten-Anstalten*, however, gradually established regular service with fixed stages along routes linking such cities as Hamburg, Stettin, and Danzig, or Cologne, Frankfort, and Augsburg. Political regulation of the lines increased, and messengers traveled by horse or wagon as well as on foot. In addition to letters, the *Boten-Anstalten* eventually carried goods and passengers.[54]

Whether traveling by horse or foot, messengers often passed through unsafe areas. The couriers carried out their duties under fear of punishment for delay or failure; if fortunate enough to complete their journey with unusual speed, they were often rewarded. At best, these "systems" do not seem to have offered the dependable service available to the merchants of ancient Kanesh more than thirty centuries earlier. The European correspondent of the later period often betrayed his lack of confidence in the postal service by writing little messages on the face of his letters for the courier's attention such as, "Per postas cito cito et fidelis" ("By post haste, haste, and be faithful").[55]

To the east, the Byzantine Empire succeeded Rome and survived until the Turkish conquest of 1453. Communications were maintained over the old Roman roads and the shipping lanes of the Adriatic Sea.[56]

Although parchment is generally associated with medieval correspondence, the use of papyrus continued in Gaul (though on a diminishing scale after the fall of Rome) until the eighth century and in Italy until the eleventh. With increasing commercial activity, paper made its timely appearance in the west. The art of paper-making, originating in China, was perfected by the Persians and introduced to the Europeans by the Moors some time before the twelfth century. Paper became the ideal medium for letter-writing. Although less permanent than parchment, paper became comparatively inexpensive. It was easily folded into a flat packet and readily sealed with wax or a paper wafer. The practice of writing on one side of a piece of paper, folding the piece with the message on the inside, and addressing the blank side of the paper remained common until the middle of the nineteenth century.[57]

THE POSTS OF
VENICE

The city of Venice was established about A.D. 600 by the Venete who had fled before the invading Huns, Goths, and Lombards. The Venetians turned to trading at an early date and eventually built one of the richest commercial empires in the world. By the eighth century, they were trading with Constantinople; after the ninth century, Venetian merchants frequented Aleppo, Damascus, Kairwan, Cairo, and Palermo; in the eleventh century, the Venetians made the Adriatic safe from pirates, subjected Istria, and erected military establishments at Zara, Veglia, Arbe, Trau, Spalato, and other points; and by the fifteenth century had extended her commercial sphere to the Istrian and Dalmatian coasts, the Ionian Islands, the Greek Morea, Cerigo, Crete, and Cyprus, with 3,000 ships plying the Adriatic and Mediterranean Seas. Inland, the Republic of Venice expanded its territory 150 miles northwest to Bergamo and about 100 miles to the east between the fourteenth and sixteenth centuries. Sustained commercial success naturally depended upon reliable lines of communication.[58]

There is evidence that a courier service had been established in Venice before A.D. 840, for in that year the Republic concluded a treaty with Lothair, the Franco-Germanic king, and guaranteed the security of the post which already existed in Venice. A more important system, however, which was to have a profound effect on European communications, was that established by Amadeo Tasso in 1290 and known as the *Corrieri Bergamaschie,* the courier service of Bergamo. Other systems, however, were established at this time. An affiliate of Tasso's system, the *Compagnia dei Corrieri Veneti* (the Company of Venetian Couriers), was established and headquartered in Venice in 1305. This company enjoyed a virtual monopoly of the incoming and outgoing foreign mails and also a substantial portion of overland mail within the territory of the Republic. The *Poste di Venezia* (the Post of Venice), operated locally in the city by 1436.[59]

By this time, Amadeo Tasso's original system was establishing more affiliates in other city-states of northern Italy and was being extended into the Holy Roman Empire. During the period 1457-1460, available records indicate the following delivery times for mail carried between Italian cities and Venice:[60]

To Venice from	Average time (days)
Rome	7 to 11
Mantova	3
Ferrara	2 to 3
Bologna	3
Florence	5 to 6

Somewhat later, during the sixteenth century, delivery schedules between Venice and other cities of the Republic indicate transit times which began to compare favorably with those of ancient Rome.[61]

To Venice from	Average time (days)	Approximate distance (miles)
Treviso	1	20
Badia	1	70
Verona	1	70
Rovigo	1	50
Brescia	2	120

All internal mail had, before 1630, been subject to two fees—the normal postal fee and a tax. In 1630 the Senate of the Republic established the following uniform rates of postage and taxes.[62]

Postage Rates (based on size of sheet and weight)

Venice to Mantova (in soldi)	Size and weight
3	¼ or ½ sheet, less than ½ oz.
5	full sheet, less than ½ oz.
14	1 ounce letter.

Letters picked up by a courier en route were cheaper than if picked up in the city. For example, if a letter addressed to Rome were posted in Venice, the rate (¼ sheet) was 5 soldi; if the same letter were picked up en route, only 3 soldi was charged.

Tax per letter (in soldi)	Weights (Venetian ounce)
1	less than 1
3	1
3	each additional

Benvenuto Cellini (1500-1571), the Italian goldsmith, sculptor, and writer, in his graphic account of how he murdered the postmaster at Siena, relates how travelers could occasionally rent post horses which is interesting as a first-hand account of some sixteenth-century postal operations as well as ethics:

After leaving Viterbo with the comrades . . . , we pursued our journey on horseback . . . . This brought us upon Maundy Thursday at twenty-two o'clock within one stage of Siena. At this place there happened to be some return-horses; and the people of the post were waiting for an opportunity to hire them at a small fee to any traveler who would take them back to the post-station in Siena. When l was aware' of this, I dismounted from my horse Tornon, saddled one of the beasts with my pad and stirrups, and gave a giulio to the groom in waiting.

I left my horse under the care of my young men to bring after me, and rode on in front, wishing to arrive half-an-hour earlier in Siena . . . . Although I went at a smart pace, I did not override the post-horse.[63]

Although Cellini returned the horse to the Siena postmaster, he forgot to remove his personal pad (*cucino*) and stirrups. The postmaster retained these personal belongings on the grounds that Cellini had ridden the horse too hard, and in the ensuing argument, Cellini shot the postmaster with an arquebuse which he had carried on the trip for protection while traveling the bandit-ridden roads.[64]

THE THURN AND
TAXIS POSTS

Courier services established by the Tasso and Della Torre families of Italy gradually grew into international services linking most countries of Europe. The families were united by marriage and, in 1450, Roger I germanized the family name to Thurn and Taxis after being knighted by Frederick III of the Holy Roman Empire and extending his courier service from Italy to the Tyrol. The couriers at first traveled by foot but later rode horses. Finally, post wagons were introduced with one, two, or four horses. The couriers carried a strip of badger skin as a badge of authority (*"Tasso"* means "badger").[65]

In 1489, Johann von Taxis was appointed as the first Imperial Postmaster of the Holy Roman Empire and established, with headquarters at Augsburg, a network of government posts in Austria with stages every five (German) miles. The service was at first restricted to the carriage of imperial mail. Other messenger systems, largely concerned with carrying business or institutional mail, were allowed to continue despite an early government decree promulgated to suppress them.[66]

In 1500 Franz von Taxis was appointed Captain and Master of the Posts at Ghent by Phillip the Fair, son of Maximilian I. Franz von Taxis, in 1505, concluded an international agreement which permitted the establishment of posts between the courts of the Holy Roman Emperor and the kings of France and Spain. Although the system already carried some general correspondence into Spain and the Empire, it was especially desired to establish reliable posts to Paris for the safe and fast carriage of diplomatic mail. An annual payment to the Thurn and Taxis system of 12,000 livres was stipulated in the agreement, but when payments lagged, Franz opened the entire service to the general public to raise revenues. This maneuver

The Thurn and Taxis posthouse at Augsburg in 1616. (From a wood engraving by Lucas Killian.)

was, apparently, established family policy originating with the older Italian operations. The new service of 1505 offered the delivery of letters under the following schedule:[67]

Between Brussels and	Time
Innsbruck	5½ days in summer
	6½ days in winter
Paris	44 hours
Granada	15 days

In 1512, Franz and other members of the family received titles of hereditary nobility. In 1615, Lamoral von Taxis and his descendants received the title of Imperial Postmaster General as an hereditary fief. Until the nineteenth century, Thurn and Taxis remained a noble house without significant landed estates—a most unusual collection of princes who owed their fortune and power to the business of carrying the mails.[68]

In 1516, the Thurn and Taxis lines were extended southward to Verona, Rome, and Naples; Brussels and Vienna were also linked. Johann Baptista von Taxis succeeded to the Postmaster Generalship in 1518, and schedules during his term of office were reported as follows:[69]

Between Brussels and	Time
Paris	36 hours in summer 40 hours in winter
Burgos, Spain	7 days in summer 8 days in winter
Innsbruck	5 days in summer 6 days in winter
Rome	10½ days in summer 12 days in winter
Naples	14 days

Under Leonard I von Taxis, who became head of the system in 1548, postal lines were established from Ghent to Liege, Treves, Spire, through Wurttemburg, Augsburg, and Innsbruck. Despite the wars of the sixteenth century and the disruption of service during the uprising in the Netherlands, additional routes were laid out to Seville and Lisbon.[70]

As the system prospered, jealous princes controlling the political destinies of their realms attempted to claim the postal service as their own monopoly and to challenge the rights of Thurn and Taxis. Shrewd members of the postmasters family more or less successfully parried these political threats until the nineteenth century, when government systems finally supplanted the Thurn and Taxis service.[71]

During the seventeenth century opposition to the family system hardened. The Thirty Years War (1618-1648), though not settling the question of the postal monopoly, did bring the problem into clear focus. While princes argued and minor adjustments were made, however, the Thurn and Taxis system carried on with 20,000 men in their employ, a "greater number" of horses in service, and four million livres per year rolling into the family treasury. Business, it seems, had never been better.[72]

But revolution swept Europe, and after 1789 the Thurn and Taxis postal system began to suffer curtailment. The right to operate in France was lost in 1801 with the Peace of Luneville. Subsequent political re-alignments and the abdication of the Holy Roman Emperor (1806) resulted in the termination of Thurn and Taxis posts in the Low Countries and Austria and other reductions in territorial service. Between 1815 and 1848, however, rights to operate posts in some states such as Electoral Hesse, Schwarzburg-Rudolstadt, and Oldenburg were recovered, and by 1848 the system was able to boast an annual income of one million marks. Under new agreements, though, part of the income was paid out as rental fees to the local governments. While in many respects unsatisfactory—the Thurn and Taxis system was by the nineteenth century one of those curious feudal remnants in a new age—the old postal family had united many German states at a time when there was no other authority to operate a single postal system. Following the expansion of Prussia in 1864-1866 and the unification of a number of duchies under a central political body, the surviving lines of a once-mighty communications system were purchased by the Prussian government, in 1867, for three million marks.[73]

EUROPEAN
GOVERNMENT
POSTAL SYSTEMS

Increasing government control of postal systems and trends toward state monopolies of postal business have been noted. The purchase of the Thurn and Taxis posts by the Prussian government in 1867 in many respects marked the end of competing systems and the resurgence of the principle that it is the state's "inherent right" to operate the posts.

The origins and universal acceptance of the "inherent right" principle seem to stem from the following factors: The government posts or messenger services originated with the rulers of the community, whether city-state or empire. Although other members of the community, such as merchants, desired to communicate, the state, during most periods of history, was best able financially to bear the expense of maintaining postal service. Communication was vital to successful government. Only the state could afford to bear the expense of an undertaking which, for the most part, could be valued for its indirect or long-range benefits. Furthermore, only governments were able to levy taxes to offset deficits incurred in operating such a service. Merchants did maintain communication lines, but only when direct profits or returns on the immediate investment were discernible. Secondly, since good lines of communication were vital to successful government, state authorities were always reluctant to permit civil organizations to carry government correspondence, especially when it is remembered that matters of state have always been regarded and treated with the utmost secrecy, even in the democratic societies. Although the power of governments was greatly weakened after the disintegration of the Roman Empire in the west, courts continued to maintain messenger services. When posts were "farmed out" for managerial purposes, the state authorities still retained the right to regulate the service. When Frederick III of the Holy Roman Empire knighted Roger I von Taxis, he not only extended certain benefits to the head of the commercial family but secured an added measure of loyalty in return for the good of the state.

Independent posts or competing systems were tolerated only as long as the functions of governments remained comparatively limited and modest in cost. But state expenses had generally increased with the political consolidations, international wars, and the evergrowing multiplicity of government activities which have characterized the periods since the Renaissance. When mail transportation as a private enterprise became actually or even potentially profitable, governments began to view such enterprises jealously, for what was "profit" to the entrepreneur was "revenue" to the government.

Governments have absorbed competing postal systems on various pretexts. One such pretext is that only the government can transport mail securely under regulated rates and schedules. While this is not necessarily true as a theory, it has been generally true in practice. The second pretext, though less often officially stated, is that the government has the right to censor or control the correspondence and goods exchanged by the members of the community, not only among themselves but with members of foreign communities. Alongside the right of censorship, the conflicting principle of "sanctity of the mails" has gained force, but the right of the individual to maintain confidential and even secret communications is frequently set aside during periods of military conflict or civil unrest. "Sanctity of the mails" is a principle which is best respected during periods of relative tranquility.[74]

The governments had assumed control of the world's posts on a virtually universal scale by the fourth quarter of the nineteenth century. By 1875, the date of the founding of the Universal Postal Union, few voices were heard to challenge the "inherent right" of governments to monopolize postal service.

The multiplicity of European states resulted in numerous postal systems serving a relatively small area of the earth's surface. The growth pattern of these messenger systems, from serving a court to nation-wide organizations carrying public and private correspondence is repeated time and again from country to country. A few examples will serve to illustrate this pattern of postal development in Europe between the thirteenth and twentieth centuries.

Gian Galeazzo (1385-1452), ruler of Milan, introduced one of the earliest postal systems in post-medieval Italy. Although Galeazzo limited this service to state dispatches, his successor, Francesco Sforza (1447-1466), expanded the system to include business and other private correspondence. The Republic of Genoa also maintained a state post. One of the earliest European postal guides which survives was published by the Postmaster General of Genoa, Giovanni del Herba, in 1563. Italy not only remained a patchwork of small states and provinces for many years, but suffered numerous invasions and occupations by France, Spain, and Austria. Wars and territorial changes constantly altered routes and postal organizations until the state was finally unified under Victor Emmanuel in 1861.[75]

Postal service in Spain originated in the thirteenth century, when private corporations of messengers were founded to serve various districts. Government courier service was established in the fourteenth century, and external communications were handled by the Thurn and Taxis posts. Despite a declaration of 1716 establishing a "royal" postal system, competing lines were permitted to operate. In Portugal, however, the posts were a royal monopoly since their founding in 1520. Private correspondence was admitted to the mails in the seventeenth century. In 1705, Portugal and England concluded a treaty regulating the exchange of mail between those nations.[76]

Switzerland was made up of thirteen cantons, each with an independent postal service, but by the eighteenth century, cooperation concerning postal affairs was apparently adequate enough to permit a "smooth flow" of mail between the cantons.[77]

In 1485, a regular courier line was established between Cracow, Poland, and Rome, via Trentschin, Pressburg, Padua, Ferrara, and Florence. In 1564, King Sigismund of Poland laid out additional routes to Venice and Milan. King Stefan Bathori granted the Italian, Sebastian Montelupi, the right to handle foreign mails in 1583, a right which was made hereditary. Polish domestic mails were opened to the public in 1647, but this service ceased with the partition of Poland by Russia, Prussia, and Austria in 1763.[78]

In Russia, communications remained extremely poor until Czar Alexis Mikhaylovich founded a messenger line between Moscow and Riga in 1665. Domestic service was not established until 1672. Peter the Great improved the service, linking Moscow with other important Russian cities, although it was not until 1711 that the Central Administration of Posts was located in St. Petersburg.[79]

State messenger service in Norway and Denmark dates from the reign of Queen Margaret (1387-1389), who ruled both countries from Copenhagen. Regular postal service, however, was not made available to the public until 1647, when the Crown granted Hanibal Sehested the authority to operate the posts. This arrangement lasted until 1711, when the monarchy assumed complete control. Messenger service in Sweden dates from the sixteenth century. The lines established by King Gustavus Adolphus in 1630 were important for maintaining communications between his court and Amsterdam, Paris, and Vienna until shortly after the close of the Thirty Years' War (1648). Swedish domestic posts admitted private correspondence in 1636. Couriers traveled on foot and schedules were strictly maintained, but in 1646, mounted couriers were introduced into Sweden.[80]

Prussia developed one of the finest postal systems in Europe. Under King Frederick Wilhelm I (1713-1740), the government posts were made available to the public; letters, parcels, freight, and passengers were carried. Numerous postal organizations served the other German states, and as late as 1800 there were still some thirty different systems in operation.[81]

The royal messenger service of France took on a more modern character in about 1477, when relay stations were established at regular intervals along the main routes. Although this service was not originally intended for carrying private correspondence, royal couriers reportedly transported some private letters as early as 1481. At first, all letters were censored to discover unfavorable references to the government. A special service was founded in 1576 to carry legal correspondence and documents between the French Parliament and inferior courts, with provisions for the couriers to carry private mail at the following rates:[82]

	Deniers
Single-sheet letter	10
Each packet of 3 or 4 letters	15
Each packet of letters weighing one ounce or more	20

These rates were applied to letters carried any distance, but the service was available only during the periods that Parliament was in session.

Under Cardinal Richelieu, the postal system was reformed (1621) and put on a regular schedule; times of arrivals and departures of couriers were fixed; and general letter rates were established in 1627, abolishing the practice (apparently current from 1621 to 1627) of privately arranged rates between the sender and the post-rider. Under the rates of 1627, single-sheet letters from Paris to Dijon were charged two sous, and from Paris to Lyons, Bordeaux, or Toulouse, three sous. Rates were revised in 1676 and varied according to fixed distance zones, the number of sheets per letter, and whether or not the letter was enclosed in an envelope. In 1703, the rates were increased to raise revenue to help pay for the wars of Louis XIV. The rates remained unchanged until 1759, when they were again increased to help defray the expenses of the Seven Years' War and to offset the general inflation then plaguing France.[83]

Although the Thurn and Taxis posts offered limited service in France, further privileges were prohibited after 1637, when postal service was declared a royal monopoly. The posts in France had been farmed since the seventeenth century in return for an annual "rental." In 1791, the last year of management under the farm system, the rental of the posts returned about twelve million francs to the French treasury. The government, hoping for greater profits, took over the direct management of the service in that year, but because of poor financial practices found that they were operating at a deficit. By 1793, four million francs were required to keep the posts operative despite an increase in postal rates two years before. Additional rate increases and censorship of correspondence led to the rise of private postal services and an alarming drop in the patronage of the state posts. Rates were then somewhat lowered, the number of zones was reduced, the service was extended to rural communes (1829), and minor adjustments in the service were made so that revenues (it was hoped) would at least equal the operating expenses. In 1839, reform proposals were advanced to drastically reduce postage rates, but little positive action was taken for ten years. On 1 January 1849 a substantially reduced table of rates became effective. Although adequate postal revenue remained a problem, the volume of letter mail increased thirty-one percent from 1848 to 1849.[84]

The early royal messengers in England—the *nuncii* or *cursores*—carried the King's letters or government dispatches when required until 1482, when Edward IV established relay stations for changing horses on certain roads to make the system more efficient during the war with Scotland. At this time, the word "post" began to appear in the English language. The term derived from the French word *posta*, a contraction of *posita* (from *ponere*), meaning "to place." These relay messengers, using the fresh horses which were "placed" along the routes, were able to travel one hundred miles per day.[85]

At first, the posts were financially maintained by the King. Although horses were kept on the main post lines, the messengers who occasionally rode secondary routes had the right to requisition fresh horses from townships without charge. Gradually, the relay system became a permanent service which also provided for the transportation of people traveling on state business, a feature which survived in England until the eighteenth century. By 1553, the law authorized ordinary travelers to rent post-horses for one penny per mile. However, abuses became frequent and people attempted to evade payment by claiming that they were traveling on state matters. The law was revised in 1603, and thereafter postmasters received two and one-half pence per mile for horse rental to state travelers showing the proper documents. Ordinary travelers were required to pay in advance any sum agreed to by the postmaster in charge of the horses.[86]

Private letters, at first, were carried by servants, hired messengers, travelers, or common carriers. As in other nations, British universities and municipalities maintained their own courier systems. Messengers in the royal service carried some private correspondence before the Crown began to regulate such traffic. In 1591, a Royal Proclamation prohibited foreign letters to be carried by anyone other than a government post-rider. A second Proclamation in 1609 reaffirmed the prohibition. The right to carry foreign letters within England—granted by a King's Patent—was disputed by claimants until November 1626, when Merchant Companies were granted the privilege to carry their own mail. This arrangement was modified about a year later to enable the government to regain more control and, if necessary, knowledge of the contents of the foreign letters during times of national emergency. Government concern with controlling foreign mail led to the adoption of a plan advanced by Thomas Witherings, Master of the Foreign Posts, whereby special couriers ("stafetti") were established on the Continent to carry mail between Calais and Antwerp with the permission of foreign governments.[87]

In 1633, Witherings proposed a reorganization of the inland posts which was carried out two years later, and in October 1635 the British government began collecting postal revenue on domestic mail under the following rates:[88]

Distance	Pence per Single-Sheet Letter	Pence per Double-Sheet Letter	Pence per Ounce
Up to 80 miles	2	4	6
From 80 to 140 miles	4	8	9
More than 140 miles	6	12	12

By 1638, the monopoly on foreign letters was not only fully established, but was claimed by the state for the transmission of domestic mail as well.

From 1653 to 1677, the British posts were farmed to individual managers for annual rentals which, during this period, rose from £10,000 for the first year to £43,000 for the last year. Rates of postage were fixed by Parliament after 1655 (reducing the high rates established by the Master of the Posts in 1644). An Ordinance of 1657 established rates comparable to those of 1635 and strengthened the government's control of the system to (1) encourage and safeguard trade and commerce, (2) provide for the carriage of official dispatches, and (3) reaffirm the right to censor mail. A supporting Act of Parliament in 1660 again claimed the right to censor mail, a right which was exercised during periods of civil unrest. Competing, and by that time, illegal carriers of mail were forcibly put down during the period 1644-1653.[89]

Unlike the French, the British continued to realize profits from the service after the government took over direct operation of the posts, receiving some £60,000 in postage in 1694.[90] In 1711, an Act of

Parliament declared that postal charges were considered to be taxes. Accordingly, this Act increased the rates of postage to help pay for war debts.[91]

Throughout this period, main postal routes radiated from London but cross-country service had remained extremely poor. After 1719, Ralph Allen, originally the postmaster of Bath, introduced better accounting methods for the existing cross-country service and added new connecting routes for expediting such mail. Largely through Allen's efforts, daily service on most of the British postal routes was available by 1741.[92]

Until 1784, mounted "postboys" had been the only mail carriers in Great Britain. In that year, however, John Palmer, another resident of Bath, saw his proposal to use coaches given a successful trial. Thereafter, mail coaches were gradually introduced on a nation-wide scale.[93]

Postage rates were increased in 1784, 1796, 1801, 1805, and 1812 for the primary purpose of increasing revenue. Under the Act of 1812, which remained in effect through 1839, basic letter rates were the highest in British history. A single-sheet letter, for example, was charged a minimum of four pence for carriage up to fifteen miles and as much as fifteen cents for transportation between 500 and 600 miles.[94]

BRITISH POSTAL
REFORM

The reduction of postage rates by Great Britain in 1840 is an important landmark in postal history for a number of reasons. Firstly, the reform was drastic. Indeed, it represented such a startling change in government policy that other nations took note of it and eventually adopted similar reforms. The traditional government viewpoint of postal charges as a source of tax revenue suffered greatly, as the viewpoint that postal revenue should merely meet the cost of maintaining the service was considerably strengthened. Furthermore, the reduction of postage and the simplification of rating methods in Great Britain were accompanied by the introduction of the world's first adhesive postage stamps.

The high rates of postage current between 1812 and 1839 discouraged the average citizen from using the government mail service and led to a number of abuses which, from an operational point of view, placed a heavy burden on the post office. Postal charges were usually collected from the addressees, but the intended recipients had the right to refuse letters and, therefore, disregard the charges. During the years high postage rates were in effect, thousands of refused letters accumulated in post offices. A traveler often told his family or friends that he would mail a letter upon reaching his destination safely. As agreed to beforehand, the letter would arrive, the traveler's handwriting would be recognized, and the recipient would refuse to accept and pay for the letter, knowing that the traveler had arrived. Sometimes, a simple code mark or misspelling might represent a definite piece of information or might indicate that the contents were important and the letter should be accepted. Since many people of importance had the privilege of sending their mail free, their franks were widely and illegally utilized for sending letters of those who did not have the franking privilege. The intricate and excessive postal rates and the widespread efforts to avoid payment of postage became objects for study and discussion among some reformers.[95]

The postal reform, only one of many reforms carried out in England during the nineteenth century, was one of the more important and lasting. Each reform had its champion, and the postal system became the particular concern of Rowland Hill, son of a schoolmaster and himself an educator who took great interest in anything that might contribute to the "progress" of mankind. After studying all aspects of the post office operations, Hill published a pamphlet in 1837 entitled *Post Office Reform: Its Importance and Practicability*, a statistical study with forceful conclusions that was widely read and enthusiastically received.[96]

Hill's statistics indicated that the average cost of distributing a letter in Great Britain was one and one-half pennies. The calculation included costs for handling the large number of newspapers and franked letters which were carried free of postage. Hill also demonstrated that the actual cost of transporting a letter from London to Edinburgh was no more than one thirty-sixth of a penny rather than the current rate of one shilling-one penny. Furthermore, he stressed the time-consuming and costly work of postal employees required to calculate mileage from one city to another, write or mark the charge upon the face of the letter, attempt to collect the postage from addressees, and to perform similar postal duties which were, according to Hill, unnecessary. He proposed a uniform rate of one penny based on the weight of a letter rather than the number of sheets. He regarded distance zones as of little or no importance. He found that the actual costs depended on the number of letters carried, that the cost per letter in a large shipment between towns many miles apart was less than the cost per letter in a small shipment carried between towns only a few miles distant. He also proposed that postal charges should be collected in advance from the sender of the letter.

Hill suggested that the government sell sheets of paper and covers (envelopes) stamped with a notice indicating that the postage had been prepaid. For those who might not have such sheets or envelopes on hand or who preferred using their own stationery, Hill proposed that the government sell "a bit of paper just large enough to bear the stamp," which could be affixed to the cover or address side of the letter by moistening the gum on the reverse side of the stamp.

Hill believed that lower rates would encourage wider use of the posts and that the greater volume of mail would maintain the gross postal revenue. Mail processing would be simplified by eliminating work of keeping records on each piece of mail that passed through the post offices.

A Select Committee of the House of Commons was appointed to report on Hill's proposals in 1837 and responded with favorable recommendations the following year. When the government did not act, however, the Radical party gained the needed votes for uniform penny postage in 1839 in exchange for their political support of the government, and the new low rates became effective on 10 January 1840.[97]

Weight per letter	Prepaid, any distance in United Kingdom
Up to ½ ounce	1 penny
Up to 1 ounce	2 pence
Each additional ounce or fraction thereof	2 pence

During the first year under the new rates, letter mail doubled. Net revenue, however, dropped one million pounds. In 1847 some 322 million letters were carried as compared with 83 million in 1839. The gross revenue of 1839 was equalled in 1850, the net revenue in 1863.[98]

Rowland Hill carried out the reforms as a special appointee to the Treasury between 1839 and 1840. The world's first adhesive postage stamps were placed on sale 1 May 1840, along with prestamped stationery, and were placed in use on 6 May. Prestamped postal stationery reportedly had made a brief appearance in Paris as early as 1653 and Sardinia in 1818. Other stamps had been used in Greece in 1831 for collecting poll taxes, and revenue stamps, in the form of embossed impressions and seals, had been used for collecting certain taxes in England as early as 1694. However, adhesive postage stamps were the invention of Hill. Under his guidance a design bearing the portrait of Queen Victoria was prepared for the one-penny and two-pence denominations. The firm of Perkins, Bacon, and Petch, bank-note printers, engraved and printed the stamps. The "bits of paper," to Hill's surprise, became more popular than the prestamped stationery.[99]

The prestamped stationery was issued as envelopes and letter sheets designed by William Mulready (1786-1863), a well-known genre painter and Member of the Royal Academy. The elaborate design depicted various benefits of the postal reform, but Mulready's work was so widely criticized that the now familiar embossed oval envelope stamp replaced the artist's line drawing within a year.[100]

Hill's innovations had far-reaching effects. The United States reformed its postal rate structure in 1845; Canada and France followed in 1849.

Rowland Hill, who promoted the reform of postage rates and fathered the introduction of the adhesive postage stamp in 1840.

Adhesive postage stamps were introduced in the United States by a private postal service in New York City in 1842. The cantons of Geneva and Zurich, Switzerland, and the government of Brazil issued postage stamps in 1843; the canton of Basle, Switzerland, and various postmasters in the United States issued stamps in 1845; and Mauritius, Trinidad (the "Lady McLeod" local), and the United States government issued stamps in 1847.[101] The first postage stamps were not perforated for easy separation, but in 1854 Great Britain introduced stamps perforated by a process developed by Henry Archer. Stamped stationery was also widely adopted. By 1870, more than thirty countries provided embossed or imprinted stamped envelopes.[102]

With the postal reforms of the 1840s, this survey of Old World postal systems closes. In the later sections which deal with postal developments in North America, the innovations of the period since 1840 are described as they occurred in the United States. The story, after the 1840s, in a general way, would be similar for many countries of the world, and no attempt has been made to describe the introduction of railway mail service, canceling machines, airmail service, and other features of the modern postal systems, in the various countries.

NOTES

See References (pp. 213-229) for complete citations

Part I: Old World Backgrounds

[1]See Muller, *The Loom of History*, pp. 54-55, 57; Frankfort, *The Birth of Civilization in the Near East*, pp. 46-64; Childe, *The Prehistory of European Society*,. pp. 34-42.

[2]See Cleator, *Lost Languages*, pp. 65-70; Kramer, *History Begins at Sumer*, pp. xviii-xx; Chiera, *They Wrote on Clay*, pp. 50-79, 222-30; Swain, *The Ancient World*, vol. 1, pp. 73-75, 94-95; Rogers, *Babylonia and Assyria*, vol. 1, pp. 354-76; Morris Jastrow, *Babylonia and Assyria*, pp. 114-19, 148, 158, et passim.

[3]Untitled Sumerian tablet translated by Kramer, pp. 19-27. Memorized messages are referred to frequently in ancient writings, e.g., Herodotus, *The Persian Wars*, vol. 1, pp. 19, 20, 21, 46, 48, et passim. See Jastrow, *Babylonia and Assyria*, pp. 487-89 for translations of state correspondence during the reign of Hammurabi (20th century B.C.), and pp. 123-63 for the general history of early city states and empires. See also Rogers, *Babylonia and Asyria*, vol. 1, pp. 429-43, for a survey of each city state

[4]Cleator, *Lost Languages*, pp. 98, 101; Lloyd, *Early Anatolia*, pp. 23, 48, 69, 113,123; Swain, *The Ancient World*, vol. 1, p. 147; Chiera, *They Wrote on Clay*, pp. 67, 224; Jastrow, *Babylonia and Assyria*, pp. 316-17, 273. Babylonian and Assyrian priests served as scribes and teachers.

[5]Lloyd, *Early Anatolia*, pp. 112-17; Chiera, *They Wrote on Clay*, pp. 69-73, 212014; Jastrow, *Babylonia and Assyria*, pp. 160-61.

[6]In Lloyd, *Early Anatolia*, p. 115.

[7]See Jastrow, *Babylonia and Assyria*, pp. 172-82, and for translations of cuneiform personal, business, and official letters see pp. 484-96. See, especially, selections IX, II (pp. 484-85) for indications that correspondents retained copies of their own letters for reference purposes. Government reports were exchanged on all matters of administration. Rogers, *Babylonia and Assyria*, vol. 2, pp. 210-25, 269 et passim, notes that Asshur-nasir-apal II (884-58 B.C.) appointed governors at cities subdued in his last campaign, an indication of firmer administration than pursued earlier. Postal service, in itself, was not sufficient to maintain control. A strong military establishment was apparently the primary unifying force.

[8]DeBurgh, *Legacy of the Ancient World*, vol. 1, p. 42.

[9]*Ibid.;* Codding, *Universal Postal Union*, p. 2.

[10]Herodotus, *The Persian Wars*, 5:52-54.

[11]*Ibid.*, 8:98.

[12]Holy Bible, Esther, VIII:10,

[13]Frankfort, *Birth of Civilization*, pls. 14-16, pp. 122-24; Lloyd, *Early Anatolia*, pl. 7, pp. 114, 123-24; Jastrow, *Babylonia and Assyria*, pp. 334-37 (for a detailed review of the use and forms of seals).

[14]Breasted, *History of Egypt*, 1964, pp. 29, 36, 38; Frankfort, *Birth of Civilization*, pp. 130-35; Kramer, *History Begins at Sumer*, p. xix.

[15]Cleator, *Lost Languages*, pp. 30-31; Swain, *The Ancient World*, vol. 1, pp. 110-12; Breasted, *History of Egypt*, pp. 38, 82-84, 479; Frankfort, *Birth of Civilization*, pp. 129-32.

[16]Alling, *Paper*, pp. 4-5; Cleator, *Lost Languages*, pp. 18-19; Seyffert, *Classical Antiquities*, 1956, p. 699; Pirenne, *Medieval Cities*, pp. 13, 19-20.

[17]See Hurt, "Stepping Stones of Postal History"; Baikie, *History of Egypt*, vol. 1, p. 11, noting that messengers used "light skiffs" on the Nile; Codding, *Universal Postal Union*, p. 2; Frankfort, *Birth of Civilization*, p. 100; Breasted, *History of Egypt*, pp. 64, 82, 193; Swain, *The Ancient World*, vol. 1, pp. 87, 147; Glanville, *Legacy of Egypt*, pp. 22, 35.

[18]See Breasted, *History of Egypt*, 1964, pp. 82-84, 141-42; Glanville, *Legacy of Egypt*, pp. 67, 76-77.

[19]Hurt, "Stepping Stones of Postal History."

[20]Herodotus, *The Persian Wars*, 1: 19, 20, 21, 46, 48, et passim; Swain, *The Ancient World*, vol. 1, p. 379; Seyffert, *Classical Antiquities*, 1956, p. 547; Harlow, *Old Post Bags*, p. 17; Hurt, "Stepping Stones of Postal History." See also, Naumann, "Letters", pp. 9-11, for a description of papyrus *scatale*, or "rolled-letters," of the Spartans.

[21]Herodotus, *The Persian Wars*, 7: 239. See also, Naumann, "Letters," p. 11, noting that wax tablets were used by salt-workers of Hall, Swabia, until 1812.

[22]See Seyffert, *Classical Antiquities*, 1956, p. 699; Alling, *Paper*, p. 5. For references to Egyptian writing on leather, see Breasted, *History of Egypt*, 1964, pp. 165, 260.

[23]Suetonius, *Lives of the Twelve Caesars*, pp. 46, 184, 217-18.

[24]*Ibid.*, pp. 122, 128.

[25]*Ibid.*, p. 85. For postal service under the Republic, see Hurlimann, "The Cursus Publicus," p. 8A.

[26]See DeBurgh, *Legacy of the Ancient World*, vol. 1, p. 284; Gibbon, *Decline and Fall*, vol. 1, pp. 279-280; Dill, *Roman Society*, 1958, pp. 204-205; Seyffert, *Classical Antiquities*, 1956, p. 547; Grant, *The World of Rome*, pp. 48-49; Mattingly, *Roman Imperial Civilization*, pp. 72, 74. Hurlimann, "Cursus Publicus," p. 8 A.

[27]Dill, *Roman Society*, 1958, p. 189, citing and commenting on Pliny, *Ad Trajan*, pp. 121, 122.

[28]See Jones, *Companion to Roman History*, p. 49; Seyffert, *Classical Antiquities*, 1956, p. 508; Richmond, *Roman Britain*, pp. 90-91; Dill, *Roman Society*, 1958, p. 206; Barrow, *The Romans*, p. 99; Mattingly, *Roman Imperial Civilization*, pp. 74-75; Grant, *World of Rome*, pp. 51, 155; Hurlimann, "Cursus Publicus," p. 8A.

[29]See Dill, *Roman Society*, 1958, p. 189.

[30]St. Paul, *Epistle to the Romans*, 16:1. It may also be noted that his *Epistle to Philemon* was delivered by Onesimus, a servant, and that the *Epistle to the Ephesians* was carried by Tychicus, "a beloved brother and faithful minister . . . ." Tychicus was, furthermore, directed to give an oral report about church affairs in Rome not covered in the letter.

[31]See Dill, *Roman Society,* 1958, pp. 206-07.

[32]Jones, *Companion to Roman History,* p. 49; Richmond, *Roman Britain,* pp. 90-91; Seyffert, *Classical Antiquities,* 1956, p. 508; Mattingly, *Roman Imperial Civilization,* p. 15; Hurlimann, "Cursus Publicus," p. 8A.

[33]Tacitus, *Annals,* ch. 3, p. 31.

[34]Richmond, *Roman Britain,* pp. 90-91; Gibbon, *Decline and Fall,* vol. 1, p. 280; Hurlimann, "The Cursus Publicus," p. 9A.

[35]See Seyffert, *Classical Antiquities,* 1956, p. 508; Jones *Companion to Roman History,* p. 49; Codding, *Universal Postal Union,* p. 3; Richmond, *Roman Britain,* pp. 90-91; Hurlimann, "Cursus Publicus," pp. 8A-12A.

[36]See Dill, *Roman Society,* 1958, p. 206; Barrow, *The Romans,* p. 98; DeBurgh, *Legacy of the Ancient World,* vol. 1, p. 284; Gibbon, *Decline and Fall,* vol. 1, p. 280; Suetonius, *Lives,* p. 34 (Julius Caesar); Grant, *World of Rome,* pp. 48-49.

[37]Jones, *Companion to Roman History,* pp. 50-51, 324; Dill, *Roman Society,* 1958, p. 206; Grant, *World of Rome,* pp. 80-81.

[38]Tacitus, *Annals,* 14:22.

[39]In parts of the ancient world where good postal service existed, the speed of the couriers was often used as a standard of swiftness which few men could exceed. The Hebrew prophet Job, for example, in casting about for a good metaphor to indicate the ultimate in speed, chose the following: "Now my days are swifter than a post . . ."

[40]China, Min. of Communications, *Report,* p. 3; China, Dir. Gen. of Posts, *Postage Stamp Catalogue,* p. ix; Hurt, "Stepping Stones of Postal History," p. 155. Cf. Ruger, "Postal Service in China," p. 289, which dates the beginning of Chinese postal service in the 12th century *B.C.*

[41]China, Min. of Communications, *Report (1921),* pp. 3-4.

[42]Marco Polo, *The Book of Ser Marco Polo,* vol. 1, pp. 433-34.

[43]*Ibid.,* p. 435.

[44]*Ibid.,* pp. 435-37.

[45]China, Min. of Communications, *Report (1921),* p. 5.

[46]*Ibid.*

[47]*Ibid.,* pp. 5-11; China, Dir. Gen. of Posts, *Stamp Catalogue,* pp. v, vii, ix.

[48]Japan, Min. of Postal Services, "History of Japanese Mail Service," p. 40.

[49]See Harlow, *Old Post Bags,* p. 24; Pirenne, *Medieval Cities,* pp. 2, 12; Meroni, *Evolution of World Posts,* p. 2; A. D. Smith, *Rates of Postage,* p. 78.

[50]Pirenne, *Medieval Cities,* pp. 165-66; Dawson, *Making of Europe,* pp. 193-94, 218-20, 227-28; Harlow, *Old Post Bags,* p. 24; Codding, *Universal Postal Union,* pp. 3-4; Pirenne, *History of Europe,* vol. 1, p. 140.

[51]Codding, *Universal Postal Union,* pp. 4-5; A. D. Smith, *Rates of Postage,* pp. 1-2, 78-79, 377-78; Harlow, *Old Post Bags,* p. 29: Henrioud, "The Franco-Swiss Postal Relations."

[52]Pirenne, *Economic and Social History of Europe*, pp. 94-95, 100; Harlow, *Old Post Bags*, p. 29.

[53]See Alves, "Mail Transportation of the Teutonic Knights," p. 1; Harlow, *Old Post Bags*, p. 37.

[54]See A. D. Smith, *Rates of Postage*, pp. 8-9; 349-350.

[55]Hurt, "Pioneers of the Posts: Posts," p. 32.

[56]See Runciman, *Byzantine Civilization, 1956, pp. 74, 134 168, 198;* Dawson, *Making of Europe*, p. 105; Vasiliev, *History, Byzantine Empire*, vol. 1, pp. 193-94. Communication by land routes in the seventh and eighth centuries was disrupted in the Balkans. See Ostrogorsky, "The Byzantine Empire, pp. 10-12; Lopez, "The Role of Trade", pp. 70-71, which notes that, while overland postal service survived on the main Anatolian highway in the seventh century, communication by water routes became more important and necessary. See also, Hurlimann, "Cursus Publicus," p. 12A.

[57]See Pirenne, *Medieval Cities*, pp. 2, 11-13, 19-20; Hunter, "Laid and Wove," pp. 587-593; Steinberg, *Five Hundred Years of Printing*, p. 26; Alling, *Paper*, pp. 5-6. For a discussion of parchment, paper, and materials and methods used to seal letters, see Naumann, "Letters," pp. 11-15.

[58]Rider, "Postal History, Venice," pp. 196-197; Pirenne, *Medieval Cities*, pp. 60ff.

[59]Rider, "Postal History, Venice," p. 197. See also Hurt, "Pioneers of the Posts: Princes," p. 141; Rider, "Handstamp Markings, Venice" pp. 2-4; Hubinont, "Establishment, International Mails," p. 2.

[60]Rider, "Postal History, Venice," p. 198.

[61]*Ibid.*

[62]*Ibid.*

[63]Cellini, *Life of Benvenuto Cellini*, p. 316.

[64]*Ibid.*, pp. 317-318.

[65]Hurt and Hollick, "Thurn & Taxis," pp. 89, 92-93.

[66]A. D. Smith, *Rates of Postage*, pp. 350-51; Hurt and Hollick, "Thurn & Taxis," p. 94; Hurt, "Pioneers of the Posts: Princes," p. 142.

[67]Hurt and Hollick, "Thurn & Taxis," p. 94. See also, A.D. Smith, *Rates of Postage*, pp. 351-52; Hurt, "Pioneers of the Posts, Princes," p. 142. Cf. Hubinont, "Establishment of International Mails," p. 4.

[68]Hurt and Hollick, "Thurn & Taxis," p. 95.

[69]*Ibid.*; A.D. Smith, *Rates of Postage*, p. 352. See also, Beck, "Postal Monopoly," pp. 76A-80A for a discussion which actually surveys certain aspects of the Thurn and Taxis posts during the period 1516-1530.

[70]Hurt, "Pioneers of the Posts, Princes," p. 143; Hurt and Hollick, "Thurn & Taxis," pp. 96-97.

[71]A.D. Smith, *Rates of Postage*, p. 352; Hurt, "Pioneers of the Posts, Princes," pp. 143-144; Hurt and Hollick, "Thurn & Taxis," p. 97.

[72]A.D. Smith, *Rates of Postage*, pp. 352-53.

[73] *Ibid.*, pp. 353-355; Hurt, "Pioneers of the Posts: Princes," pp. 144-147; Hurt and Hollick, "Thurn & Taxis," pp. 98-100.

[74] See Codding, *Universal Postal Union,* p. 6, for his conclusion that governments have asserted the right of postal monopoly to gain postal revenues as taxes and to control the exchange of information and ideas, especially to prevent communication between enemies of the state, Codding cites Great Britain, Postmaster-General. *The Post Office: An Historical Summary* (London: 1911), p. 121, as a blunt reiteration of the right of political censorship by a 20th century government. Government control of the exchange of ideas and information is, of course, an obvious phenomenon. See also, Hurlimann, "Cursus Publicus," pp. 12A-13A, which summarizes the historical connection between ancient and modern government posts from a purely institutional point of view. Governments, according to Hurlimann, never surrendered their right to control the exchange of mail.

[75] Belfiore, "Italian Postmarks", Harlow, *Old Post Bags,* pp. 101-02; Banci, *Catalogo Prefilatelico Del Lombardo-Veneto,* p. 13.

[76] Hurt, "Stepping Stones," p. 156.

[77] Harlow, *Old Post Bags,* pp. 103-04; cf. Hurt and Hollick, "Thurn & Taxis," p. 100-101.

[78] Harlow, *Old Post Bags,* pp. 95-96; Mueller, "Outline for Postal History, I," p. 8.

[79] Sokolow, "Historical Facts, Russian Post," pp. 173-179, for a history of the earliest post offices, the so-called *Jams;* Ibid., no. 12 (December 1896), pp. 187-199, for the period 1665-1880. Dates cited by Harlow and Hurt do not agree with those reported by Sokolow. Cf. Harlow, *Old Post Bags,* pp. 94-95; Hurt, "Stepping Stones," p. 156.

[80] Mueller, "Outline for Postal History, I," pp. 7-12; Fisher, "Postal History of Norway," pp. 8-24; Harlow, *Old Post Bags,* pp. 96-99. See also, Sweden, Post Office, "The Swedish Posts Before 1636, I," p. 114, which notes that the Swedish state had an organized service for carrying diplomatic correspondence between Sweden and Holland as early as 1618. The regular Swedish post between Hamburg and Markyard was opened to public correspondence in 1620 (*Ibid.,* p. 115).

[81] Harlow, *Old Post Bags,* pp. 104-05.

[82] A.D. Smith, *Rates of Postage,* pp. 79-80; Harlow, *Old Post Bags,* p. 45. The date of the establishment of the French posts by Louis XI, as reported by both authors (and others), has been corrected to 1477 instead of 1464. See Codding, *Universal Postal Union,* p. 5. See also, Henrioud, "Franco-Swiss Postal Relations," *Union Postale,* pp. 198-200, for an interesting discussion of Royal Mails exchanged between France and Switzerland.

[83] A.D. Smith, *Rates of Postage,* pp. 80-81; Mueller, "Outline for Postal History, I," p. 8.

[84] Mueller, "Outline for Postal History, I," p. 8; A.D. Smith, *Rates of Postage,* pp. 81-88.

[85] Smith, *Rates of Postage,* pp. 1-2; Hemmeon, *History of the British Post Office,* pp. 3-4; Codding, *Universal Postal Union,* p. 5.

[86] A.D. Smith, *Rates of Postage,* pp. 3-6; Hemmeon, *History of British Post Office,* pp. 4-6.

[87] A.D. Smith, *Rates of Postage,* pp. 6-9; Hemmeon, *History of British Post Office,* pp. 6-12; Hurt and Hollick, "Thurn & Taxis," p. 97.

[88] Clear, *Thomas Witherings pp. 3-7; A.D. Smith, Rates of Postage,* p. 9; Hemmeon, *History of British Post Office,* pp. 13-15.

[89] Hemmeon, *History of British Post Office,* pp. 21-26; A.D. Smith, *Rates of Postage,* pp. 9-15.

[90] A.D. Smith, *Rates of Postage,* p. 15.

[91] Kay, *Royal Mail,* pp. 33-34; A.D. Smith, *Rates of Postage,* pp. 15-16.

[92] Kay, *Royal Mail,* pp. 35-39; Hemmeon, *History of British Post Office,* pp. 35-37; A.D. Smith, *Rates of Postage,* pp. 18-19.

[93] See Kay, *Royal Mail,* pp. 46-60; Hemmeon, *History of British Post Office,* pp. 40-42.

[94] A.D. Smith, *Rates of Postage,* pp. 21-22; Kay, *Royal Mail,* pp. 66-71.

[95] For a detailed discussion, see Hemmeon, *History of British Post Office,* pp. 196-201.

[96] See Codding, *Universal Postal Union,* p. 8, noting that three different editions of Rowland Hill's pamphlet were published in 1837. Detailed discussions, summarized hereunder, may be found in *Ibid.,* pp. 8-11; A.D. Smith, *Rates of Postage,* pp. 23-30; Kay, *Royal Mail.,* pp. 71-77; Hemmeon, *History of British Post Office,* pp. 59-62. Hill's pamphlet, *Post Office Reform* in London by W. Cowles & Sons. See also, Melville, *A Penny all the Way,* for a complete discussion of the concept of "penny postage," including good discussions about Dockwra's London Post and the "Ocean Penny Postage" movement.

[97] Great Britain, *Acts,* 2 and 3 Victoria, Cap. 52. See A.D. Smith, *Rates of Postage,* pp. 30, 339; Kay, *Royal Mail,* p. 77.

[98] A.D. Smith, *Rates of Postage,* p. 31.

[99] See the excellent discussions by Williams and Williams, *The Postage Stamp,* pp. 16-19; Todd, *British Postage Stamps pp.* 47-81; Marshall, *The British Post Office, From Its Beginnings to the End of 1925* pp. 17-31.

[100] See Todd, *British Postage Stamps,* pp. 72-73; Williams and Williams, *The Postage Stamp,* p. 17; Marshall, *British Post Office,* pp. 165, 182, 202; Evans, Mulready Envelope, passim.

[101] A.D. Smith, *Rates of Postage,* pp. 53-55, 73, 86-87; Williams and Williams, *The Postage Stamp,* p. 19; Phillips, *Stamp Collecting* p. 14.

[102] Ascher, *Grosser Ganzsachen-Katalog,* passim.

PART TWO

COLONIAL POSTAL SERVICE IN NORTH AMERICA

EARLY COLONIAL
POSTAL SERVICE

There were no formal postal arrangements available to the early American settlers. Feelings of mistrust or hostility often existed between colonies; populations were small; overland trails were extremely poor; and commerce between the early colonies was negligible.[1] Clinging to the eastern coast, the colonists were at first in little need of good overland communications. Letters between the new settlements and the homelands accounted for the greatest volume of mail for a considerable period.

Government correspondence was carried by warships.[2] Private citizens entrusted their letters and packets to masters of merchant vessels. Mail from overseas was deposited at coffee houses or taverns on both sides of the Atlantic. Recipients looked for their own mail at such places. Those wishing to send letters deposited them in bags located at the same establishments or handed the letters to the captain. On the sailing date the bag was closed and taken aboard. The captain of the vessel received a penny for each letter, collected from either the sender or addressee.[3]

This traditional and, at best, makeshift method was first dealt with by the General Court of Massachusetts by legislation passed on 5 September 1639.

The order designating Richard Fairbanks' tavern in Boston as the place where overseas mail was to be serviced was the first American legislation concerned with postal matters. The order stated that Fairbanks would handle such letters for the fee of one penny each but specified that persons sending letters were not to be compelled to deposit them with Fairbanks. Local or domestic letters were not mentioned.[4] When in 1677 the General Court received complaints about the lack of control of overseas letters placed in coffee houses, there again was no mention of domestic mail.[5] The Dutch at New Amsterdam also found need to regulate the transmission of overseas letters. A letter from the Directors as early as 1652 suggested that Peter Stuyvesant supervise the mails, but there is no certainty that the suggestion was put into practice for, in 1659 (effective June 1660 at New Amsterdam), the Directors made it mandatory for the Secretary of the Colony to regulate the mails.[6]

Virginia became the third colony to deal with postal matters but the act passed by the Assembly in 1657 merely provided that each plantation owner was responsible for the transmission of official government letters across his own property. Neither overseas nor private overland mail was dealt with.[7]

The Dutch colony of New Netherlands fell to the British in 1664. Subsequent hostilities between Great Britain and the Netherlands endangered New York. With this breakdown of overseas control, New York Governor Francis Lovelace, in January 1673, established the first overland intercolonial postal service between New York City and Boston. Although the primary responsibility of the post-rider was to carry official intercolonial correspondence, private letters and packets were also to be carried under instructions from the Governor. This monthly service was short-lived, for on 9 August 1673 the Dutch recaptured New York. Although peace brought the return of British rule early the following year, intercolonial service was not resumed.[8]

In 1674, twenty-four routes were established for transporting official correspondence in Connecticut. Pennsylvania, in 1683, established weekly postal service for private letters between Philadelphia, the Falls of the Delaware, Chester, New Castle, and "Maryland," with no terminal for the latter being specified.[9]

Although Thomas Dongan, Governor of New York, failed to have adopted his 1684 plan for establishing a postal service from Nova Scotia to the Carolinas, he succeeded in reviving Lovelace's New York-Boston route under the Dominion of New England (1685-1689). Although the Dominion collapsed in 1689 when news reached the colonies that James II had fallen, Boston and New York immediately appointed postmasters, indicating that the Boston-New York overland mails had reached considerable importance in these commercial centers.[10]

INTERCOLONIAL POSTS
UNDER THE
NEALE PATENT

In 1692, King William III of England granted Thomas Neale a patent empowering him to establish an intercolonial postal system in North America. Neale, a court favorite and Master of the Mint in Great Britain from 1679 to 1699, never came to America. Instead, he appointed Andrew Hamilton as his Deputy Postmaster in America.[11]

The Patent was to have been effective for twenty-one years. Although it granted Neale a monopoly of the postal service, it paradoxically allowed private letters to be carried by special messengers. The Patent did not grant Neale the monopoly of overseas letters. Neale was to keep all profits except the token fee of six shillings eight pence annual rent payable to the Exchequer of England. American postage rates were to be patterned after those in force in England but were not specified in the Patent.[12]

Andrew Hamilton had resided in New Jersey since 1685 as agent for the proprietors and as Governor Merchant of Edinburgh, Scotland. After becoming Neale's deputy, Hamilton attempted to secure support for the new system from colonial legislatures and enjoyed more success in the northern and middle colonies than in the southern ones. Hamilton and Robert West of England assumed control of the Patent on Neale's death in 1699. In 1703, Hamilton died, and the Patent was then managed by Hamilton's widow and West. In 1707, with about six years remaining of the Patent's term, the British Government preempted it for £ 1,664.[13]

The colony of New York was the first to respond to Hamilton's overtures and passed an act establishing postal service on 11 November 1692. The provisions of the Act included the establishment of a General Letter Office at New York City and a fine of £ 100 for those convicted of competing with the authorized system. The act also required that all overseas letters be brought to the General Letter Office. Contradictory to the terms of the Patent, mail service up or down the Hudson River was not to be provided by Neale's posts. Overseas postage was fixed at nine pence per single-sheet letter; single-sheet letters from Boston to New York were charged nine pence; from New York to Maryland, nine pence; and any place less than 80 miles distant, four and one-half pence. New York renewed the act five times, with minor changes only in the last renewal (1708) after the Patent had been purchased by the Crown.[14]

Pennsylvania's legislature passed acts on 15 May and 1 June 1693, establishing posts under the Patent. This legislation, recorded as a single act, did not grant Neale a monopoly of overseas postage. Rates per single-sheet letters between Pennsylvania and Europe or other overseas destinations were two pence; New York and Philadelphia, four and one-half pence; Philadelphia and Connecticut, nine pence; Philadelphia and Boston, fifteen pence; Philadelphia and points beyond Boston, nineteen pence; Philadelphia and points within eighty miles, four and one-half pence. Post-riders were granted free ferriage and required the posts to carry all government correspondence free of charge. The postage rates were found to be somewhat inadequate, and in 1697 postage was increased so that all letters from overseas, whether single or packet, were charged four pence and overland rates were raised, for example, to eight pence per single-sheet letter to or from New York, to eighteen pence per single-sheet letter to or from Boston, and to two shillings per single-sheet letter to or from points beyond Boston. Rates to the south, fixed by the Act of 1693, were not specified in the Act of 1697.[15]

New Hampshire passed a postal act on 5 June 1693, granting Neale's system a monopoly, but providing for a £ 5 fine for each failure of the mails. This Act exempted also innkeepers who were postmasters from excise charges on ale and liquor sold in their commercial capacity.[16]

The legislation passed by Massachusetts on 9 June 1693, also granted Neale a postal monopoly, imposed a fine for every failure of the posts, granted free ferriage, and provided for the free carriage of official correspondence, but annual grants were made to compensate for this "free" service. Single-sheet letters sent overseas were charged two pence each; between Boston and Connecticut, nine pence; to or from New York, twelve pence; to or from Pennsylvania, fifteen pence; to or from Boston and other points in Massachusetts, either three or four pence. Massachusetts, always to be counted on to provide unusual aspects, stipulated that an added fee of one penny would be charged for every letter or packet uncalled for after forty-eight hours to cover cost of delivery to the addressee and also stipulated that letters be marked "with a print" to show the day, month, and year received at the office.[17] The Act, although disallowed by the Privy Council in England, was nevertheless enforced by the colonial authorities.[18]

Connecticut provided for the establishment of Neale's posts with legislation passed on 10 May 1694. Free ferriage was granted to post-riders but, as in New Hampshire, no postal rates were specified.[19]

Virginia considered establishing postal service in January 1693, but refused to grant Hamilton authority to establish Neale's postal service.[20] The legislature of Maryland also failed to provide for service under Neale's Patent, and Governor Francis Nicholson's Proclamation of 1695 which attempted to establish service in Maryland, failed to bring the posts to that colony because of political opposition.[21] Rhode Island, North Carolina, and South Carolina were without service, although South Carolina made a fruitless attempt in 1702.[22]

Intercolonial service under the Neale Patent began 1 May 1693, from Portsmouth, New Hampshire, to Philadelphia, Pennsylvania. In spite of numerous and much publicized complaints about the service, the advantages were apparent. When Pennsylvania increased the postage rates in 1697, it took care to go on record as being "sensible of the benefit of the said office to Trade & Commerce & to the Province & Territories in General."[23] In 1698, the government of Connecticut took special steps to keep the post roads and bridges in good repair.[24]

In 1704, Lord Cornbury observed that no regular posts existed west of Philadelphia and that special messengers provided the only overland means to communicate with Maryland or Virginia.[25] There were always complaints that letters were sent by private, illegal means.[26]

The initial cost of establishing service in the colonies was very high during the first four years of service. Receipts from the postage of 1699, however, equalled all expenses except Hamilton's salary.[27] Despite special cash grants to Hamilton to compensate for losses, the managers of the posts under the Patent never seem to have realized a profit. There was considerable belief, however, that the system could have become a sound business venture without too much tinkering with rates and that profits would have been possible if the monopoly had been strengthened to eliminate the traffic in letters carried "out of the mails." Despite the efforts of Mrs. Hamilton and West to retain the Patent, the Crown forced its purchase of the colonial system in 1707.[28]

THE ROYAL POSTAL SERVICE
IN THE COLONIES
1707-1753

John Hamilton, son of Andrew, was appointed Postmaster General for America by the Crown upon purchase of the posts. In 1710, Parliament passed an act which reorganized postal service throughout the Empire and thereafter, all postal matters came under control of the Postmaster General of England, with deputy postmasters general appointed for the colonies. John Hamilton served in America until 1721, when he was succeeded by John Lloyd of Charleston, South Carolina. In 1730, Alexander Spotswood, a former Lieutenant-Governor of Virginia, succeeded to the Deputy Postmaster Generalship, followed in turn by Head Lynch in 1739, Elliott Benger in 1743, and Benjamin Franklin (with William Hunter) in 1753.[29]

New Jersey had established postal service in 1709 and placed its posts under Hamilton's supervision. Hartford, Connecticut, received its first regular postal service in 1714.[30] In the fall of 1717, a route was laid out from Philadelphia to Williamsburg, Virginia, but the Virginia legislature again prevented the establishment of postal service in that colony. The rates of postage established under the Act of Queen Anne, 1710,were thought to be excessive and "the people were made to believe that the Parl't [Parliament] could not Levy any Tax, (for so they call ye Rates of Postage,) here without the Consent of General Assembly."[31]

Beginning in 1714, service was actually reduced. The weekly schedules that post-riders had attempted to maintain between Boston and Philadelphia on a year-round basis since 1693 were revised to accommodate only one trip every two weeks during the winter months.

In 1727, the route was extended southward from Philadelphia to Annapolis, Maryland, and, finally, in 1732, Spotswood succeeded in establishing service to Williamsburg via Annapolis and Newport. He also established monthly service from Williamsburg to Edenton, North Carolina.[32]

On the Philadelphia-Williamsburg run, the post-rider was scheduled to leave Philadelphia every Thursday, reaching Annapolis on Monday and Williamsburg on the following Thursday, completing the circuit to Philadelphia on the next Wednesday, or two weeks in all. This schedule was too difficult to maintain and, in 1738, the same circuit was placed on a twenty-four day schedule. In 1734, the route south of New York had been altered to utilize better roads and ferries and, as a result, Trenton, New Jersey, received its first posts. By 1747, irregular service was extended from Williamsburg to Charleston, South Carolina.[33]

Between 21 October 1702 and 20 July 1711 Edmund Dummer, Surveyor-General of the Navy, had provided armed packet service between Portsmouth, England, and Barbados. While not providing direct service to the continental colonies, the successful operation of the line proved the feasibility of fast, safe transatlantic mail service.[34]

About 1704 English merchants were urging the Treasury to inaugurate a direct line of packets to the American mainland. In 1710, William Warren received a contract to establish packet service between Bristol and New York. Although little is known of Warren's packet service after the first round trip made by Captain Shorter in the brig *Royal Anne,* it is apparent that sailings ceased after two or three years.[35] Transatlantic mail of the private citizens and businessmen remained in the hands of merchant vessels and government dispatches overseas continued to be carried by warships.[36]

Benjamin Franklin began a long association with the postal service in 1737, when he became Postmaster of Philadelphia.[37] During the sixteen years he held this office, he became thoroughly familiar with the nature of the service in which he was to become the Deputy Postmaster General for America.

Postage rates established under the Neale Patent continued in force through 31 May 1711. The Act of Queen Anne (1710) established new rates of postage effective in North America on 1 June 1711. Under this Act, rates were as follows:[38]

Per single-sheet letter (less than 1 oz.):

London to New York	1 shilling
New York to the West Indies	4 pence
New York to Philadelphia or New London	9 pence
New York to Boston or Portsmouth	1 shilling
New York to Williamsburg or Piscataway	1 sh. 3d.
New York to Charleston, South Carolina	1 sh. 6 d.
Philadelphia to Boston	1 sh. 9 d.
General: Up to 60 miles	4 pence
60 to 100 miles	6 pence

Multiple sheet and packet rates:

2 sheets	double above for single
3 sheets	triple above for single
4 sheets or 1-ounce packet	quadruple above for single

The Act required shipmasters to deliver all letters, with the exception of bills of lading and similar papers, to the colonial post offices upon arrival in port. Shipmasters were to receive one penny for each letter delivered.

Postage rates were high. The charge of one shilling for overseas letters was based on the assumption that the Bristol-New York packet ships would continue to sail. Under such an arrangement, ships of this special service would carry mail and little else and would be expected to cross the ocean in the fastest possible time. But the packet service of 1710 was not retained for more than two or three years, and the rate schedules calling for one shilling per packet letter were meaningless until 1755, when the Falmouth-New York packets began sailing. Shipmasters often "forgot" to call at post offices. The subterfuges practiced in all parts of the literate world at that time to avoid paying postage became common in America. Postage rates were just another form of taxation, as stated by the home government, and were considered as such by the colonists.[39]

COLONIAL POSTS DURING THE ADMINISTRATION OF BENJAMIN FRANKLIN 1753-1774

Benjamin Franklin and William Hunter were named joint Deputy Postmasters General for America in 1753.[40] When Hunter died in 1761, John Foxcroft succeeded him,[41] serving jointly with Franklin until Franklin was dismissed by the British government in 1774.

In the summer of 1753, shortly after assuming office, Franklin made a personal inspection tour of the posts north of Virginia.[42] He made a second tour of the posts in 1763 and Foxcroft traveled over the southern lines the following year. A great deal of Franklin's time was spent in England while he served as Deputy Postmaster General, residing abroad from June 1757 to November 1762, and from November 1764 until after Hugh Finlay replaced him as Postmaster General on 31 January 1774. During his absence, able administrators, such as James Parker, Comptroller, did much to keep the American postal system running as successfully as local conditions and the high, inflexible rates of postage permitted.[43]

The new administration of Franklin and Hunter improved the schedule of mails between New York and Philadelphia. By October 1754, three riders left each of these cities three days per week, each rider completing his trip in thirty-three hours. By February 1755, letters could be sent and answers received between Philadelphia and Boston in three weeks instead of six.[44]

Franklin also reformed the system of carrying newspapers by post. According to custom, single copies of newspapers were exchanged between printers free of postage. Many printers, however, were also postmasters, and as such occasionally refused to carry papers printed by competitors. Other printers found it difficult to reimburse post-riders directly for carrying papers to distant subscribers, and unpaid bills had accumulated. To remedy these conditions, Franklin and Hunter admitted all newspapers to the mails under the following rates, effective 1 June 1758:[45]

Per subscription per year:	Sterling (or equivalent in local currency)
Up to 50 miles	9 pence
50 to 100 miles	1 shilling 6 pence
Every additional 50 miles	9 pence
Single papers exchanged between printers	free

Accounting procedures were revised so that every possible penny would be collected from postal patrons.

In 1765, after the acquisition of Canada and Florida as British possessions, the colonial postal system was divided into two districts. The Northern District extended from Canada to Virginia and remained under the administration of Franklin and Foxcroft. The Southern District included North and South Carolina, the Floridas, and the Bahama Islands, with headquarters at Charleston, South Carolina. Deputy Postmasters General for the Southern District were Benjamin Barons (1765-1766), Peter DeLancey (1766-1771), and George Roupell (1771-1784), respectively.[46]

The postal Act of 1710 (see p. 49) was reformed partly as a result of protests over the high inland charges on letters exchanged with Canada between the time of British occupation in 1760 and formal acquisition by the Treaty of Paris in 1763. The Act of 1710 was still in force, and when it became applicable to Canada, postage on a single-sheet letter from Montreal to New York became two shillings and from Quebec to New York three shillings. Rates were revised under the new Act, which became effective on 10 October 1765, for each single-sheet letter:[47]

Distance	Rate
Up to 60 miles	4 pence
60 to 100 miles	6 pence
100 to 200 miles	8 pence
each additional 100 miles	2 pence
New York to	
Montreal	1 shilling
Quebec	1 shilling 3 pence
Overseas ship letters (at port)	
Inbound	2 pence
Outbound	1 penny plus inland charges
Outbound packet letters	1 shilling plus inland charges

"Ship letters" were those carried by merchant vessels. The high rate of one shilling became applicable only to those letters carried by armed packet vessels. Under the previous Act, the one shilling rate was legally applicable to all overseas letters, but for many years there had been no packet service and the excessive rates had led to widespread evasion of the one shilling rate demanded by law.

The inclusion of packet rates under the Act of 1765, however, was based on service which had been successfully established ten years before. While the need for dependable packet service had been widely recognized, the British Treasury had not acted until Braddock's defeat (9 July 1755) indicated that the French were quite strong on the frontier and that if good communications were to be maintained under wartime conditions, a fast and dependable line of communications ships would prove to be the best solution. This, at least, was the basic reason for establishing a packet line; but in actual practice, performance and philosophy did not always coincide.

The packet line between Falmouth, England, and New York began operations on 18 September 1755, employing four armed vessels of 200 tons each with crews of thirty per vessel. They carried mail only—no cargo

—and, at times, a few passengers. The ships were to sail monthly, with each ship expected to make a round trip every four months. There were periods, however, when sailings were extremely irregular, as in the years 1756 and 1757, when only a total of four trips were completed. The vessels, under control of the Admiralty, were at times slower than merchant vessels.[48]

In 1755, a Halifax-Boston packet line was put into operation, and in 1764, the Falmouth-West Indies packet route was altered to include Charleston, South Carolina, via Pensacola and Fort St. Augustine. Within the year, however, direct Falmouth-Charleston service was inaugurated, with overland couriers being dispatched southward to St. Augustine via Savannah, Georgia. Smaller vessels also connected Jamaica, Pensacola, and Charleston making round trips every eighty-three days.[49]

In 1763, Franklin traveled to Quebec to establish overland postal service. The resulting route included Quebec, Three Rivers, Montreal, St. John, the Richelieu River and Lake Champlain, Crown Point (or Fort Frederic), Albany, and New York, the packet-line terminal. Thirty hours were consumed between Quebec and Montreal, with nine to ten days required between Montreal and New York. Franklin appointed Hugh Finlay as Deputy Postmaster for Canada. Finlay, a devoted and thorough administrator, soon accelerated the Montreal-New York schedules to once a week and, by 1765, to twice a week. Canadian routes remained in operation until interrupted by hostilities in May 1775.[50]

Besides the inauguration of service between New York and Canada, Franklin and Foxcroft, during 1762-1764, attempted to tighten administrative practices throughout the Northern District. Night post-riders were introduced on the New York-Philadelphia route, enabling letters and answers to be exchanged between those cities in two days. Night riders between Boston and New York, in 1764, reduced the exchange schedule from two weeks to four days. Letters and answers could be exchanged between Philadelphia and Boston in six days rather than three weeks.[51]

When the end of hostilities between England and France (1763) led the Lords of the Treasury to contemplate suspending the transatlantic packet service, Franklin and Foxcroft persuaded them to retain the service for the benefit of commerce. New and less expensive ships of 130 tons were secured for the New York packet line.[52] The southern packet line was also similarly improved, and, until 1840, Admiralty packets remained an essential part of British transatlantic communications.

Increasing communications between merchants and a growing literate population contributed largely to the financial success of the pre-Revolutionary postal service. Revenues collected for the period 1757-1760 enabled the colonial post to show a profit for the first time, amounting to a surplus over expenditures of £1,221.[53] Until the Revolution, the American posts returned surpluses to the British Treasury, a phenomenon in which Franklin took great pride.

The posts south of Virginia had remained undeveloped. Lieutenant Governor Tryon of North Carolina, beginning in 1764, attempted to inaugurate regular posts through securing financial support from the legislatures and exerting pressure on the Deputy Postmasters General for the Southern District[54] (see p. 52). Barons died before accomplishing anything, and DeLancey, after January 1769, managed to send four or five riders from Charleston to Virginia. Service remained virtually non-existent and as late as 1771 the legislature of North Carolina passed an act to support the establishment of a regular postal service. The act, however, was not approved by authorities in England. Georgia also lacked dependable overland posts. Even as late as 1774, the southern service remained irregular because it lacked sufficient financial support for such matters as paying trustworthy riders and postmasters.[55]

Indeed, there seems to be a general deterioration of the service during the ten years preceding the Revolution. Hugh Finlay's special survey of all routes in America during 1773-1774[56] revealed that post riders had become careless about maintaining schedules and performed many extra services en route for their personal profit, all to the detriment of post office business. Private overland carriers were depriving the post office of much revenue, especially in the north, and vessels were carrying a great number of letters without depositing the mail at post offices as required by law.[57]

Finlay found at Portsmouth, New Hampshire, that a coach had been introduced in the mail service "some years ago," i.e., before 1773. The coach had at first carried mail illegally but was incorporated as part of the regular royal service to avoid a loss in revenue. Despite this semi-weekly royal service, other coach lines between Portsmouth and Boston had made considerable inroads into the postal revenues by illegally carrying letters.[58]

Finlay also found that certain postmasters had "gone to the country" instead of being on duty and found other postmasters extremely lacking in bookkeeping abilities. He met one rider, near Saybrook, carrying merchandise and money and driving horses and oxen to market while on duty as a post-rider. This business, carried on by a certain Mr. Herd, was so good that Finlay jotted in his journal: "He has made an Estate by his riding," and, "tis ridiculous to see His Majestys carrier, metamorphis'd to a snail paced Carrier."[59] While at Wilmington, North Carolina, in January 1774, Finlay observed that "at present it is so long before an answer can be had between Charles Town [Charleston, South Carolina] and New York (they say it requires ten weeks) that no body in either of these two places thinks of writing by Post."[60]

The high rates of postage were regarded by the majority of Americans as undesirable taxes. With indifferent local postmasters in charge of the mails and service that seemed to deteriorate or remain undeveloped, as in the south, potential patrons preferred to utilize other, and undoubtedly cheaper, means to send letters. The feelings of hostilities between colonists and representatives of the Crown which began to emerge contributed to commonplace evasion of paying postage or illegally sending communications "out of the mails."[61]

NOTES

Part II: Colonial Postal Service in North America

[1]See W. Smith, "The Colonial Post-Office," p. 259; Staff, *Transatlantic Mail*, p. 19; (A.A.S.H.O.) *Historic American Highways*, p.25.

[2]See Staff, *Transatlantic Mail*, p. 20.

[3]*Ibid.*, p. 20. Difficulties preventing the establishment of early intercolonial posts are discussed by: A.D. Smith, *Rates of Postage*, pp. 49-50; Holmes, *Stagecoach Days in the District of Columbia* (1952), p. 1; Burgess, "Early American Postal History," pp. 245-246. Even after 1639, the residents of Boston found that overseas letters were inadequately handled at places of public deposit. See, "The Petition of sundry Merchants respecting Letters" to the General Court in Boston, 23 May, 1677, in Coll. Mass. Hist. Soc., 3rd ser., vol. 7, no. 3, pp. 49-50.

[4]General Court Records, 5th, 9 mo., 1639, in Coll. Mass. Hist. Soc., 3rd ser., vol. 7, no. 1, p. 48. Provisions for regularizing the service required for carrying official letters were established in 1673. See, General Court Records, 6 January, 1673 in *Ibid.*, p. 49.

[5]"Petition of sundry Merchants," in Coll Mass. Hist. Soc., 3rd ser., vol. 7, no. 3, pp. 49-50.

[6]New York, *Documents, Colonial History*, vol. 14, pp. 186, 446, 475.

[7]Hening's *Statutes at Large* (of Virginia), vol. 1, p. 436, cited by W. Smith, "Colonial Post-Office," p. 265 and, quoted in full, by Palmerlee, "The American Posts," pp. 53-55.

[8]Gov. Francis Lovelace to Gov. Winthrop, 22 January, 1673, in New York, *Documents, Colonial History*, vol. 2, pp. 196, 198, quoted in full by Palmerlee, "American Posts," (7 September, 1957), p. 54; Letter of instructions, Gov. Lovelace to courier, January 22, 1672, in Staff, *Transatlantic Mail*, pp. 21-22. See also, W. Smith, "Colonial Post-Office," p. 259; A.A.S.H.O., *Historic American Highways*, p. 25.

[9]Connecticut, *Public Records, 1665 to 1678*, pp. 242-44, for the Order of the General Court at Hartford, 8 October, 1674; Watson, *Annals of Philadelphia and Pennsylvania*, vol 2, pp. 391-92, for the establishment of the post in Pennsylvania, cited by Rich, History of *United States Post Office*, p. 7.

[10]See W. Smith, "Colonial Post-Office," p. 259, citing Great Britain, *Calendar of State Papers, Colonial, America and West Indies, 1681-1685,* no. 1848; New York, *Documents, Colonial History,* vol. 3, pp. 349, 355, 682; Sewall, *Letterbook, entry for March 6, 1685, in Coll. of Mass. Hist. Soc.,* 6th ser., vol. 1, p. 25; *Massachusetts Acts and Resolves, Public and Private, of the Province of Massachusetts Bay,* 17 vols. (Boston: 1869-1910), vol. 6, p. 37, cited by Rich, *History of U.S. Post Office,"* p. 11.

[11]See Rich, *History of U.S. Post Office,* p. 12; Thomas Neale to Lords of the Treasury (undated) in A.D. Smith, *Rates of Postage,* pp. 391-392. The Neale Patent is partly quoted by Woolley, "Early History of the Colonial Post Office," p. 275.

[12]Woolley, "Early History of the Colonial Post Office, p. 275; W. Smith, "Colonial Post-Office," p. 261.

[13]See Neale to Lords of the Treasury (undated) in A.D. Smith, *Rates of Postage,* pp. 391-392; Petition of Andrew Hamilton and Robert West to the King (undated), in *Ibid.,* pp. 398-399. See also, *Ibid.,* p. 62; Rich, *History of U.S. Post Office,* pp. 14, 22; Bayles, "Postal Service in the Thirteen Colonies," p. 435.

[14]New York, *Colonial Laws,* vol. 1, pp. 293-296, 346, 347, 410, 525, 526, 580, 581, 612-615.

[15]*Duke of Yorke's Book of Laws,* pp. 224, 262; Pennsylvania, *Colonial Records, 1683-1790,* vol. 1, p. 524.

[16]New Hampshire, *Provincial Documents, 1686 to 1783,* vol. 2, pp. 100-101; vol. 3, pp. 11, 18, 30; Act of 5 June, 1693, quoted by Woolley, "Early Colonial Post Office," pp. 283-284.

[17]Act of 9 June, 1693, in *Coll. Mass. Hist. Soc.,* 3rd ser., vol. 7, no. 5, pp. 52-54.

[18]See W. Smith, "Colonial Post-Office," p. 262; Rich, *History of U.S. Post Office,* pp. 15-16.

[19]Connecticut, *Public Records, August, 1689, to May, 1706,* vol. 4, pp. 123, 246-247, 468.

[20]Virginia, *Journals 1659/60-1693,* pp. 430, 431, 434, 435, 436, 437, 438, 439, 444, 489; Beverley, *History and Present State of Virginia,* 1947, p. 101.

[21]Maryland, *Archives, 1693-1696/97,* pp. 346, 513; Rich, *History of U.S. Post Office,* p. 16.

[22]Rich, *History of U.S. Post Office,* p. 16.

[23]*Duke of Yorke's Book of Laws,* p. 262.

[24]Connecticut, *Public Records of Connecticut,* 1689-1706, vol. 4, pp. 246-47.

[25]Lord Cornbury to the Lords of Trade, 30 June 1704, in Rich, *History of U.S. Post Office,* pp. 18-19.

[26]E.g., Memorial of Andrew Hamilton to the Lords of the Treasury (c. 1699), in A.D. Smith, *Rates of Postage,* pp. 392-95; Petition of Duncan Campbell, Postmaster of Boston, to the General Court, 8 March 1694, in *Coll. Mass. Hist. Soc.,* 3rd ser., vol. 7, no. 7, p. 56; Memorial of John Campbell to the General Court, 26 May 1703, in *Ibid.,* no. 10, pp. 61-63.

[27]See North American Post Office Accounts, May 1693-May 1697 (Lords of the Treasury); statement of R. Cotton and T. Frankland, 27 April 1699; Memorial of Neale

to the Lords of the Treasury, 28 April 1699; and Petition of Hamilton and West (undated), in A.D. Smith, *Rates of Postage*, pp. 396-99. For a summary, see *Ibid.*, p. 62.

[28]*Ibid.*, pp. 62-63.

[29]The Act of 1710 became effective in 1711. For appointments of the Deputy Postmasters General for America, see W. Smith, "Colonial Post-Office," p. 267; W. Smith, *Post Office in British North America*, p. 25; Roper, *U.S. Post Office*, pp. 25-26; Great Britain, General Post Office, *Orders, 1737 to 1774*, entry for 13 August 1743, vol. 1, p. 79; *Ibid.*, 10 August 1753, vol. 1, p. 180; Butler, *Doctor Franklin*, p. 34.

[30]See W. Smith, *Post Office in British North America*, p. 19; Bayles, "Postal Service," p. 441.

[31]Alexander Spotswood to the Board of Trade, 24 June 1718, in Spotswood, *Official Letters*, vol. 2, pp. 280-281.

[32]See Bayles, "Postal Service," pp. 439-440; Butler, *Doctor Franklin*, pp. 31-32.

[33]See W. Smith, *Post Office in British North America*, p. 25; Bayles, "Postal Service," pp. 439-440; Butler, *Doctor Franklin*, pp. 31-32, 34-37.

[34]See Robinson, *British Mails Overseas*, pp. 35-37; Staff, *Transatlantic Mail*, pp. 28-29.

[35]Staff, *Transatlantic Mail*, p. 32; Robinson, *British Mails Overseas*, pp. 37-38, which reports an attempt in late 1709, but notes specifically only the arrival of one of William Warren's packets at New York in 1710. McCusker, "New York City and the Bristol Packet," pp. 4-5.

[36]See Spotswood to the Council of Trade, 15 October 1712, in Spotswood, *Official Letters*, vol. 2, p. 1; to Earl of Dartmouth, 11 February 1713, *Ibid.*, p. 5; to the Lords Commissioners of Trade, 11 February 1713, *Ibid.*, p. 9.

[37]See Franklin, *Papers Franklin*, vol. 2, p. 178, for his comment on appointment as Postmaster of Philadelphia.

[38]Act of 9th Anne (1710), as received in Massachusetts, is reproduced in full in *Coll. Mass. Hist. Soc.*, 3rd ser., vol. 7, no. 18, pp. 71-79. See also, W. Smith, "Colonial Post-Office," pp. 267-268; W. Smith, *Post Office in British North America*, p. 19; A. D. Smith, *Rates of Postage*, p. 63; Staff, *Transatlantic Mail*, p. 32; Sampson, *Colonial Postmark Catalog*, p. 4.

[39]See Spotswood to Board of Trade, 24 June 1718, in Spotswood, *Official Letters*, vol. 2, pp. 280-281; A. D. Smith, *Rates of Postage*, p. 63; Staff, *Transatlantic Mail*, pp. 32-34.

[40]Great Britain, General Post Office, *Orders, 1737 to 1774*, entry for 10 August 1753, vol. 1, p. 180.

[41]See Butler, *Doctor Franklin*, p. 71, citing Great Britain, General Post Office, *Commission Book, 1759-1854*, pp. 23, 26. Although the precise reasons or circumstances surrounding the dismissal of Franklin from office are unclear, there seems to be some truth in the matter that the Crown wanted officials in the postal service who were less loyal to the colonists and that there was some weight to Franklin's suggestion that the Crown was considering using the control of the postal service to censor intercolonial correspondence and perhaps spy on those believed to be disloyal to the home government. See Butler, *Doctor Franklin*, Chapter 9.

[42]See Butler, *Doctor Franklin,* p. 46; *Franklin, Papers of Franklin,* vol. 4, p. 512, n.

[43]Franklin's son, William, also served as Comptroller. See Butler, *Doctor Franklin,* p. 48; W. Smith, "Colonial Post-Office," pp. 270, footnote 42.

[44]Butler, *Doctor Franklin,* p. 49, citing *Pennsylvania Gazette,* 1 January 1754 and 10 October, 1754. Cf. Bayles, "Postal Service," p. 446.

[45]See Rich, *History of U.S. Post Office,* pp. 36-37; Butler, *Doctor Franklin,* pp. 56-59.

[46]See Hecht, "U.S.-Canadian Postal Relations," p. 234; Staff, *Transatlantic Mail,* p. 36; Rich, *History of U.S. Post Office,* p. 39; W. Smith, "Colonial Post-Office," p. 272. Roupell's term of office is reported as ending in either 1782 or 1784.

[47]A.D. Smith, *Rates of Postage,* pp. 63-64; Sampson, *Colonial Postmark Catalog,* p. 4. See also, Hecht, "Postal Relations," *N.Y. Hist.,* vol. 38, no. 3 (July 1957), p. 244; Staff, *Transatlantic Mail,* pp. 39, 174; Rich, *History of U.S. Post Office,* p. 40.

[48]Great Britain, General Post Office, *Orders, 1737 to 1774,* entry for 17 October 1755, vol. 2, p. 14; W. Smith, "Colonial Post-Office," pp. 271-272; Staff, *Transatlantic Mail,* p. 35; Robinson, *British Mails Overseas,* pp. 44-45.

[49]*Ibid.,* pp. 47-48; W. Smith, "Colonial Post-Office," pp. 272-273; Staff, *Transatlantic Mail,* p. 35.

[50]See Hecht, "Postal Relations," p. 234, for an excellent account. See also, Staff, *Transatlantic Mail,* pp. 36, 39.

[51]See Rich, *History of U.S. Post Office,* pp. 34-35; W. Smith, "Colonial Post-Office," p. 271; Butler, *Doctor Franklin,* pp. 86-90.

[52]Butler, *Doctor Franklin,* pp. 90-95.

[53]See W. Smith, "Colonial Post-Office," pp. 270-271; Rich, *History of U.S. Post Office,* p. 37.

[54]*Ibid.,* pp. 112-18; Rich, *History of U.S. Post Office,* pp. 34, 39.

[55]See Butler, *Doctor Franklin,* pp. 118-20.

[56]Finlay, Journal.

[57]Finlay, Journal, entry for 2 October 1773, pp. 24-25.

[58]*Ibid.,* entry for 5 October 1773, pp. 25-27.

[59]*Ibid.,* entry for 11 November 1773, pp. 54-55.

[60]*Ibid.,* entry for 20 January 1774, p. 100.

[61]E.g., *Ibid.,* pp. 78-79, 80, 99, 100-01, 103, et passim.

PART THREE

THE
UNITED
STATES

THE REVOLUTION AND
POSTS UNDER THE
CONTINENTAL CONGRESS

After royal authorities barred the newspaper of William Goddard from the mail, he hired riders (August 1774) to carry his papers from Baltimore to New York via Philadelphia. As early as February 1774, Goddard had solicited the support of colonial legislatures, and by May 1775 he had inaugurated successful routes from Portsmouth, New Hampshire, to Williamsburg, Virginia. As the royal posts were driven from the roads or ceased to function, Goddard's system served the colonists until the Continental Congress assumed control of postal operations on 26 July 1775 with effective service being instituted under its sole management by September 1775.[1]

As the new independent system got under way, the reduced postage rates —twenty percent less than those under the Act of 1765—were withdrawn and the old colonial rates were continued in force.[2] The financial instability of the Revolutionary period was reflected by the frequent increases in postage rates, in a general way paralleling the steady depreciation of American Continental paper currency. Postage rates were raised by fifty percent in 1777; the rates of 1777 were doubled in April 1779. The initially reduced rates of 1775 increased by twenty times in December 1779; and in May 1780, by forty times. In 1782 the reduced rates of 1775 were restored, and in 1788 the rates of 1782 were reduced by twenty-five percent. On 1 June 1792 new postage rates were effected pursuant to the Act of Congress of 20 February 1792 under the new Constitution.[3] The rates throughout these years remained high, despite the comparative reductions of 1782 and 1788.

Benjamin Franklin was elected Postmaster General by the Continental Congress on 26 July 1775. Franklin named his son-in-law, Richard Bache, as Secretary and Comptroller, and William Goddard as Riding Surveyor, a disappointment to Goddard who had expected to be named Postmaster General. Franklin was appointed Commissioner to France before the end of 1776, and Bache became Postmaster General on 7 November 1776 holding the office until 28 January 1782 when Ebenezer Hazard became head of the service.[4]

The Royal inland mails, of course, virtually ceased to function, although mail arriving from abroad was handled by the authorities in the ports remaining under British control. The North American packets continued to sail, but many were captured or lost to the colonists or their allies. In 1778 Philadelphia briefly became the American packet port, and in 1780 the packets sailed to Charleston. Franklin arranged for French packet service and eventually, by 1785, concluded arrangements for French and British packets to serve the former British colonies. Interestingly enough, Foxcroft, Franklin's former associate, had remained loyal to the Crown throughout the War and was appointed as British packet agent at New York after hostilities ended. Hugh Finlay, who had conducted the important survey on the eve of the Revolution, retained a primary concern for the Canadian posts. After a relatively short-lived breakdown of postal service in Canada during the War, the royal posts again began to operate under Finlay's direction. He was appointed Deputy Postmaster General of Canada, Nova Scotia, and New Brunswick, an office he held until 1800. After hostilities, Canadian mails to and from overseas were dispatched exclusively over the old New York route until 1787, when a 633-mile line was opened between Halifax and Quebec. Nevertheless, British packet ships continued to call at New York, with service to and from Canada via Albany provided by the United States.[5]

Under the Articles of Confederation, Congress became the only authority to establish and operate a postal service in the United States. Postal regulations were revised and consolidated under one Ordinance in 1782 to insure that the safety of the people and the commercial interests of the country were provided for by "the communication of intelligence with regularity and despatch from one part to another of the United States."[6]

During the War, the most important task of the postal service was to maintain efficient and rapid communications between Congress and the armies. The regular service for civilian purposes became a secondary concern. Mail service was often interrupted because of the changing military situation. The volume of civilian mail fell. Congress found it difficult to finance post office operations with the depreciated currency, and riders began to carry mail for their own profit. Despite financial problems, Congress established a separate system of couriers for government correspondence over the route from Cambridge, Massachusetts, to Philadelphia. Express riders traveled day and night. In 1776, this special service was improved so that three trips per week were made. The southern colonies were kept in communication with Congress by three "advice boats." Early in 1777, the American system was again divided into two districts, with the principal overland route established from Falmouth, Maine, to Philadelphia, via Portsmouth, Boston, Hartford, Fishkill, and Easton. The southern district included the route between Philadelphia and Savannah, via Annapolis, Williamsburg, Halifax, Wilmington, and Charleston. Regular service, however, remained poor throughout the War. The Inspector of Dead Letters, an office established in 1777, controlled censorship and reported to Congress subversive plans discovered in letters coming to the Inspector's attention.[7]

Following Postmaster General Hazard's suggestion, postal laws and regulations were revised and codified under the Ordinance of 18 October, 1782. Postal service was made the monopoly of the central government for lines wholly within the boundaries of individual states as well as interstate routes. Censorship of letters was restricted to time of war or when specifically ordered by the President or Congress. Under moderate rates established by the Postmaster General, newspapers were to be carried by the riders, who received a percentage of such revenues. These charges and commissions were not fixed by the Ordinance, but it was clearly indicated that postal revenues were primarily intended to meet the expense of the service, with surpluses, if any, to be applied to the improvement of the system after previous deficits had been repaid to the Treasury.[8]

Service had begun to improve shortly before Hazard took office in 1782. The southern route to Savannah was in operation and stage coaches were on regular schedule over the more important northern sections of the route, with mails traveling between New York and Philadelphia in twenty-two hours, three times a week. New contracts for the year 1786 provided for the transportation of mail by coaches from Portsmouth, New Hampshire, to Savannah, Georgia. "Cross posts," or secondary postal routes, and new lines to the settled regions of the interior were encouraged by legislation in 1788.[9]

The first significant westward extension of the posts was attempted in 1787, but the actual inauguration of postal service to Pittsburgh was delayed until 3 July 1788. Westward mail from Philadelphia to Chamberstown via Lancaster, Yorktown, and Carlisle was carried by post-riders once a week, and from Chamberstown to Pittsburgh via Bedford once every two weeks.[10]

Samuel Osgood replaced Hazard after the adoption of the Constitution, taking office on 27 September 1789. At that time, there were seventy-five post offices in the United States and about 2,000 miles of post roads.[11]

GROWTH OF
THE POSTAL SERVICE
1789-1845

Rates of postage established by the Ordinance of 1782 were continued in force until 1792. A slight adjustment was made in 1799, reducing the number of distance-zones from nine to six. In 1815, to increase revenues to alleviate the expense of the War of 1812, postage rates were raised fifty percent but were reduced in 1816 and revised again that year to consolidate the number of zones to five. The increase of 1815 was the last instance of the use of postage rates as a war tax by the Government until World War I. Except for a slight increase for letter postage of the 151 400-mile zone, rates remained the same until the postal reform of 1845. The postage charges were based on mileage and the number of sheets per letter rather than on weight. Charges remained high—single-sheet letters traveling more than 400 miles after 1816 were charged twenty-five cents. Letters were generally sent unpaid, with postage being collected from the addressees. Although the Act of 1794 provided for local delivery service for the additional payment of two cents per letter, the service remained optional and apparently few postmasters made provision for local delivery. In large cities, some carriers were employed, as they were in Boston, where between 1829 and 1849 from one to eight city postmen carried local mail under the supervision of the postmaster. As a rule, however, patrons went to their post office to mail their letters and call for incoming correspondence.[12]

In 1792, mail over the principal route from the District of Maine to Virginia was carried three times a week. Mail "south of Virginia" was conveyed only once a week in winter and twice a week in summer. Although Postmaster Timothy Pickering noted that between six and seven thousand miles of post roads were in operation in 1792, Pittsburgh and Albany marked the western limits of postal service.[13] But in that year energetic efforts resulted in an extension of lines through New York to Canajoharie via Schenectady, through Vermont, western Connecticut, central Pennsylvania, the Carolinas, and western Virginia through the

Cumberland Gap to Danville, Kentucky. Service west of Pittsburgh was extended overland to Wheeling, with special boats providing mail service to settlements on the Ohio River as far west as Limestone, Kentucky, and overland service from that place to Cincinnati by August 1794. Zane's Trace across southern Ohio eventually provided a more reliable route, and the boat service was discontinued in 1798. As settlements grew, service within Kentucky was extended and in 1794 Knoxville, Tennessee, received its first mail over a route from Abingdon, Virginia. By 1799, more than 16,000 miles of post roads had been established.[14]

Western post-riders found it difficult to maintain schedules over the wilderness routes. During the winter, the post-riders required seven days more than the scheduled fifteen and a half to carry mail over the 646-mile route between Philadelphia and Lexington, Kentucky. In 1799, Postmaster General Joseph Habersham lengthened the unrealistic schedule, realizing that accidents to horse and rider and the lack of bridges to cross flooded streams in a sparsely settled country greatly delayed the mails.[15] As late as 1810, Samuel Lewis, the post-rider between Cincinnati and Chillicothe, was still fording streams on the bridgeless roads. On one occasion, "several days" were lost when Lewis was struck on the head by a log while thrashing about in a flooded creek to recover the mail bag, temporarily lost while Lewis had been swimming and leading his horse.[16]

In 1800, new north-south routes between western cities began to link settlements previously served by east-west routes only. Knoxville and Nashville, Tennessee, were connected with Natchez, Mississippi; Washington, Kentucky, and Chillicothe, Ohio, were joined; and new post roads connected Cincinnati, Louisville, Vincennes, Indiana, and Cahokia, Illinois. By 1803, Cleveland and Detroit were receiving mail and in 1804 St. Louis was served. Southern mails reached Augusta, Georgia, in 1803, and routes were placed in operation for the newly acquired Louisiana territory in 1804. Overland mails to New Orleans presented unusual difficulties to riders traveling the Indian trails through unsettled areas. Part of the original eastern New Orleans route was located in Spanish west Florida, and much attention was given to finding a better route.[17]

Special express mails were run over principal routes for military dispatches during the War of 1812, from about April 1813 to 27 February 1815. Civilian letters were carried by these expresses, but newspapers and pamphlets were sent by previously established and generally slower postal routes. Although this service was established in the south, lines north of Washington, D.C., were regarded as more critical.[18]

Stage coaches had been introduced west of the mountains in 1806 and by 1822 were operating between Washington, D.C., and Nashville on eleven-day schedules, running at night as well as during the day. Under Gideon Granger, Postmaster General from 1801 to 1814, post-riders were directed to carry lights at night on some wilderness routes to maintain round-the-clock schedules.[19] Postal markings and manuscript notations indicate that transit time between Nashville and Philadelphia was sixteen days in 1813; between Lexington and Louisville, Kentucky, one-day service was possible in 1815.[20] In a letter written at New York on 6 February 1815, the writer notes that news of the Battle of New Orleans (8 January 1815) had just reached the city.[21] As late as 1824, Washington-New Orleans mails via Knoxville and Natchez still consumed twenty-four or -five days in transit.[22]

The Postmaster General authorized mail contracts for steamboat service between New Orleans and Natchez as early as June 1813. River mail contracts, however, were not in force from 1819 to 1837. In the latter year steamboat mail service was renewed between New Orleans and Louisville with schedules requiring tri-weekly service and allowing six days for down-river runs and ten days for up-river runs. Branch service to St. Louis was also included.[23] Meanwhile, since 1824, a steamboat line had been utilized for a portion of the "Great Mail" route between New Orleans and Mobile.[24] In fact, steamboats had become so common by 1823 that Congress passed an act that year declaring all steamboat routes to be "post roads," thereby subjecting all mail matter carried by steamboats on domestic waterways to Federal regulation. Oddly enough, the great inland canals were not important elements in the mail transportation system. The draft animals on the tow-paths were too slow and if any mail contracts were concluded with canal boat operators they were listed under the heading "Modes of Transportation Not Specified."[25]

As postal routes followed the pioneers westward, complaints about poor roads and against stagecoach drivers who "forgot" the mail pouches were commonplace. Nevertheless, Little Rock, Arkansas, received mail in 1821; Rock Island, Illinois, and Hannibal, Missouri, were served in 1826; and mails reached Dubuque, Iowa, in 1836.[26]

By 1834, railroads were offering reasonably reliable service over short lines. Although some mail contractors had utilized this service as soon as advantages over coach service became apparent, it was not until 1838 that Congress declared all railroads to be "post roads" and specifically authorized mail contracts with railroads companies.[27] Beginning in 1837, Route Agents, employees of the Post Office Department, traveled aboard steamboats and trains alike to service the pouched mail between towns and to receive letters directly from patrons en route.[28]

Rail lines, however, did not develop into continuous systems fast enough to provide the efficient service demanded by commercial interests of the south and west. In 1836, a special express service was inaugurated which is now termed the "Eastern Pony Express" to distinguish it from the more publicized and dramatic "Western" Pony Express which followed twenty-four years later.[29] The express service of 1836-1839 utilized riders on horseback and round-the-clock schedules between the major cities of the east and St. Louis, New Orleans, Mobile, and Charleston. Normal contract routes were not eliminated. Instead, the primary purpose of these expresses was to carry news of price fluctuations, especially for the cotton market, and to expedite the dissemination of news by carrying special news slips instead of bulky newspapers generally exchanged by most printers. Government dispatches and private letters (prepaid at three times the normal postage rates of 1825) were also carried.

Express schedules between New York and New Orleans stipulated that southbound trips were to be completed in six days and seventeen hours and northbound trips to be completed in six days, twenty-three hours, a substantial reduction compared with the thirteen- to fourteen-day schedules normally performed by contractors employing stagecoaches on most of the route.

From the beginning, this express system utilized the railroad between New York and Philadelphia and the steamboat line between Mobile and New Orleans, thereby being combined with the ordinary mails over these sections without a saving in transit time. The time gained by the riders on horseback was often lost when the southern steamboat connection failed, and delays on the western lines were also frequent. Eventually, the increased use of railroad service on ordinary contract routes shortened schedules to a degree which did not justify the expense of the special service. By July 1839, when the southern express was discontinued, normal mail schedules between New York and New Orleans had been reduced to ten days.

Between 1789 and 1845, the number of post offices in the United States had grown from seventy-five to 14,183. In 1790, the first full year of operations under the Constitution, revenues amounted to $37,935 and expenditures totaled $32,140. In 1845, revenues amounted to $4,289,842, compared with $4,320,732 in expenditures.[30]

During this period, unlike the colonial period, official policies carried out the concept that the main purpose of the postal organization was to serve the public rather than function as a primary source of revenue.[31] In reply to Meriweather Morris, Postmaster of Columbia, Virginia, who had requested additional but unauthorized compensation, Timothy Pickering wrote:

> There are many Offices in which the profits are really not adequate to the trouble, yet for the accommodation of the people they are kept up. I hope you will be induced to continue in yours for the convenience of your Neighborhood. Half the post offices in the United States would be broken up, if the postmasters were not influenced by motives other than those of a pecuniary nature.[32]

Although postage rates were high, expenses were great in providing service to an ever-growing population, seemingly always moving westward. Even the rate increase of 1815 may be considered reasonable when it is remembered that express routes virtually never produced revenue equal to the expense. Nevertheless, the cost of receiving a letter remained a luxury to many a citizen.

Local postmasters generally charged patrons on a monthly basis rather than collect the fee for each letter, a practice which was perfectly acceptable to officials.[33] Letters were carried "out of the mails" at every opportunity, and even some Federal office holders who lawfully exercised the franking privilege were prone to abuse their right to send mail free of postage. Pickering once noted that a Member of Congress had placed 119 free letters amounting to five and a half pounds in a single mail. Always ready to add a barb to his comments, Pickering observed that "if every member were to load the mail in the same manner, it would take 15 horses to carry the mails of a single day.[34]

Slowly, the increased mail volume led to innovations in postal practices, carriage by trains and steamboats being among the more obvious. But innovations less apparent began to appear. The use of postmarking handstampers, for example, first introduced in America in the eighteenth century, became more prevalent. Besides saving the time required to write town names and dates at busy offices, stampers produced more legible postmarks (when applied correctly). As early as 1792, the Postmaster General remarked that, "with respect to stamps [postmarking devices] for the post office, they are so useful, I wish every office were furnished with them."[35] After 1800, a marked increase in the use of stampers is evident, with the "modern" circular format rather than the straight-line style becoming prevalent. There was a great variety of styles at first, however, and beautiful oval or pictorial markings were used by some postmasters. Handstampers for indicating postage rates were used by a few offices as early as the late 1820s to eliminate the task of writing rates by hand, but the complex rate structure discouraged widespread adoption of these devices.[36]

The Letterbooks of the Postmaster General indicate that procurement of supplies was often an informal affair. Saddle-bags and portmanteaus were sent out from the General Post Office, but local purchases by postmasters and carriers were readily authorized if supplies were exhausted at headquarters. The security of the mails was considered to be of utmost importance, and the Letterbooks reflect great concern over lost mail pouches and robberies. Yet, the Postmaster General did not have authority to reimburse patrons for their losses. In reply to a complaint about money stolen from the mails, Pickering wrote:

> I know of but one effectual Security—To cut bank notes into two parts—send one and wait an acknowledgment of its receipt, before the other is forwarded. This is the plan recommended by the General Post Office in London, to guard against the like evil there.[37]

Although the precise legal nature of the postal organization was rather unclear during the first years under the Constitution, the Postmaster General remained under the direct supervision of the President. The establishment itself was referred to as the "General Post Office" until December 1821, when headings in the Letterbooks were changed to "General Post Office Department." The term "Post Office Department" appeared in 1825, two years after President James Monroe had requested the first annual report from the Postmaster General. The Postmaster General became a member of the Cabinet in 1829 under President Andrew Johnson.[38]

THE PRIVATE EXPRESS COMPANIES 1840-1863

While the frontiers had been moving westward, the population of cities had grown. The cost of providing mail service in thinly settled regions was long regarded as adequate reason to maintain high postage rates. But in the more densely populated areas of the country, it was discovered that a lower scale of rates could be profitable. This "discovery" was made by private companies.

Letters had always been carried "out of the mails" by individual post-riders, stagecoach drivers, railroad employees, and travelers. The term "out of the mails" denoted the illegal transportation of letters which should have been carried in the government's mail under the postal monopoly. Parcels were not considered mail matter. In the early 1840s the attention of the Post Office Department was directed particularly to the express companies when their services were extended to encompass the carriage of letters between cities. William F. Harnden, a former conductor on the Boston & Lowell Railroad, played a large role in establishing the Nation's express business when, in 1839, he inaugurated a Boston-New York service. By 1844 more than forty companies were operating in the Boston area alone.[39] Hale & Company was among the largest concerns carrying intercity mail, providing service from New England to Washington, D.C. and branch service to Buffalo. Letters were picked up by company carriers and delivered to the doors of addressees in distant cities in less time and for less money than required for U.S. Mail.[40]

In an effort to minimize these inroads, the Post Office Department established in 1842 the "U.S. Express Mail" between Boston and New York and between Albany and New York. Mail was serviced on these routes on accelerated schedules at no extra cost. Furthermore, some mail agents were authorized "to carry mail on their own account, money, packages, specie and other matter not mailable by law."[41] This service was expanded to embrace other routes, utilizing rail and steamboat lines and remaining in operation on some routes until shortly before the Civil War.[42] When postage rates were reduced by Congress in 1845, the private intercity letter express companies no longer offered competition, and subsequent court decisions established the monopoly of the Post Office Department with respect to carrying mail in the United States.[43]

Private collection and delivery services within cities, however, remained in operation after 1845. In 1842, Alexander M. Greig and Henry T. Thomas had established the City Despatch Post in New York to carry letters within the city. The first adhesive postage stamp in the United States was issued by this private company on 1 February 1842. Boxes for the deposit of letters were located in public places and registry service was offered at three cents in addition to postage for letters with valuable contents, another service not offered by the Post Office Department. The stamps, especially useful in prepaying postage on letters deposited in the boxes, were sold at three cents each or $2.50 per hundred.[44] This local post flourished. By July 1842, Greig's carriers were handling about 450 letters per day while the government carriers at the New York Post Office were handling only 250 per day. By purchasing Greig's post, the New York Postmaster estimated that the combined service would produce an annual revenue of about $2,400. This purchase was made and the postage stamps continued in use. In 1844 John T. Boyd opened a rival local system in New York with improved schedules of delivery. Boyd soon offered better service for less money, charging two cents per letter instead of the Government rate of three and a half or four cents under the revised Federal rates of 1845. The Act of 1845 had unfortunately increased the local (intracity or "drop") postage to two cents while retaining the two-cent carrier fee in an effort to compensate for the anticipated losses in nationwide revenue when lower intercity rates went into effect.[45] The U.S. City Despatch Post of New York, the government's first major effort in city delivery service, gave way to private competition and ceased operation on 28 November 1846, ironically a victim of the first postal reform act.[46]

Local posts continued to operate without serious competition from the government—Barnard's City Letter Express of Boston, D.O. Blood & Company of Philadelphia, and Swart's City Dispatch Post of New York were typical.[47] Although private "penny posts" survived in some cities until 1863, the government had placed itself on an equal footing in 1851 under revised rates which lowered the drop fee to one cent and carrier fees to "one or two cents" per letter. The Post Office Department embarked on a comprehensive city delivery program and issued two different one-cent "Carrier" stamps in 1851. Many carriers, however, used locally designed and prepared "semi-official" adhesive stamps even though they performed their duties under the supervision of U.S. city postmasters. While some carriers received salaries from the Department, many received compensation directly from the fees they collected.[48] For the fiscal year ending 30 June 1855, government carriers in New York, Philadelphia, Boston, Baltimore, and New Orleans handled 8,624,611 letters, circulars, handbills, newspapers, and pamphlets.[49] The Act of 3 April 1860 established a standard rate for drop letters delivered by carriers at one cent each.[50] The dual system of carrier compensation was abolished when all carriers became Federal employees and free carrier service was instituted in forty-nine cities in 1863.[51]

POSTAGE RATE REFORMS
AND GOVERNMENT
POSTAGE STAMPS
1845-1863

The reform of postage rates carried out by Great Britain in 1840 and the actual loss of revenue to private competition led to a reexamination of the basic rates of postage which had remained essentially unchanged since 1816.[52] Postmaster General Amos Kendall sent George Plitt of the Department to study the British reforms and, although Plitt's report supported reform, Charles A. Wickliffe, Postmaster General from 1841 to 1845, opposed a reduction of rates, fearing that lower postage rates would not stimulate enough additional use of the mails to avoid a crushing deficit. Nevertheless, Cave Johnson, who succeeded Wickliffe, offered support for a reduction and on 3 March 1845 an Act of Congress established a lower, simplified scale of postage rates.[53]

The new rates became effective 1 July 1845. Letter rates, for the first time, were based on weight exclusively rather than the number of sheets. A "single" letter was considered as one weighing up to ("not exceeding") one-half ounce. Distance zones were reduced from five to two in number. Letters up to a half ounce were charged five cents for carriage under 300 miles, and ten cents for over 300 miles. Prepayment of postage remained optional. The drop-letter rate, as previously noted, was increased from one to two cents. Packets weighing more than three pounds were not to be accepted in the mails.[54]

Unlike Great Britain, the United States did not introduce adhesive postage stamps or stamped stationery when the reformed postage rates became effective. Since the majority of letters, however, were rated either five or ten cents after 1 July 1845 there was widespread adoption of handstampers bearing the numerals "5" and "10" at post offices across the nation and a gradual decline in the use of pen and ink for indicating postage rates. Furthermore, some postmasters locally issued their own postage stamps before the government's first general issue of adhesives appeared in 1847. The "Postmasters' Provisionals" which have been preserved were issued at Alexandria, Virginia (August 1846); Annapolis, Maryland (stamped envelopes, c. 1846); Baltimore, Md. (several varieties, beginning March 1846); Boscawen, New Hampshire (a handstamped type-set design, c. 1846); Brattleboro, Vermont (summer of 1846); Lockport, New York (handstamped, c. March 1846); Millbury, Massachusetts (a woodcut, c. July 1846); New Haven, Connecticut (handstamped envelopes, 1845); New York, New York (14 July, 1845); Providence, Rhode Island (24 August 1846); St. Louis, Missouri (November 1845).[55] It is interesting to note the number of small-town postmasters who prepared these early postage stamps.

The provisional stamps, valid for indicating prepayment of postage at the issuing post offices, were not used in great numbers. The one exception, the New York City provisional issue, was used on some letters posted in several other cities but addressed to New York. The use of these issues was sanctioned by the postal authorities in Washington, but, in a general way, the public apparently was reluctant to buy postage stamps prepared by secondary officials. The need for the full authority of the Federal government to guarantee the validity of the stamps soon became apparent.[56]

Congress, in an act approved 3 March 1847, provided for the first issue of United States adhesive postage stamps, to be issued to the public on 1 July of that year. The firm of Rawdon, Wright, Hatch & Edson of New York City was awarded the contract to manufacture the stamps.[57] Dies were engraved, transfer rolls were made, two printing plates were prepared bearing one hundred each of the five- and ten-cent stamps, and the stamps were printed on thin bluish paper without perforations. The five-cent denomination bore a portrait of Benjamin Franklin in brown and the ten-cent stamp carried the portrait of George Washington in black. The use of the stamps was not compulsory. Between 3 June 1847 and 9 December 1850 some 4,400,000 five-cent stamps and 1,050,000 ten-cent stamps were delivered by the contractors. However, only 3,712,000 five-cent and 891,000 ten-cent stamps were distributed to postmasters. On 1 July 1851 the date of issue for new postage stamps under different rates of postage, the issue of 1847 became invalid and patrons were given an opportunity to redeem the unused stamps of the first issue.[58]

After the rates were lowered in 1845, there was agitation for a further reduction and the elimination of the 300-mile zone. As in Great Britain, the first year of operation under the reduced rates produced a deficit. Unable to curtail service to eliminate the deficit and unwilling to increase the postage rates again, the government was only able to establish a rate of forty cents

The 5-cent denomination depicting Benjamin Franklin was the first general issue of United States postage stamps to become valid in 1847. A 10-cent stamp, with a portrait of George Washington, was also issued at the same time.

for letters carried between points in the east and on the Pacific Coast in 1847. In 1848, letters carried between post offices on the Pacific Coast were charged twelve and one-half cents. The rates established in 1845, 1847, and 1848 continued in force until the rather complex rate structure of 1851 became effective.[59]

The reform of 1845, despite the deficit, was deemed a success. Agitation for lower rates continued and the government officials remained predominantly firm in their regard of the Post Office as a public service which should be developed for the benefit of the public. A.D. Smith has observed that "the need for some further reduction was well illustrated by the fact that the ordinary charge for transporting a barrel of flour from Detroit to Buffalo was at this time the same as the charge for carrying in the same conveyance a letter weighing half an ounce, viz. 10 cents."[60] Accordingly, the Act of 3 March 1851 was passed. It included the interesting provision for enabling those who prepaid their letters to do so for less money than those who sent their letters "collect." This Act revised the letter rates.

> From and after June 30, 1851, in lieu of the rates of postage now established by law, there shall be charged the following rates:
>
> For every single letter in writing, marks, or signs, conveyed not exceeding 3,000 miles, if prepaid, 3 cents; if not prepaid, 5 cents, and for any greater distance double said rates; double letter, double rates; treble letter, treble rates; quadruple letter, quadruple rates; and every letter or parcel not exceeding half an ounce in weight shall be deemed a single letter, and every additional weight of half an ounce or less shall be charged with an additional rate. Drop letters, 1 cent each. Advertised letters, 1 cent in addition to the regular postage.[61]

"Advertised letters" were those left uncalled for at post offices and which were listed in the local newspapers by the postmasters. The additional fee for such letters covered the expense of placing the ads.

On 1 July 1851 a new basic issue of stamps was introduced consisting, at first, of two denominations of one and three cents. Franklin's portrait was used for the one-cent stamp and Washington's for the three-cent. The firm of Toppan, Carpenter, Casilear & Co. produced this issue under contract. Again, the stamps were issued without perforations and had to be cut from the sheets.[62] This inconvenience was remedied in 1857, when United States stamps were perforated for easy separation.[63]

The rates of 1851 were simplified in 1855 with the elimination of the prepayment option. On 1 April 1855 prepayment of domestic postage became compulsory, with rates of three cents for half-ounce letters carried up to three thousand miles and ten cents for letters carried more than three thousand miles. On 1 January 1856 prepayment by means of postage stamps for domestic letters became compulsory.[64]

Embossed stamped envelopes were issued in the United States on 1 July 1853. Stamped envelopes have been produced under contract since that time, the first contractor being George F. Nesbitt and Company. The "first issue" or design series was produced in three-, six-, and ten-cent dominations, with the ten-cent issue appearing in 1855 to meet the need of the new 3000-mile rate.[65]

DOMESTIC
REGISTRY SERVICE
1855

It has been noted that the safety of the mails had troubled postal officials at all times. In a general way, the early "surveyors" of the posts, beginning with Finlay and Goddard, concerned themselves with this problem. It was not until Chester Bailey of Philadelphia was assigned specific duties relating to depredation cases that the Department embarked on a program to safeguard the contents of the mails. Between 1807 and 1822, Bailey was assigned to cases dealing with external robberies and thefts committed by postal employees. With the appointment of E. Hayward as General Agent, 1 December 1829, the origin of the Postal Inspection Service may be dated. In its first form, the agency was known as the Office of Inspection and, within a year, as the "Office of Instruction and Mail Depredations." Numerous reorganizations of the agency and increases in the Office's staff followed, but other measures were required to prevent the loss of valuable mail.[66]

The earliest practical attempts to curb internal thefts of letters with valuable contents apparently were carried out at Philadelphia between 1845 and 1851. By informal agreements with postmasters in different parts of the country, the postmaster at Philadelphia kept a register of letters enclosing currency, securities, or other important papers. Little is known of the actual methods employed in handling these "registered" letters, but special handstamped markings of the initial letter "R" are found occasionally associated with notation in manuscript such as "Reg'd" or "Registered." Similar notations are found on some mail exchanged between New Orleans and Mobile. Post offices at Detroit and Cleveland actually applied the words "Money Letter" to some pieces. These services, however, were not authorized by the Department and were offered at no cost to patrons.[67]

The Act of 3 March 1855, which made prepayment of postage on domestic letters compulsory, also established the domestic registry system in the United States. As such, this was the first "special service" of the U.S. postal system. Registration began with a fee of five cents per piece (in addition to postage), applicable only to letter mail, and provided no indemnification or liability for loss. For the year ending 3 December 1855 Postmaster General James Campbell reported:

> A just estimate of the value and ultimate success of the plan of registration adopted cannot be formed from the short experience had of it. Its operation brings to the immediate knowledge of the department not only every failure, but every delay in the transportation and delivery of registered letters; and in carefully observing its operation, with a view to such modifications as may be

required, I have, in each day's report, found abundant proofs of its usefulness, and also of the necessity of perfecting it by such means as experience may suggest.

By arrangements with Prussia and Bremen, the registry system had been extended to letters conveyed between the United States and Germany.[68] Between 1863 and 1868, the registry fee was established at twenty cents in addition to postage, and on 1 June 1867 prepayment of the fee in stamps became compulsory. Registry service was gradually extended to include all classes of mail matter. An indemnity, not exceeding $10,000, was introduced in 1898 and, thereafter, increased. The fees, since 1868, have varied considerably over the years, with eight or ten cents remaining usual until the 1920s.[69]

WESTWARD EXPANSION
AND THE
POSTAL SERVICE
1835-1861

The remarkable growth of the postal service of the United States during the fifteen year period prior to the Civil War is apparent in table 1.[70]

Table 1.   Growth of United States Postal Service, 1845-1860

Year Ending 30 June	Number of Post Offices	Annual Miles				
		Rail-road	Steam-boat	Coach	Mode not Specified	Total
1845	14,183	3,900*		140,040*		143,940
1850	18,417	6,886	9,725	40,776	121,285	193,751
1855	24,410	18,333	14,619	49,203	145,753	227,908
1860	28,498	27,129	14,976	54,577	143,912	240,594

*Mileage of railroad and steamboat mail routes was reported as a combined total; mileage for transportation of the mails by horse, sulky, and coach routes was reported as a combined total.

The increase of nearly 100,000 miles of post roads between 1845 and 1860 was largely due to the westward movement of population.

In the early 1830s, on the eve of Texas independence, American settlers in that region found that mail service in northern Mexico was far less efficient than the worst service offered in the United States. The postrider from Mexico City consumed three weeks on the trail to San Antonio and an additional four days to Santa Fe. By 1833, the Americans in Texas were sending their mail overland to the Gulf, where it was placed on ships bound for New Orleans. On 20 October 1835 the revolutionary Texas government provided for the establishment of an independent postal system with John Rice Jones as Postmaster General. The first route was established about 3 November 1835 between San Felipe de Austin, Texas, to Cantonment Jessup in the United States. The postal organization was instituted by Texan .law on 13 December 1835 and a series of routes began to criss-cross the new Republic. The Act of 6 February 1840 reorganized the routes and enumerated thirty-six different lines with weekly service. Jones made attempts to follow the postal practices current in the United States, even obtaining sample forms and blanks from Washington. The postage rates established on 30 October 1835 were based on the sheet-and-mileage-zone formula, with the highest rate for a single-sheet letter being 37½ cents for a distance of more than 200 miles. Periodic rate revisions followed and, on the whole, the postage in Texas was quite high. Officials of the government were given the franking privilege and publishers were permitted to exchange up to fifty newspapers free of postage with other publishers.[71]

Generally speaking, the Texas postal system was absorbed without difficulty by the United States after several initial problems had been

Revenue	Expenditures	Postage Stamps Issued	Stamped Envelopes and Wrappers Issued
$4,289,842	$ 4,320,732	None	None
5,499,985	5,212,953	1,540,545	None
6,642,136	9,968,342	72,977,300	23,451,725
8,518,067	14,874,601	216,370,660	29,280,025

resolved. An act of 29 May 1846 established United States postal routes in Texas and a contract was let to transport mails between New Orleans and Galveston once every five days in two steamships, the *Galveston* and *New York*. Shortly after this service started, the *New York* was lost in a storm. The special agent of the Post Office Department, Daniel J. Toler, who was carrying special instructions for the improvement of postal service in Texas, perished with the *New York*. The *Galveston,* at that time, was engaged in carrying troops, and so the restoration of efficient service over the 3,186 miles of postal routes in Texas was delayed.[72] Between 1846 and 1851, the number of post offices in Texas grew from 119 to 328.[73] By 31 May 1861 mails in Texas were carried over 19,664 miles of routes, including 2,095 miles by steamboats and 180 miles by railroad, serving 923 post offices.[74]

Elsewhere, other Americans had begun to populate the vast territories west of the Mississippi. The Mormon settlement in Utah was served by private carriers and travelers as early as 1847. In April 1848 a private express company made an attempt to establish service between various communities in California and Independence, Missouri, but after one trip the gold excitement put an end to the enterprise. United States military authorities provided courier service between their posts and at times made this service available to the public. While employed by the Army, "Kit" Carson enjoyed the distinction of carrying the first overland mail from coast to coast in 1848. Federal post offices were established at Astoria and Oregon City in 1847, at San Francisco in 1848, and at Salt Lake City in 1849, but the actual transmittal of mail between these western towns and the eastern United States was difficult to accomplish. At the close of 1847, the Department had received no bids on advertised mail contracts to Oregon and had received no reports from the postmasters or special agent assigned to inaugurate the service. The opening days of the San Francisco post office coincided with reports of gold strikes, and all hands aboard the *California,* the first mail steamship to arrive, deserted the vessel in port to search for gold, thus delaying the first eastbound mail scheduled under a new contract.[75]

Although other routes were established, the most significant east-west mail service between 1849 and 1858 was the "Ocean Route," carried on under three contracts which covered the route from New York City to Panama, the section overland across the Isthmus of Panama, and the Pacific section from the west coast of Panama to San Francisco and Oregon. After the delay at San Francisco noted above, the first eastward service over the route commenced on 12 April 1849 when the *Oregon* steamed from San Francisco to Panama City. The *Oregon's* crew had been retained aboard the vessel by force. In 1855 the transit across the Isthmus was improved with the completion of the Panama Railroad, and by 1858 mail was transported between New York and San Francisco in a little more than three weeks. For awhile, Cornelius Vanderbilt's steamships competed with the contractors by offering faster service via the Nicaraguan Isthmus, but his line failed to win a mail contract and the supremacy of the Pacific Mail Steamship Company continued. Another contract line offered semi-monthly mail service after October 1858 between New Orleans and San Francisco via the Isthmus of Tehuantepec, Mexico. This route, however, was discontinued in 1859.[76]

Although a post office had been established at Salt Lake City in 1849, the initial bi-monthly mail service to Council Bluffs, Iowa, was performed by Almond W. Babbitt at his own expense. Such an arrangement naturally, was unsatisfactory. Overland mail under contract was inaugurated from Independence, Missouri, to Salt Lake City in 1850 on a thirty-day schedule by pack animals, but vast stretches of territory without post offices and severe winter weather prevented the schedules from being maintained. In 1851, a route was established between Salt Lake City and Fort Laramie via Fort Bridger. Monthly service (in good weather) was established, also in 1851, between Salt Lake City and Sacramento, via Folsom, Placerville, and the Carson Valley. The mail route between Independence, Missouri, and Santa Fe, New Mexico, was established in 1847, with regular monthly coach service starting in 1850. By 1854, twenty-five-day mail service was performed over a coach line between San Antonio and Santa Fe, with improvements resulting in weekly service in 1858.[77] In 1851, the number of post offices in the newly settled regions were reported as follows: California, 21; Minnesota, 17; Nebraska, 3; New Mexico, 6; Oregon, 40; and Utah, 6.[78] In 1859, the mail service in the western states and territories could be characterized in part as seen in table 2.[79]

Table 2. Mail Service in Western United States and Territories, 1859

| States and Territories | Number of Post Offices | Annual Miles | | | | | Letter Postage Paid |
		Rail-road	Steam-boat	Coach	Mode not Specified	Total	
Texas	714	82	2,322	4,095	13,918	20,417	$ 8,273
California	318	22	1,285	4,946	1,606	7,859	54,987
Oregon	98	-	144	125	719	988	3,007
New Mexico Terr.	22	-	-	347	80	427	347
Utah Terr.	46	-	-	917	533	1,450	1,463
Nebraska Terr	86	-	-	536	1,236	1,772	1,114
Kansas Terr.	209	-	-	3,164	2,558	5,722	2,473
Washington Terr.	44	-	340	-	416	756	1,084

Service on the overland routes improved considerably. In 1858 it was reported that mail between St. Joseph, Missouri, and Placerville, California, via Salt Lake City, Utah, was carried once a week in thirty-eight days each way. Postmaster General Aaron V. Brown stated that "this service has been performed with remarkable regularity, insomuch as to merit special commendation."[80]

Public criticism of the service performed by the Pacific Mail Steamship Company gradually developed and the proposals to build a transcontinental railroad had been discussed since 1852. Although the sectionalism grounded in the slavery issue prevented the selection of a rail route, an Act of 3 March 1857 authorized the establishment of an improved transcontinental mail route between a "point on the Mississippi river as the contractors may select" and San Francisco. Postmaster General Brown, from Tennessee, selected a route—despite the stipulations of the Act—which began at St. Louis, Missouri, and at Memphis, Tennessee, converged at Little Rock, Arkansas, and proceeded to Preston, the "best" crossing of the Rio Grande above El Paso, over "the new road being opened and constructed under the direction of the Secretary of the Interior," to Fort Yuma and San Francisco, California. Brown secured the agreement of the bidders to adjust their proposals to apply to this route and then awarded the six-year contract to John Butterfield and his associates on 16 September 1857. The annual payment to Butterfield amounted to $600,000 for semi-weekly service in stage coaches and celerity wagons. The first coaches were of the Concord type, which could accommodate four passengers, their baggage, and five to six hundred pounds of mail. Larger vehicles were secured later. By 1860, teams could be changed every ten or fifteen miles along the route.[81]

Butterfield's service on the "Southern Route" began 15 September 1858 with the simultaneous departure of coaches from San Francisco and St. Louis. The initial trips were completed ahead of the scheduled twenty-five days. Celebrations for both the departures and arrivals at the terminals were held, and, until the beginning of the Civil War, service remained satisfactory. By 1860, more letter mail was carried by Butterfield coaches than by the steamers.[82]

The Southern Route, however, was roundly criticized by northern interests. Brown used eighteen pages of fine print in his *Annual Report* for 1858 to justify the selection of the route in answer to his numerous critics.[83] He improved the other western routes and attempted to exhibit no partiality for north or south, but the issue was debated for years until northern and western interests secured the passage of the Act of 2 March 1861. The new law stipulated that the mail contract on the Southern Route was to be changed on 1 July 1861 so that the operators of the Butterfield line could transfer their service to the Central Route. Denver and Salt Lake City were to be served with mails at least tri-weekly. The law also required that the four-year million-dollar contract was to provide service for transcontinental letter mail six times a week, "to be carried through in twenty day's time, eight months of the year, and in twenty-three days the remaining four months of the year.[84] The law also required that a pony express be provided over the route until the transcontinental telegraph was completed—actually a continuation of the pony express service already in existence at the time. Although the transfer of the Butterfield line to the Central Route had been strongly urged in 1860, the operations in Texas were interrupted on 1 March 1861 by rebellious forces flexing their muscles on the eve of the Civil War. The revised overland stage service commenced on the new Central Route, in accordance with the law, on 1 July 1861.[85]

THE WESTERN
PONY EXPRESS
1860-1861

Private express lines were a principal feature of western communications during the early period of settling the Far West. While the government provided mail service on "principal routes," the express companies offered supplemental and rival service over such lines as, for example, the Nicaraguan Route. As the adventurous miners moved over the hills and mountains, the express operators followed quickly to maintain service between the camps and isolated towns and the nearest post office. The carriage of letters, gold dust, newspapers, and parcels was a lucrative business—undoubtedly more dependable than prospecting itself. Such express services were offered by both individuals or small organizations as well as the large national companies such as the Adams, American, National, and Wells Fargo concerns.[86]

In many respects, the most dramatic visions of the American postal service are associated with the words "Pony Express." The western pony express, however, was not a service originally established by the United States Post Office Department.

William H. Russel and John S. Jones organized the Leavenworth & Pike's Peak Express Company to provide stage service from Leavenworth to Denver when gold was discovered in Colorado. Russell had secured the Hockaday contract to carry U.S. mail from the Missouri to Salt Lake City and, on 28 October 1859 reorganized the Leavenworth & Pike's Peak line under the auspices of Russel, Majors & Waddell (a freighting firm) to form the Central Overland, California & Pike's Peak Express Company (C.O.C. & P.P.Ex. Co.). When the Salt Lake City-Placerville mail contract with George Chorpenning was annulled on 11 May 1860, the C.O.C. & P.P. Ex. Co. became the sole contractor for the Central Route. Both sections of the route brought a combined annual pay of $260,000 for carrying the mail, compared with the $600,000 paid to the Butterfield interests for carrying mail on the Southern Route. Aware that the public controversy over the virtues of the Southern and Central Routes would lead to revised postal legislation, the firm of Russell, Majors & Waddell decided to dramatically keep the Central Route before the public's attention and gamble to win a more lucrative mail contract to carry all or most of the transcontinental mail. Abraham Lincoln's nomination heightened the sectional controversy, and Russell, Majors & Waddell launched their anti-Southern Route campaign with the inauguration of a Pony Express service.[87]

Russell, Majors & Waddell set about organizing the new Pony Express in the early spring of 1860. Horses were purchased and dispersed at stations along the Central Route. Small riders were hired and special equipment was secured. The saddles were extremely light in weight and were covered by a *mochilla*—a rectangular sheet of leather with a small locked pouch for mail in each of the four corners and with cut-outs for the saddle horn and seat. When horses were changed at relay stations, the *mochilla* was quickly removed from the first horse and thrown over the saddle of the second

A Pony Express rider passes pole-setters erecting the overland telegraph line in the summer of 1861. (After a painting by George M. Ottinger.)

horse, eliminating the need to change the letters from pouch to pouch or to waste precious time in loosening and tightening saddle cinches. The saddle and *mochilla* had a combined weight of only thirteen pounds. Two minutes were allowed for each stop at the relay stations, which were spaced about fifteen miles apart and under the care of two men. The riders and station attendants were armed, but riders relied mainly on the speed of their mounts to escape the pursuit of hostile Indians.[88]

On 3 April 1860 the Pony Express was inaugurated. The rider from the east, "Billy" Richardson, departed from St. Joseph, Missouri, at 6:30 p.m. with the mail for San Francisco. Exactly six days later, the westbound pony arrived at Salt Lake City, Utah, passed through Carson City, Nevada, at 2:30 p.m. on 12 April and arrived at Sacramento, California, at 5:30 p.m. on the 13th. Horse and rider boarded the steamboat at Sacramento and arrived at San Francisco at 1:30 a.m. on 14 April amid cheers, band music, and speeches. The express from San Francisco to St. Joseph also accomplished the trip within the scheduled ten and a half days.[89]

Letters and newspaper slips carried over the route were at first charged $5.00 per half ounce, but in April 1861 the fee was reduced to $2.00 per half-ounce. On 1 July 1861, in accordance with the stipulations of the Overland Mail Act, the express fee was reduced to $1.00 per half-ounce.[90] Letters were generally written on tissue to conserve weight and remain within the half-ounce rate. Between November 1860 and April 1861, an average of forty-one letters per trip were carried to San Francisco; between April and July 1861, the average became sixty-four per trip; and after July until the end of service in October, the average rose to ninety per trip. Eastbound express mails were heavier, with one trip in April 1860 accounting for 205 letters. About 350 letters per trip were carried eastward during the final month and a half of operations.[91]

Indian disturbances interrupted Pony Express service from the latter part of May to the latter part of June 1860, but service was resumed on a semi-weekly schedule and remained efficient until October 1861. Winter lengthened the scheduled time to fifteen days, but the schedule was seldom maintained. News dispatches carried between the temporary telegraph terminals of Fort Kearny and Fort Churchill, Nevada, varied in transit time from eleven to seventeen days during the winter of 1860-1861. With the coming of better weather, Pony Express service improved and construction of the telegraph line was resumed. On 26 October 1861 the transcontinental telegraph was completed with the meeting of the two lines at Salt Lake City and the Pony Express came to an end.[92]

Although the law of 2 March 1861 provided for the relocation of the "Butterfield line" to the Central Route, Russell, Majors & Waddell made a working agreement to continue the operation of the St. Joseph-Placerville Pony Express mentioned in the act and to operate the daily mail coaches between the Missouri River and Salt Lake City. The Butterfield line, known simply as the Overland Mail Company and at that time headed by William B. Dinsmore, operated the Western Division of the stage line between Salt Lake City and Placerville. The fifty-mile portion to Sacramento was operated by the Pioneer Stage Line under agreement with Dinsmore's company.[93]

The receipts from the entire Pony Express operation amounted to only $91,404. Russell, Majors & Waddell had lost an estimated half million dollars on the enterprise and owed about $200,000 to Benjamin Holliday alone. Russell resigned as president, the original company was reorganized, and a struggle for financial survival ensued. Finally, Holliday acquired possession of the C.O.C. & P.P. Ex. Co. in March 1862.[94]

THE CIVIL WAR
1861-1865

The interruption of the main overland mail line in March 1861 heralded the beginning of new problems for postal officials throughout the country. Although there was a certain amount of administrative confusion in Washington at the beginning of the Civil War, mail service in the North remained efficient and was even improved upon to a remarkable degree. On the other hand, postal matters in the Confederacy were in a nearly constant state of deterioration throughout the War.

John H. Reagan of Texas was appointed as the Postmaster General of the Confederate States of America about a month after the Confederacy was organized in February 1861. Reagan maintained the existing post offices in the South and, during the initial phase of the War, post office business was conducted as usual with U.S. money and U.S. postage stamps. Mail continued to be carried from North to South until hostilities interrupted some of the service and until the United States prohibited these exchanges on and after 1 June 1861. Of the 28, 586 post offices in the United States at this time, United States Postmaster General Montgomery Blair reported that 8,535 post offices in the "disloyal" states had made no quarterly returns for the third quarter of the fiscal year (January-March) 1861. He made special mention, however, that 167 offices in (western) Virginia remained loyal and within the United States postal organization.[95]

In addition to prohibiting the exchange of mails between the North and South, the United States Government demonetized current issues of postage stamps and brought out a new series of stamps in different designs, making the old issue worthless as a government obligation. The demonetization was carried out in stages as new stamps became available. The country was divided into zones for this purpose and the western regions, naturally, were the last to receive the new stamps.[96] Furthermore, to put the South entirely on its own resources, the Confederacy was unable to secure diplomatic recognition and failed to negotiate postal treaties with foreign governments. The effective naval blockade which the U.S. Government maintained made it extremely difficult for the South to communicate with the "outside world," despite the daring exploits of the swift vessels which occasionally ran the blockade.[97]

Postage rates of the United States continued in force in the Confederacy until 1 June 1861 when high rates (essentially the U.S. rates of 1845) became effective. Letters carried less than 500 miles were charged five cents per half-ounce; those carried more than 500 miles were charged ten cents. These rates were soon found inadequate and on 30 June 1862 the postage for half-ounce letters carried less than 500 miles also became ten cents. Local, or "drop," letters were charged two cents per half ounce.[98]

The lack of postage stamps became a nagging problem to people who had become accustomed to them during the fifteen-year period prior to the War. The Confederate government set about securing stamps in London from the firm of Thomas De La Rue & Co., but such matters could not be taken care of rapidly enough. The shipments of new stamps and printing plates from England were greatly delayed. When the new postage rates became effective on 1 June 1861, postmasters were without valid stamps of any kind. They reverted to the old practices of indicating postage by applying rate markings to the covers. Some postmasters sold provisional adhesive stamps or stamped envelopes of their own creation, valid only at the issuing offices. Later, after Confederate stamps had been issued, some postmasters had recourse to such provisional measures whenever the supply of government stamps became exhausted. Finally, the government issued lithographed stamps in October 1861, in themselves a type of "provisional" issue pending the arrival of typographed stamps and the printing plates from London. As luck would have it, the first shipment of stamps from De La Rue fell into Union hands. In April 1862, however, some of the five-cent London stamps were placed on sale. Subsequent printing plates from London were on Richmond presses in August. Nevertheless, this particular issue inadequately served its purpose, for the increase of postage rates from five to ten cents rendered the issue inappropriate after 30 June 1862 and, of necessity, many of the five-cent stamps were used in pairs. Undaunted by such problems, the postal authorities secured truly beautiful and well executed stamps printed from recessed-engraved plates by the Richmond firm of Archer & Daly. The stamps were made available between April and June 1863, in two-, ten-, and twenty-cent denominations. The supply of stamps was again threatened in 1864, when Union forces menaced the capital and the stamp production operations were moved to Columbia, South Carolina.[99]

The Confederacy was not as liberal in matters concerning official mail as had become traditional before hostilities. The only correspondence carried free of postage was that of the Confederate post office department. Southern soldiers and congressmen were permitted to send their letters "postage due."[100]

By mutual agreement between the Confederacy and the Union, prisoner-of-war letters were exchanged at designated points. Civilian letters, under a flag of truce, were also exchanged on occasion, but this practice was not encouraged. These classes of mail were subject to censorship.[101] The exchange of mail by private express companies between Union Louisville and Confederate Nashville was an interesting development of the early days of the War, but these exchanges lasted only until 26 August 1861 when the Federal government prohibited such intercourse.[102]

Despite the long struggle of arms, from April 1861 to mid-1865, every military success of the North was a damaging blow to Southern communications. A chronological table of military events partly tells the story: "Feb. 23, 1862—Nashville, Tenn., occupied by Federal troops . . . Mar. 14, 1862—New Bern, N.C., occupied by Federal troops as permament base . . . Apr. 24, 1862—Fall of New Orleans, La. . . ."[103] When the Union forces gained control of the Mississippi River, regular east-west mail service was disrupted. Special Confederate government "express" service was provided under contract in 1863 to restore communications between the divided regions. Twice a week, couriers evaded Union troops over bridle and cattle tracks, which led through swampy wilderness areas to reach the water's edge, rowed their skiffs quietly under the cover of darkness between the Union gunboats on the river, and landed on the opposite shore. This critical service was carried out between the alternate terminals of Shreveport or Alexandria, Louisiana, and Meridian or Brandon, Mississippi. Letters carried by the nerveless expressmen were charged postage of forty cents per half ounce.[104]

The war that had started with band music and a rush of volunteers became a drudgery of casualty lists, draft calls, and shortages. The envelopes bearing pictures of heroes, patriotic slogans, and Confederate flags (there seemed to be an endless variety) gave way to home-made envelopes of ledger paper, wallpaper, and envelopes used twice over.[105] Blockaded, divided, and short of supplies, the people of the Confederacy felt the mounting pressure of Union forces before the end of 1864. Savannah fell December 21; Columbia and Charleston fell 17 February 1865; and Wilmington, North Carolina—like Charleston and Savannah, once the proud haven for blockade runners—fell 22 February. After Richmond was lost and Lee surrendered, significant Southern resistance soon ended. The government collapsed in May and fighting ended in June 1865.

The Civil War brought increased use of the mails in the North, and the problem of congestion at main post offices was considerably heightened. The Department appointed special agents to speed the distribution of mails at critical points such as New York, Cleveland, and Cairo, Illinois, and, before the end of hostilities, was well on the way toward developing a new system of nation-wide mail distribution which was actually needed long before the start of the War. The Confederacy represented a loss of only eleven states with a population of nine million people, more than one third of whom were slaves, while the twenty-three Northern states had a population of nearly twenty-two million people, mostly free. Although Southern guerillas had interrupted service on such lines as the Hannibal-St. Joseph route, Northern communications were never permanently damaged. The loss of considerable numbers of mail bags in Southern hands and the increased volume of mail represented an unusual and unexpected expense, but costs were reduced in other areas. A new contract with the National Bank Note Co. for producing postage stamps represented an estimated saving of thirty percent over the former contract.[106]

The scarcity of small change in the North led to the Act of 17 July 1862, which directed the Secretary of the Treasury to furnish "postage and other stamps of the United States" for currency. Before the public fully understood how this plan was to be carried out, there was a "run" on post offices in the North and "extraordinary quantities" of stamps were purchased, some local supplies being exhausted. People began "cleaning" cancelled stamps and the Department set about searching for better cancelling ink, new handstampers for "the destruction of the postage stamp," and cancelling machines to do a better job of "killing" the stamps.[107] Better ink was found, but the stamp-destruction devices were unsatisfactory. The original "Postage Currency" plan entailed pasting postage stamps on Treasury paper but, as eventually carried out, beginning on 21 August 1862 resulted in printed notes bearing facsimiles of current stamps. Postage Currency remained in use until 1876.[108]

Letters addressed to suspended Southern post offices represented a unique and heavy burden on the Dead Letter Office, which was responsible for returning undeliverable mail to senders. Some 46,697 letters addressed to "rebel states" were processed between 1 November 1861 and 1 November 1862. In the same period, 3,198 Southern letters were forwarded "postage due," since valid stamps were not available in the South. Furthermore, 13,463 letters intended for Southern addressees were returned to foreign countries bearing the "Mails Suspended" marking.[109] Contrary to expectation, these problems remained as the War continued. In 1863, Northerners addressed at least 21,200 letters to Southern destinations. Military authorities forwarded 3,114 Southern "flag of truce" letters for delivery in the North after performing the customary censorship.[110]

As the War came to an end, the U.S. Post Office Department began restoring service which had been suspended. By 15 November 1865, 241 mail routes had been placed in operation over 18,640 route miles. By 1 November 1866 only 3,234 of the 8,902 prewar Southern post offices had been restored to the Federal system. In 1867 the Department indicated that a great number of Southern post offices had been discontinued to enable the U.S. Auditor to close the accounts of the "late postmasters." Reestablishments were indicated thereafter as "new" post offices, with the *Annual Report* for 1867 failing to use the term "reestablished."[111]

Using statistics, the cost of the War to the Federal post office operation can only be approximated as shown in table 3.[112]

Table 3.   United States Post Office Statistics, 1860-1867

Year Ending 30 June	Number of Post Offices	Revenue	Expenditures	Postage Stamps issued	Stamped Envelopes & Wrappers issued
1860	28,498	$ 8,518,067	$14,874,601	216,370,660	29,280,025
1861	28,586	8,349,296	13,606,759	211,788,518	26,027,300
1862	28,875	8,299,821	11,125,364	251,307,105	27,234,159
1863	29,047	11,163,790	11,314,207	338,340,385	25,548,750
1864	28,878	12,438,254	12,644,786	334,054,610	28,218,800
1865	28,882	14,556,159	13,694,728	387,419,455	26,206,175
1866	29,389	14,386,986	15,352,079	347,734,325	39,094,725
1867	25,163	15,237,027	19,235,483	371,599,605	63,086,650

The nearly 9,000 Southern post offices were carried on the records of the Department throughout the War as those not submitting quarterly returns until the Auditor's adjustment was made in 1867. The subtle drop in revenues and expenditures at the beginning of the War is quite insignificant; however, the increase of more than six million dollars in annual revenues between 1861 and 1865 is remarkable. Postal reforms and improvements initiated by the North during the War were carried out under a basically sound financial operation, with postal revenues comparing very favorably with the expenditures. Unlike the South which suffered so badly during the War, the North was able to introduce improvements of such importance that the whole character of the Federal postal system was thereafter changed.

UNIFORM POSTAGE
AND FREE CITY
DELIVERY SERVICE
1863

In the midst of war, agitation for lower postage continued. Blair reviewed such proposals carefully, considered the reformed system of Great Britain to establish some guidelines for improvement, and recommended uniform postage and a reform of rate schedules for printed matter. The Act of 3 March 1863 established a uniform letter rate of three cents per half-ounce regardless of distance, thus eliminating the ten-cent transcontinental rate. Furthermore, it established rates according to "Classes," with three major categories of mail being initially defined. Printed matter rates were simplified and reduced. Weekly newspapers, for example, were charged five cents per quarter and book postage was established at four cents per four ounces. A general weight limit of four pounds per mailable article was also established.[113] The new law became effective 1 July 1863.

The same law created free letter carrier service in forty-nine of the larger Northern cities and towns. Across the Union 449 carriers were employed. Blair reported that, "in the city of New York there are now, daily, five deliveries from the office, and six collections of letters for the mails from the depositories [letter boxes] in the various parts of the cities. During the quarter ending 30 September 1863 there were delivered by carriers 2,069,418 letters, and 1,810,717 collected for the mails and city delivery, being an increase of 968,825 letters (about 25 percent) over the preceding and last quarter under the old system."[114] While most of the carrier offices were initially located in the northeastern quarter of the country, it is interesting that Louisville, Kentucky, was included in the new system. New York employed 137 carriers and Philadelphia, 119, but Chicago was not represented until the following year.[115] By 1864, delivery service was established in sixty-six cities with 685 letter carriers.[116] The following year, the service was discontinued at twenty-two of the smaller offices, but free delivery in larger cities was improved with an increased number of carriers.[117] In 1866, Postmaster General Alexander W. Randall, in making a plea for higher pay for postal employees, stated that "the letter carriers claim peculiar consideration. They travel every day from early in the morning until late at night, in heat and cold and rain and snow, all through the cities, distributing letters and papers without compensation enough to pay house rent."[118] Compensation was increased. In the same year, the southern cities of Memphis and Nashville were given carrier service. By November 1867 Randall could observe:[119]

This mode of delivery continues to grow in public favor, as is shown by the increase of postages on local matter, the reduction of the number of post office boxes, and the large decrease of advertised letters in several of the cities where the system has been more efficiently conducted. Experience, so far, justifies the belief that it will supersede the present system of box delivery, increase correspondence, especially in large cities, and not only pay its expenses, but yield a revenue to the department.

By 1880, 2,628 carriers operated from 104 offices and, by 1890, 9,066 carriers served 454 offices.[120]

DOMESTIC MONEY ORDER SERVICE 1864

The domestic money order system was inaugurated in 1864 under the Act of 17 May. Although registry service had rendered the mails more secure, the money order system largely eliminated the need to enclose currency in letters. Money orders were intended to discourage depredations and thefts. Furthermore, the new system partly met the demand for a convenient means whereby Union soldiers and their families could exchange money. This service was initially introduced at only 141 larger post offices but was eventually extended to virtually all offices, branches, and stations. Although the amount of the first money orders was limited to thirty dollars, this was increased to $100.00 by 1883. As inaugurated, the system was specifically designed to safeguard the transmission of small sums of money. Dead Letter Office statistics had shown that the average amount of money enclosed in letters was $4.53 in 1862 and $5.18 in 1864. Nominal fees for the initial service were fixed: for amounts from one to ten dollars, the fee was ten cents; for amounts up to twenty dollars, fifteen cents; and for thirty dollars, twenty cents.[121] The amount of domestic money orders issued in 1865, $1,360,122, had risen to $100,352,818 by 1880.[122]

THE RAILWAY POST OFFICE SYSTEM

In addition to introducing uniform postage rates, free city delivery service, and money order service during the War, the intercity mail transportation system was greatly improved. Railroads had made significant technological advances during the twenty years preceding the War and the Department began to reap important benefits. Although night travel by railroad was unusual in the 1830s, the locomotive headlight was becoming a common piece of equipment by the 1840s and lighted cars were being used quite frequently by the 1850s. Although eleven different track gauges had been introduced in the north, the "standard gauge," 4 feet, 8½ inches, was the more common by 1860. The telegraph was first employed for controlling rail traffic in 1851, and the gradual adoption of the telegraphic train order system resulted in safer transportation and improved schedules. Improved motive power, rails, and roadbeds resulted in higher speeds.[123] The growing importance of railroad transportation and the declining significance of the mail coach is indicated by the *Annual Report* for 1863, when transportation of the mails "By Coach" was deleted as a statistical category. Thereafter, coach transportation was incorporated under the statistical heading of mails carried with "Certainty, celerity, and security"—an all-inclusive and rather secondary category compared with railroad and steamboat mails.[124]

At the beginning of the Civil War, the Route Agent system had been essentially the same as it was since its introduction in 1837. Route Agent service on a main line was described in *Niles Register*, 18 May 1838 as follows.[125]

> Mail cars constructed under the direction of the Post Office Department are now running on the railroads between Washington and Philadelphia. They contain two apartments: one appropriated to the use of the great mails, and the other to the way mails; and a post-office agent. The latter apartment is fitted up with boxes, labeled with names of all the small offices on or near the railroad lines. It has also a letter box in front, into which letters may be put up to the moment of starting the cars, and anywhere on the road. The agent of the Post Office Department attends the mail from the post offices at the ends of the route, and sees it safely deposited in his car. As soon as the cars start, he opens the letter box and takes out all the letters, marking them so as to designate the place where they are put. He then opens the way-mail bag and distributes its contents into the several boxes. As the cars approach a post office, the agent takes out the contents of the proper box and puts them into a pouch. The engineer slackens the pace speed of the train, and the agent hands the pouch to a postmaster or a carrier, who stands beside the track to take it, receiving from him at the same time another pouch with the matter to be sent from that office. This the agent immediately opens and distributes its contents into the proper boxes. Having supplied thus all the way offices, the agent, when arrived at the end of the route, sees the mail safely delivered into the post office.

Although most Route Agents did not have an entire car for their work, the duties were primarily the same on all lines. Mail for points beyond the end of the line was simply pouched for the terminal post office or the nearest Distributing Post Office. Mail was not usually exchanged with other rail routes and the need for additional sortings at the Distributing Post Offices (D.P.O.s) represented unnecessary delays. A modified "Express Agent" system was introduced in 1857 to enable some Agents to accompany certain mails over connecting lines to specified terminals. Nevertheless, Express Agents did not separate mail for connecting routes or for points beyond the D.P.O.s.[126]

The D.P.O.s had been established in 1810 to accelerate mail transportation in the stagecoach era. By 1859, there were fifty D.P.O.s serving as redistribution points. But because postmasters of D.P.O.s received commissions for the mail handled in their offices, abuses in the routing of letters became apparent and as a letter passed from one D.P.O. to another, the postage fee was often committed to pay commissions rather than the cost of actual service. Furthermore, the redistribution of letters from route to route had to be performed together with the other task of making up city mails for carrier routes and local mails for suburban and regional offices. The Express Agent system was deemed too costly and was curtailed in 1859, despite the fact that Philadelphia-Chicago mails had been carried through in thirty-six hours. In 1860, however, mail was carried at night between New York and Boston, resulting in improved schedules. Night service was extended to Washington, "so that mails and passengers leaving Boston at 2 p.m. arrive at Washington by 9:30 a.m., or in less than twenty-three hours."[127]

If the D.P.O. system had presented problems in peacetime, they were small in comparison with the troubles at the start of the War. Realizing that the mails could be worked while in transit aboard trains, William A. Davis, an assistant postmaster at St. Joseph, Missouri, personally inaugurated a system of performing D.P.O. work in a modified baggage car on the Hannibal & St. Joseph Railroad in July 1862. After deadheading eastward to Palmyra, Davis opened the pouches normally destined for the St. Joseph D.P.O. and made up the California mails before the train arrived at the western terminal, making a connection with the earliest possible coach departure from St. Joseph. The service was in the nature of an experiment with the full approval of the Post Office Department.[128]

The large number of Route Agents—370 were employed in 1862—were unable to relieve D.P.O. congestion as long as they were unable to sort the "through" mails in transit. When the War was in its early stages, George B. Armstrong, in charge of the Chicago D.P.O., was assigned the task of clearing the tremendous quantity of mail for the army that had accumulated at Cairo, Ill. A man of vision, Armstrong had considered a reform utilizing "traveling post offices" in 1854, long before his wartime assignment. Experiences at Chicago and Cairo convinced him that a drastic reform was needed. A.N. Zevely, Third Assistant Postmaster General, was also searching for ways to speed the mails. In 1864 Zevely placed New York City clerks on board some trains entering that city to sort mail in transit for immediate distribution on arrival for carrier and suburban routes. In the same year, Zevely was placed in charge of distribution reform experiments for the entire nation. He requested certain railroads to furnish special cars and asked Armstrong to submit a detailed plan in writing. Armstrong urged that post offices be reclassified according to their functional nature, i.e., terminals, junctions, star route offices, etc.; that all possible packaging of mails to D.P.O.s be discontinued and that the letters be grouped and tied according to a common office of destination or route junction; and that the transit of letters should not be interrupted—a goal to be accomplished by the use of traveling post offices wherein all possible sorting should be done after only the essential groupings had taken place at the terminals.[129]

Armstrong's plans were carried out. He placed the first "Railway Post Office" car (R.P.O.) in operation between Chicago and Clinton, Iowa, on the Chicago & North Western Railroad on 28 August 1864. The through mails were sorted for advance connections and local exchanges as well. Thus the Railway Mail Service was created, a reform so simple that one wonders why it had not evolved from the Route Agent system years before. Postmaster General William Dennison modestly reported on 15 November 1865:[130]

> Railway post offices have been established on several leading railroads, and arrangements are in progress for their introduction on other lines. The result, so far, encourages the hope that the system, by accelerating the transmission of correspondence, and lessening the number of distributing offices, will be of permanent advantage to the postal interests of the country.

Until the new service was firmly established and understood by all postal employees, some confusion was noticeable in mail handling, particularly before the number of D.P.O.s was substantially reduced. But problems were rapidly solved. Railway Mail Service officials supervised the make-up of outgoing mails at large offices. Trackside mail cranes were developed to reduce hazards in exchanging mail "on the fly" on nonstop runs. Especially constructed "full-length" forty-foot R.P.O. cars were introduced on some lines in 1867. Route Agents formed a separate body of employees but were usually assigned to branch lines. It was not until 1882, that Route Agents were incorporated into the R.P.O. clerk force. In 1867, clerk strength at eight D.P.O.s had been reduced and congestion at all main offices was noticeably relieved.[131] The nation's postal system had undergone a revolutionary change.

Railroads also revolutionized transcontinental communications. Wells Fargo had fallen heir to much of the old western coaching business, even carrying the transcontinental mails as a subcontractor to the Holladay and Dinsmore interests. The end of an era, however, was recorded by Postmaster General John Creswell in his *Annual Report* for 1869.[132]

> The contract or agreement entered into on the 21st October, 1868, between the Post Office Department and Messrs. Wells, Fargo & Co., for the transportation of the United States mails between the western terminus of the Union Pacific railroad and the eastern terminus of the Central Pacific, for the term of one year from October 1, 1868, or until the two railroads should meet,

at the rate of $1,750,000 per annum, subject to deduction *pro rata* for every section of fifty miles of railroad completed and reported to the department ready to carry the mails, expired on the 9th of May, 1869, the railroads having effected a junction and reported ready to carry mails through on the 10th.

Improved railroad mail service rendered another coach route (the "Smoky Hill Route") between Cheyenne Wells and Denver unnecessary after June 1869. At the same time, a third route was affected:[133]

The contract made on the 28th October, 1868, with Wells, Fargo & Co., to carry the mails for one year . . . from Cheyenne City to Denver, one hundred and two miles, . . . was re-let . . . This is all that remains of the old overland mail service, and this will doubtless be superseded in a few months, a railroad between Cheyenne City and Denver being now in rapid course of construction.

Under the old overland coach contracts, transcontinental mails had consumed twenty days between Sacramento and the Missouri during four winter months and sixteen days during the remaining eight months. The new railroad service dramatically reduced transit time:[134]

San Francisco to	Average time			Fastest time		
	days	hrs.	mins.	days	hrs.	mins.
Washington	6	23	15	7	7	11
New York	6	15	20	7	2	23
Boston	7	4	0	7	19	25
Chicago	5	7	30	5	14	55
St. Louis	5	1	30	5	16	23

In the same year, 1869, the important New York-New Orleans mails were dispatched twice daily via Lynchburg and Knoxville, averaging about ninety hours in transit, and via Louisville in about ninety-one hours per trip. Three daily New York-Chicago mails were also being carried by railroad in less than thirty-one hours per trip.[135]

The rapidly increasing importance of mail transportation by railroad is indicated in table 4.[136] In 1860, there were 27,129 miles of railroad mail routes; in 1874, there were 67,734 miles of railroad mail routes.

The growing supremacy of the railroads over other forms of mail transportation, especially steamboats, is clearly apparent. The railroads offered faster transportation and more direct service to many more centers of population, whether on navigable waters or not. The smallest hamlet on a railroad line could be served, even though the mail trains did not stop there. Domestic waterway mail service, which had been so important before the Civil War, dropped sharply before the end of the century. In 1860, there had been 14,976 miles of steamboat routes; in 1870, 20,695 miles; in 1880, 23,320 miles; and in 1890, 10,456 miles.[137]

Table 4.   United States Domestic Mail Transportation, 1862-1874

	Annual Miles			
Year	Modes not Specified*	Steamboat	Railroad	Total
1862	28,641,587	2,013,710	22,777,219	53,432,525
1864	30,901,281	2,112,134	23,301,942	56,315,357
1866	37,816,486	3,411,962	30,609,467	71,837,914
1868	45,540,587	3,797,560	34,886,178	84,224,325
1870	45,350,641	4,122,385	47,551,970	97,024,996
1872	48,184,137	4,308,436	62,491,749	114,984,322
1874	52,088,206	4,078,725	72,460,545	128,627,476

*Includes stage coach and Star routes.

POSTAL CARDS
AND THE
FREE MAIL REFORM
1873

Two important improvements were carried out under the administration of Postmaster General John Creswell. Postal cards, first introduced by Austria in 1869, were authorized in the United States by the Acts of 8 June 1872 and 9 January 1873. Creswell reported:[138]

The delivery of the cards on requisitions was commenced on the 1st of May last. As predicted, they have been favorably received. They have supplied a public want, and have made a new and remunerative business for the Department.

Between 1 May and 30 September 1873, 64,302,300 postal cards had been issued. The first U.S. cards were prepared in denominations of one cent each, a postal rate which was to remain unchanged until 1952, with but one exceptional and brief increase to two cents during the war years 1917-1919. The postal card became quite popular and, in a sense, represented a measure of success for the champions of "penny postage." Although messages on cards cannot be confidential, many billions have been used. In 1880 alone, more than 272,550,000 were issued. The related convenience —the "private mailing card," or post card on which an adhesive stamp is affixed—was not authorized under the one-cent rate until 1898.[139]

The traditional right of government officials to send correspondence without postage was reexamined in the early 1870s, when obvious abuses and the bulk of free mail matter had reached ridiculous proportions. Free matter had to be collected, sorted, transported, and delivered, just the same as other mail. Postal officials complained about the unexpected "dumping"

The steamboat *City of Providence* of the St. Louis and New Orleans
Anchor Line. Note the legend "U.S. Mail" on the wheel housing.
(Photograph from the Library of Congress.)

of Congressional mail in great quantities at the most inconvenient times.
Postmaster General Creswell protested vigorously against the existing free
franking system and in the *Annual Report* for 1872 stated:[140]

> In my three previous reports, I have urgently recommended the immediate
> and unconditional repeal of the franking privilege. The experience of the past
> year has strengthened my conviction that its abolition is absolutely necessary
> to an efficient, economical, and vigorous administration of our postal system.
> . . . It will appear that the actual cost of free matter, if charged with the
> regular rates of postage, was then [1871] 12,543,327.72 annually. During the
> late presidential canvass, the quantity of such free matter was largely
> increased, and I think it safe to say that the free matter carried during the past
> year, if taxed at ordinary rates, would have yielded a revenue of three and a
> half millions of dollars, a sum larger than the entire deficiency of the year.

The free franking of mail was abolished as of 1 July 1873. Special postage
stamps and stamped envelopes were prepared, bearing the names of the
various Departments and denominations corresponding with current postage rates. The Departments purchased the stamps with their own
appropriated funds. During the first full year under the new system, the Post
Office Department derived $1,769,301 from the sale of official stamps and
envelopes to other government agencies.[141]

While the reform seemed to be a noble effort, the basic law was eroded
within a short time. In 1875, for example, *The Congressional Record,* parts
thereof, and speeches and reports included in the *Record* were restored to
the free mail category if franked by a Member of Congress or a Delegate.
Other printed public documents were allowed free under the franking
system, together with seeds distributed by Congressmen, Delegates, and the
Commissioner of Agriculture. In 1877, the present system of mailing official

correspondence was inaugurated. The Act of 3 March provided for the use of the endorsement, including the words "Official Business" and the name of the Department or Agency. The Act also stipulated that anyone sending private correspondence under the free "Official Business" endorsement would be subject to a fine of $300. The penalty notice was imprinted on the stationery which, within a short time, became known as "penalty envelopes." The franking privilege was restored to Senators, Representatives, and other office holders, and the work of Creswell and his fellow reformers was largely nullified. For a while, the Department stamps were still valid because the restoration of the free franking system was gradual. Within a short time, however, penalty envelopes and authorized franking rendered the stamps useless. On 5 July 1884 the short-lived "official" stamps were declared obsolete.[142]

Creswell had also fought for other reforms and a wider range of activities for the Federal postal service. In 1873, Creswell used eleven pages of his *Annual Report* to develop an eloquent plea for Congress to establish a postal savings system, citing the success of the British postal savings banks which had been introduced in 1862. The Panic of 1873 had just begun with the failure of three leading securities firms and a ten-day holiday for the New York stock exchange. "The events of the past few weeks," wrote Creswell, "have awakened a lively interest in a plan heretofore submitted, for securing the savings of the great body of the people by a pledge of the credit and faith of the United States."[143] Creswell's plan was well developed, but a postal savings system was not inaugurated until 1911 Marshall Jewell, took office in 1874, had an opposite view. Furthermore, he abandoned Creswell's proposal to make the telegraph business a national monopoly as it was in some other nations. Jewell curtly announced "that the time has come when a resolute effort should be made to determine how far the Post-Office Department can properly go in its efforts to accommodate the public, without trespassing unwarrantably upon the sphere of private enterprise."[144] Jewell also promised a policy of strict economy. Business firms were failing, mills were closing, unemployment was growing, and the enterprises of the Department were to be affected by the depressed conditions until about 1878.

INTERNATIONAL POSTAL REFORM: THE UNIVERSAL POSTAL UNION 1874

During the nineteenth century, the international mails had become increasingly important, not only because they had grown in volume but because the postal administrations of most nations continued to concern themselves with acquiring complete control over every aspect of the exchange of correspondence. The steam engine had also revolutionized transoceanic transportation. In 1840, Cunard steamers had replaced the British sailing packets and in 1865 the Pacific Mail Steamship Company had inaugurated scheduled transpacific mail service under a U.S. contract.[145]

The old "ship letter" method of transporting international mail gradually gave way to a new system. Although the British packet postage rates had always been higher for the premium service, a series of bilateral postal treaties further complicated international postage rate structures. The United States concluded its first postal treaty with the state of Bremen in 1847, although the rates did not become effective in the United States until 1 March 1848. Thereafter, treaties with other nations were concluded so that, by 1862, eight different arrangements were in effect. Under the treaties, rates were fixed, accounts with foreign countries were kept and adjusted, and the postage collected was distributed between the countries in proportions fixed by the conventions. Rates were generally determined according to the domestic postage applicable in the country from which the letter was sent, the rate paid for conveyance by ship ("sea postage"), the rate charged by each country through which the letter passed in transit to its destination, and, finally, the domestic postage of the country in which the letter was delivered. The "sea postage" and intermediary transit charges varied according to the route or nationality of the vessels, and it was often possible to send letters by several routes to the same destination. A letter addressed to Australia, for example, could be sent by six different routes, and the postage would be 5, 33, 45, 55, or 60 cents or $1.02 per half ounce, respectively.[146]

In reviewing these conditions, N. M. Brooks, Superintendent of Foreign Mails in 1895, observed that:[147]

> The inconvenience and annoyance occasioned to persons having correspondents in foreign countries by this condition of affairs may be easily imagined. But, in addition, the complicated accounts necessary to be kept with the several foreign countries with whom we had postal treaty relations, and each of which had to be credited with its portion of the sum prepaid on each article (not on the aggregate weights of the mails), and the minute details required to be entered in the Letter Bill sent with each mail, are almost beyond belief; for these accounts were kept by the "rate" and according to the standard weight of the creditor country, so that the credits were by the English ounce, the French gram, and the German "loth," and the unit of rate was with some countries one sheet of paper, with some a quarter of an ounce, with some a third of an ounce, with some a half-ounce, and with some two-thirds of an ounce. As the scope and volume of the foreign correspondence increased, the rates, conditions, and accounts became more and more complex, until it became absolutely necessary to simplify both, as under the then existing conditions a person could not tell without considerable inquiry how much postage to prepay upon a letter he wished to reach its foreign destination as

soon as possible; and the time necessary to carefully scrutinize each article before closing the mail, and to make on the Letter Bill, with the necessary minute detail, the separate credits to be given to the various foreign Offices furnishing the sea or land transportation, required the mails to be closed an unreasonably long period before the steamer sailed.

Rowland Hill's postal reforms in Great Britain had inspired many to agitate for international postal reform. In 1841 and 1842, J. von Herrfeldt, a German economist, called for faster transportation, a shortening of routes, frequent exchanges, and lower and simplified rates. In 1850, the postal treaty between Prussia and Austria had resulted in the founding of the Austro-German Postal Union, which eventually included all fifteen German postal administrations. A private organization, the International and Colonial Postage Association, began a campaign in 1851 to reform the international postage rate structures, and despite its collapse after several years of promising activity, did much to propagandize the need for improvement. At the suggestion of Postmaster General Blair of the United States in 1862, fifteen countries sent delegates to Paris to deliberate on ways to simplify the exchange of international mail. While no binding treaty resulted from the conference, the recommendations which were adopted served as a basis for subsequent reform. Within two years after the Paris Conference, the United States renegotiated nine postal conventions along guidelines established at Paris. In 1865 twenty European nations created the International Telegraph Union for the regulation of telegraphic communications. The success of the Union inspired Heinrich von Stephan, Director of Posts of the North German Confederation, to call an international postal conference. Although the Franco-Prussian War delayed the meeting, the first international postal congress opened at Berne, Switzerland, on 15 September 1874.[148]

The Congress required only three weeks to draft and sign a treaty which, in one step, eliminated the confused procedures of the past, simplified and standardized international rates, and created a single unit to control the exchange of mail between member nations. The permanent organization was at first known as the General Postal Union, but the name was changed to the Universal Postal Union in 1878. Since its founding, the U.P.U. has held meetings at regular intervals and maintained a permanent headquarters. By 1885, fifty-four countries had joined the Union and by 1906, seventy-one. The Congress of 1874 established a basic letter rate ranging from 20 to 32 centimes per 15 grammes. A relatively small surtax was permitted for letters carried more than 300 miles by sea. Postal cards were to be charged half letter postage and rates for mail matter such as books, newspapers, and other printed matter were placed on a weight basis. Prepayment of postage on international mail was encouraged by doubling the postage for unprepaid matter. Mail was to be sent by the most expeditious means available.[149]

The new rates between twenty member nations became effective on 1 July 1875 but France, the twenty-first member, did not adhere to the articles of the convention until 1 January 1876. United States letter mail addressed to member nations was rated at a uniform five cents per half ounce.

In 1876 Postmaster General James N. Tyner reported:[150]

> The General Postal Union treaty concluded at Berne, October 9, 1874, has been in operation since July 1, 1875, with the most satisfactory results. Our people have enjoyed the advantages of the cheap and uniform postage-rates which have been established to all parts of the civilized world, and the Post-Office Department has also been financially benefited by the greater simplicity of postal operations under its provisions, as well as by the entire suppression of postage accounts on the Postal Union correspondence.

In the 1840s, the marked improvement in carrying transatlantic mails had become increasingly important as more steamships began to carry international correspondence. The average westward crossing of the fast sailing ships varied from 30 to 36 days; average westward trips of three Cunard steamships varied from 16 to 17 days. Eastward averages for the sailing vessels ranged from 20 to 24 days; averages for the Cunarders varied from nearly 14 to 16 days. In 1859, post offices were provided on certain Cunard steamships for sorting, postmarking, and rating mail while in transit.[151]

Although foreign mails had been carried occasionally under contracts and a conscious effort had been made to provide American steamship companies with the best opportunities for carrying mail, direct subsidies for American lines were difficult to execute, as in 1885, when Department officials found it impossible to implement a poorly worded law intended to assist American shipping.[152] The traditional American method of dispatching overseas mails was to send them by the first or fastest ship. In 1886 the practice was defended:[153]

> Although the Department has sedulously preferred the steamships of the United States wherever they sail, the greater proportion (about nine-tenths) of the foreign mails have been necessarily transmitted in foreign bottoms. No instance has arisen of declination by any such vessel to carry whatever quantity of mail has been offered it for the sea postage only . . . Our transatlantic service has been especially excellent, and may be pronounced without doubt the most expeditious and satisfactory of any upon the seas.

The system continued and was described in more detail in 1895:[154]

> As a rule, the mails for transatlantic destinations have been assigned to steamers for their conveyance upon the plan that has been in vogue for many years; that is to say, in the case of two steamers leaving New York for Great Britain at or about the same time the mails have been assigned to the steamer which, according to the record of its three voyages just preceding the assignment, delivered the mails in the shortest time in London.
> The record upon which these assignments are made is based upon "trip

reports" made to this office by the agents of the vessels upon the termination of each voyage, in connection with statements furnished weekly by the British Office, showing the exact time of the arrival of the mails at the London post-office.

During the year 1895, the average eastward crossings of the five lines carrying mail between New York and England varied from 162 to 242 hours, with the Cunard liners compiling the best annual average. The fastest transit of mails between New York and London via Queenstown in fiscal year 1894-1895 was turned in by the Cunarder *Lucania*,156.7 hours.[155]

At the turn of the century, steam transportation on the high seas and reformed U.P.U. rates had greatly expedited and stimulated correspondence between widely scattered peoples. The airplane would further revolutionize international correspondence, and thanks to an efficient postal union, the rates for international airmail after World War II would reach reasonable and relatively uniform levels to make air communication available to nearly everyone.

RISE OF THE
FAST MAIL TRAINS
1875-1917

George S. Bangs succeeded Armstrong as General Superintendent of the Railway Mail Service in 1873. Under Bangs, numerous improvements in Railway Post Office (R.P.O.) procedure were carried out, including the separation of mail by states before being placed aboard trains and the publication of a "Schedule of Mail Trains."[156] Perhaps the most dramatic innovation in mail transportation since the running of the Pony Express was the introduction of the "Fast Mail" trains. Following Bangs' suggestion, the New York Central & Hudson River and the Lake Shore & Michigan Southern Railways (N.Y.C.-L.S.) cooperated with the Department in placing a train of four especially constructed postal cars in service between New York and Chicago on a greatly improved schedule. This line received the greatest publicity, but the Pennsylvania Railroad also inaugurated a Fast Mail train between New York, Cincinnati, Indianapolis, and St. Louis at the same time.

Superintendent Bangs and about one hundred other officials and prominent citizens rode in a drawing-room coach on the inaugural run of the N.Y.C.-L.S. train. The Fast Mail pulled out of Grand Central Station early on the morning of 16 September 1875 carrying 43 pouches of letters, 663 sacks of papers and additional bundles of newspapers, comprising a total of 33 tons of mail to be handled, worked, and distributed in transit.

"The Flight of the Fast Mail" over the tracks of the Lake Shore
and Michigan Southern Railway in 1875. Note the mail pouch on the
track-side crane to be picked up by the catcher arm of the first
mail car.

All the operations performed on the slower R.P.O. trips were carried out
without a mishap, and the 900-mile run was completed in twenty-six hours.
At the end of the trip, the exhausted engineer fainted. The Pennsylvania's
New York-St. Louis run was completed in thirty-three hours.[157]

Although the first Fast Mail service was conducted as an experiment, its
success was unquestioned. The New York Central had constructed twenty
cars for the new service. But Congress, on 12 July 1876, ordered a ten
percent reduction in pay to railroads for carrying the mails. Irate with this
decision—the nation had not fully recovered from the financial crash of
1873—the railroads discontinued the Fast Mail service on 22 July 1876.[158]

The officials of the Department were extremely disappointed. Postmaster
General Tyner noted "serious embarrassments" because of the reduction
and reported that railroads had retaliated by providing poorer facilities and
slower mail schedules than before the inauguration of Fast Mail service.
"To be thus compelled to go backward in the work of insuring speedy
transmission and perfect delivery of the important business correspondence
of the country," commented Tyner, "is a source of mortification to all the

officers of this Department whose duties are connected with mail-transportation."[159] He insisted that letter mail should be carried through between important points "within the same time required to convey passengers between the same points over the speediest lines of communication."[160] The public also protested.

However, by 1881, the N.Y.C.-L.S. Fast Mail cars had received a new coat of paint and were in service again. The Pennsylvania Railroad restored its *Limited Mail,* the Illinois Central inaugurated a fast run between Chicago and Cairo, and the Chicago, Milwaukee & St. Paul also instituted fast mail trains. In 1884, the Chicago, Burlington & Quincy inaugurated the Fast Mail service between Chicago and Council Bluffs Iowa. Coast-to-coast Fast Mail service was inaugurated in November 1889, when the last link between Omaha and San Francisco was made, providing a scheduled time of 108 hours, 45 minutes between New York and San Francisco. The first train had run as late as thirty-eight minutes between Green River and Ogden, Utah, but all the lost time was made up by Engineer William "Wild Bill" Downing. Downing set a new speed record and gave the officials aboard such a frightening ride that the General Manager of the Union Pacific attempted to stop the train.[161]

The Fast Mail trains continued to render great service. They were not only a dramatic reality but furnished writers and songsters with countless images and symbols of speed. What could be more romantic than the moan of the whistle or more exhilarating than the sight and sound of an onrushing mail train hanging its plume of black smoke low near the horizon?

The excellent service of the railroads continued until the United States went to war in 1917. Air brakes, steel-underframe cars, improved signalling, and better car lighting and heating gradually benefited the Railway Mail Service. But when the first World War ended, a new transportation revolution was on the nation's threshold.

LETTER RATE REDUCTIONS—
THE ZENITH OF U.S.
POSTAGE RATE REFORM
1883 AND 1885

With the return of more prosperous times in the early 1880s, Congress was prepared to consider more postage rate reforms. With the introduction of the penny postal card in 1873 and the reduction of most overseas letter rates to a uniform five-cent rate, there seemed little reason to retain the "high" charge of sending a domestic letter at three cents.

Therefore the Act of 3 March 1883, "reduced the postage on first-class matter to 2 cents a half ounce or fraction thereof on and after October 1,

1883." Two years later, effective 1 July 1885, first class postage became two cents per ounce.[162] The two-cent letter rate established by these acts remained unchanged until 1932 except for the period 1917-1919, during World War I, when first class postage was increased to three cents per ounce.

The Act of 1883 also revised the money order system by raising the limit to one hundred dollars. Postal Notes were authorized between 1883 and 1894 as a cheaper and more convenient means for sending small sums of less than five dollars.[163]

SPECIAL DELIVERY
1885

"Special delivery" was introduced in 1885 at a limited number of offices, for an additional ten cents. The service was available at any free-delivery office, or at any city, town, or village with a population of 4,000 or more, according to the Federal census, and consisted of immediate delivery within the carrier district at free-delivery offices or within one mile of the post office in other qualified locations. Special delivery was made between the hours of 7:00 a.m. and 12:00 midnight. Some 555 post offices qualified for the service. Distinctive ten-cent stamps were prepared, showing a uniformed, running messenger carrying a letter in his hand. The legend on the stamp read "Secures immediate delivery at a special delivery office."[164]

The Act of 4 August 1886 made the service available for all classes of mail and at all post offices. On 10 August 1886 the Postmaster General issued an order making Special delivery available from free-delivery offices on Sunday, and all other offices if open on Sunday. Special delivery was also made available on holidays. Old supplies of the stamp remained on sale and were used until a new issue was prepared. The picture of the messenger was retained but the legend was changed to read: "Secures immediate delivery at any post office."[165]

EXTENSION OF THE
U.S. POSTAL SYSTEM
1867-1917

The expansion of the United States did not end with the settlement of California, Oregon, and Washington. The acquisition of additional territory created some interesting problems for officials in Washington, D.C., concerned with the domestic postal service.

The purchase of Alaska, ratified on 26 May 1867 presented the first problem. Although formal transfer of the territory was not made until October 1867, the first U.S. post office in Alaska was authorized on 23 July 1867 at Sitka, with John H. Kinkead (who later became the first American governor there) serving as postmaster. The Russians had not established a post office and, therefore, there were no routes, offices, or equipment to take over. The first formal arrangement to carry mail to Alaska from San Francisco by steamer resulted in at least one trip before the end of 1867. In 1869 contract steamship service on a monthly schedule connected Sitka in Alaska with Port Townsend, Washington Territory. This arrangement was renewed in 1880, when only 6,812 letters were mailed from Alaska Territory. The Army garrisons, maintained from 1867 to 1877, were given mail service. Other postal services were slow to develop until the 1880s. When gold was found in the Juneau area, Alaskan postal development accelerated. In the eighties and nineties, the private express companies provided the postal services which the Department could not or did not supply. Wells Fargo, The Pacific Express Company, The Northern Express Company, and the powerful Alaska Commercial Company—which dominated the fur and seal pelt trade—were the leading express companies, performing the same services previously rendered in California and other western mining areas.[166]

In 1896, following new gold strikes, the Department began to establish inland routes. It was found that miners "and others" at Circle City were paying as much as a dollar per letter for carriage by private express lines. The establishment of a U.S. mail route, however, met with considerable difficulty. The first carrier from Juneau to Circle City, for instance, had to cut timber and construct a raft to travel from the Chilkoot Pass region to Lake Bennett, where he again paused to construct a boat to reach Circle City with the mail. Once at Circle City, the carrier—a certain N.A. Beddoe—elected to continue downriver to the Bering Sea rather than pole his boat upriver to the Chilkoot region. Upon reaching the coast, he boarded a steamer bound for Seattle, delivered the Circle City mail there, boarded a second steamer at Seattle with the U.S.-Alaskan mail, and returned to his original starting point at Juneau, "having traveled," as Beddoe reported, "6,500 miles in addition to the regular trip, and saving thereby over a month of time in the delivery of the return mail; and I owe it to myself to say that I was the last man into the Yukon and the first one out this season, which is evidence that no unnecessary delay occurred."[167]

As gold strikes brought more people to the interior, better service than Beddoe's was attempted. An international exchange was established between Dyea, Alaska, and Dawson City, Canada, in September 1897.[168] In 1898, although steamship service improved, the overland mails broke down. "Temporary" service was provided by Department agents in 1899 when the contractor failed to carry the mails over the long Juneau-Skag-way-Circle-St. Michaels route. By 1900, however, reasonable service was being provided over several inland routes, with winter service—performed by dog sled—being restricted to letter mail only.[169]

The acquisition of the Hawaiian Islands represented yet another extension of postal service which, when annexation took place on 12 August 1898 posed relatively few problems to postal officials. American residents had become so numerous in the islands by 1849 that two articles of a treaty drafted that year were concerned with the exchange of mails between Hawaii and the United States. The kingdom became a member of the Universal Postal Union in 1882 and the five-cent international postage rate became effective between the mainland and the islands. After 1887, following the adoption of a liberal constitution, events in Hawaii bore a striking resemblance to those which had transpired in Texas earlier in the century. Queen Liliuokalani was deposed, a Republic was proclaimed, and annexation to the United States was requested in 1893, only to be deferred until 1898, when Admiral Dewey's activities during the Spanish-American War changed political thinking in Washington.[170]

Oddly, Postmaster General Charles E. Smith reported on 21 November 1898:[171]

> The acquisition of Hawaii has not thus far been followed by any change in our postal relations with that *country*. The absorption of its postal system into our own and the exercise of our control, like the incorporation of other features of its local administration, have awaited the report of the Congressional committee and the legislation which will follow . . . . Hawaii already has a good mail service which is more than self-sustaining.

The postage stamps of the Republic of Hawaii remained in use on mail to the United States and foreign countries by order of Postmaster General Smith. Furthermore, postage rates between Hawaii and the mainland remained as before, including the five-cent overseas letter rate. The Hawaiian system was incorporated into the U.S. postal system on 14 June 1900, at which time Hawaiian stamps became invalid but were accepted in exchange for U.S. issues until 14 December 1900.[172]

The military mail problems resulting from the Spanish-American War and the incorporation of former Spanish colonies into the U.S. postal system required special attention from Department officials. Beginning with Camp Black, New York, in May 1898, military post offices were established at all training centers. The offices were generally treated as branches of nearby cities. Postal service followed the troops into Cuba. Spanish postal authorities were replaced by American personnel and civilian services were continued wherever possible. In Puerto Rico, the same course of action was followed, with postal matters coming under the direction of a superintendent detailed from the Railway Mail Service, acting in conjunction with the military commander. Two military postal stations were established at Manila and Cavite in the Philippines under the supervision of a superintendent from San Francisco. Although Americans supervised the larger offices in occupied areas, former postmasters who had served under Spanish rule were retained. Other local officers were installed in the smaller post offices. The postal officials were subjected to the same hazards as the troops, and a number of employees died of fever or were hospitalized.[173]

Fast mail steamers were converted to naval duty under authority of the Act of 3 March 1891. The *St. Louis, St. Paul, New York* (rechristened *Harvard*), and the *Paris* (rechristened *Yale*), all formerly in the Atlantic mail service, became armed auxiliary cruisers.[174]

Although the war was brief, U.S. forces remained in the various islands and required continuing postal service. At the same time, civilian mails became the responsibility of the United States. The old Cuban postal system was remodeled after that of the United States but was, from the first, maintained quite independently of the U.S. Post Office Department. During U.S. military control, the Cuban postal organization had its own bureaus, auditing system, and financial basis. Major E.G. Rathbone was designated as Director-General of Posts, but most of the other offices were held by Cubans. Equipment and facilities were found to be obsolete and a general overhaul was carried out. Money-order and registry services were instituted and new routes were opened. The Spanish postal administration had also operated the telegraph system, but this was placed under the temporary administration of the U.S. Signal Corps. An overall improvement was reflected in the significant increase in the use of the mails by Cuban civilians.[175]

During the period of U.S. military rule, postage stamps, postal cards, and stamped envelopes of the United States were surcharged for use in Cuba in lieu of those issued under Spanish authority. The U.S. Bureau of Engraving and Printing also prepared a distinctive series of stamps in 1899. The U.S. administration of Cuba ended in 1902.[176]

Puerto Rico remained a permanent possession but its postal system, like that of Cuba, was reorganized along lines which would have kept it quite independent of the Department. Within a short time, however, a severe hurricane struck the island and postal operations and revenues were so drastically reduced that the Department paid the deficit from its own appropriations. Although overprinted U.S. stamps and postal stationery were used in Puerto Rico, they were supplanted by ordinary postal issues of the United States within a short time after the new administration became established. Three free-delivery city offices were created in 1900, and in 1902 it was reported that forty-seven postal routes, totaling 3,491 miles, were in operation on the island.[177]

In 1899, a United States post office was opened on Guam under jurisdiction of the Navy Department, but in 1901, Guam's postal operations became part of the regular United States postal organization and ordinary United States postage stamps replaced those bearing the "Guam" overprint. In 1899, the Philippines postal system became independent of the San Francisco office. The Philippines were supplied with overprinted United States postage stamps until 1906, when a distinctive series was supplied. Under F.W. Vaille, Director-General of the Posts for the Philippines, service was rapidly extended. Puerto Rico, Guam, and the Philippines were given the benefit of United States domestic postage rates as "practical evidence that they were under the flag of the United States."[178] Postal receipts in the Philippines exceeded expenditures during the first two years of U.S. postal operation.[179]

During fiscal year 1900-1901, a fourth class United States post office was opened at Tutuila, Samoa Islands, and Pago Pago was served under a revised transpacific mail contract negotiated in November 1900 with the Oceanic Steamship Company as a feature of the San Francisco-Sydney service.[180]

The establishment of postal service in the Panama Canal Zone is rather unique in the annals of the American posts. Under Major General George W. Davis, first Governor of the Zone, a new postal system began to take form with the designation of nine post offices and the appointment of postmasters on 21 June 1904. The posts of The Republic of Panama had ceased to function in the Zone and an unsatisfactory messenger service had filled the vacuum during the administrative changeover. Governor Davis acted quickly to procure overprinted postage stamps of Panama for temporary use in the Zone. These stamps were basically the 1892-1896 issue of the Department of Panama, Colombia, which had been overprinted by the new Panamanian government. The "Canal Zone" overprint was, therefore, a second overprint on an issue which was (in each altered form) subsequently valid under three different governments. "Domestic" postage rates of the Canal Zone were applicable to mail addressed to the United States, Guam, Philippine Islands, Hawaii, Puerto Rico, Tutuila (American Samoa), Canada, Cuba, Mexico, and Panama. By June 1904, the new Canal Zone postal system was organized and ready for operation.[181]

> The Canal Zone postal administration is unique in its establishment and operation. It has its own postal regulations, yet the United States regulations are applicable. Its postal laws are contained in both the Federal Statutes and the Canal Zone Code. It does not belong to the Universal Postal Union but adheres to its policies. It is not within the United States Post Office Department, but like that organization, is a unit of the United States Government. Its stamps are engraved and printed by the United States Bureau of Engraving and Printing in Washington.[182]

On July 1904 two inspectors from the United States Post Office Department traveled to the Zone to assist in the establishment of the new postal system. They brought two million United States stamps overprinted "Canal Zone

Panama" to be used in place of those purchased from the Republic of Panama, but in September, after the Republic had protested the use of these overprinted United States stamps, an agreement—known as the "Taft Agreement"—was reached whereby the Zone was to purchase overprinted Panamanian stamps at forty percent of face value. Following abrogation of the Taft Agreement in 1924, overprinted United States stamps were again placed in use. In 1928 distinctive stamps, printed especially for the Zone by the Bureau of Engraving and Printing, were introduced as a "Permanent Issue."[183]

The United States postal establishment was extended to include the Virgin Islands in 1917. The Islands were given all facilities of the U.S. system, including domestic postage rates for mail between the Islands and the mainland, parcel post (including insurance and COD features), and money order service.[184]

GENERAL DEVELOPMENT
OF THE SERVICE
1867-1900

Postmaster General D. McK. Key surveyed the fiscal deficiencies characteristic of the period in his *Annual Report* for 1878. In suggesting ways to eliminate unnecessary expenses, Key noted that fourth class postmasters automatically retained commissions in proportion to business conducted at the offices, "whether there be an appropriation by Congress for it or not." Secondly, Key was critical of laws regulating payments to railroad companies. Railway mail appropriations had been reduced, despite the fact that the weight of mails carried was increasing. In order to increase revenue to meet costs which would soon increase, Key suggested that Congress again abolish the free franking privilege or drastically restrict its use. He also requested that rates be increased for advertising matter and "merchandise" mailable under the four-pound weight limit.[185]

In 1879, a fourth "class" of mail matter was created as a new "catch-all" category. First Class still embraced ordinary letters and postal cards; Second Class matter consisted of newspapers and magazines; Third Class matter was limited to circulars, miscellaneous printed matter, and books; and Fourth Class included anything not defined in the other three classes and which would not "destroy, deface, or otherwise damage the contents of the mail bag, or harm the person or any one engaged in the postal service." The four-pound limit was retained and prepayment of one cent per ounce of Fourth Class matter was required. Congress did not restrict the transmission of official matter free of postage as recommended.[186] Expenditures continued to exceed revenues (see table 5).[187]

Table 5. United States Post Office Statistics, 1875-1895

Year	Number of Post Offices	Revenues	Expenditures	Annual Miles Railroad	Annual Miles Total
1875	35,547	$26,791,314	$33,611,309	75,154,910	133,822,216
1880	42,989	33,315,479	36,542,804	96,497,463	178,236,996
1885	51,252	42,560,844	50,046,235	151,910,845	238,478,773
1890	62,401	60,882,098	66,259,548	215,715,680	327,409,493
1895	70,064	76,983,128	87,179,551	267,177,737	402,606,058

During the twenty-year period 1875-1895, expenditures exceeded revenue in all but two years, 1882 and 1883. After rates were reduced to two cents in 1883, revenues did not equal those of the preceding year under the three-cent rate until 1887. Meanwhile, expenditures had continued to rise. Postmaster General Key had remarked that "it was not expected that the [Post Office] department should be self-sustaining, but that the deficiencies in its revenues should be met by appropriations from the general treasury."[188]

In a practical step to economize on the procurement of postage stamps, the long-standing policy of securing them through contracts from private bank note companies under contracts was changed when the Department awarded a contract to the Bureau of Engraving and Printing to produce all postage stamps on 20 November 1893. The Bureau's estimate of $139,487 was substantially lower than the lowest bid of $146,454 from a commercial firm and that of $162,401 submitted by the American Bank Note Company, the last contractor to produce stamps under the previous policy. This action not only represented an immediate economy but inaugurated the present program of producing stamps on government premises by government personnel. With the manufacture of postage stamps a major function of the Bureau, great strides were made in the development of equipment especially designed for this work. Benjamin R. Stickney, an outstanding mechanical engineer of the Bureau, developed web-fed rotary printing presses in 1914. The Stickney presses, built in two sizes, had a capacity to print 10,000 to 10,500 small sheets or 8,000 large sheets of postage and revenue stamps per day. Stickney also developed improved perforating and coiling equipment and was later called upon to install his rotary printing presses in Cuba, Czechoslovakia, and Sweden.[189]

The manufacture of embossed stamped envelopes had continued to be carried out under private contracts, but in 1910 the production of postal cards became a function of the Government Printing Office in Washington; D. C.[190]

Postmaster General John Wanamaker, the Philadelphia mercantile king, became head of the Department in 1889. In the *Annual Report* for 1890 he summarized the achievements of the postal system after a century of operation under the Constitution. He noted that among the great accomplishments of the three decades before 1890 were the growth of mail routes (exclusive of city carrier routes) to about 428,000 miles, the doubling of the number of post offices, the growth of the free delivery service in 454 cities, and the extension of the money order system to 9,382 offices. The steady improvement of the Railway Post Office system, the transcontinental railroad service, the opening of communications with China and Japan, and the establishment and undisputed success of the Universal Postal Union were regarded as exceptional achievements. Wanamaker also praised the progressive reduction of postage rates, observing that U.S. rates, taken altogether, represented "perhaps a lower and simpler tariff of postage than [was then current in] any other country in the world."[191] Furthermore, he observed that "the postal establishment of the United States has arisen from a condition of insignificance to be the largest of all the nations of the world."[192] More than 150,000 postal employees in 1890 were handling an estimated 8,000 letters per minute. In 1789, the U.S. mails had consisted of but about 1,000 letters per day.

In 1890, Wanamaker stated the goal which was to dominate the work of the Department until World War I: "To make the mails go faster, more safely, and more frequently."[193] All mail schedules had been reviewed, and there had been a considerable improvement in deliveries. Nevertheless, Wanamaker envisioned a greatly improved system of public communication and pleaded for a Government-controlled telegraph system.[194]

> The swiftest mail is not fast enough . . . .The post-office should do more than employ fast mails and stage coaches . . . .We strain every muscle and nerve trying to gain an hour or two on this collection or that delivery. We worry the railroads with importunities for new trains or faster ones that shall save perhaps three or four hours . . . .
>
> There are mail routes of thousands of miles in the new States and thinly settled parts of the older country where every mile entails a certain loss to the Department; but the priceless privilege of communication by post is maintained though every other channel of intercourse is closed . . . . In one form or another the public imperatively demands cheaper telegraphy, and the Post-Office Department can supply it at less cost than any corporation . . . . The Government of this and every other country controls the mail service and stoutly claims that the general welfare is promoted by managing the transmission of correspondence.

Despite Wanamaker's eloquent pleas, the postal telegraph never became a reality in the United States. The Department continued to face the problems of collecting, moving, and delivering correspondence without being able to incorporate electrical communications systems into the postal service. As the volume of mail increased, new burdens on the existing system became apparent. Facilities required enlargement, new mail-handling machinery was introduced, and new methods of transporting mail were developed. The movement of city mail became more troublesome, and rural service, which had remained the same since Colonial times, cried out for a complete overhauling.

RURAL FREE DELIVERY
1896

The number of post offices in 1895—more than 70,000—was to reach its peak within a short time. While many other statistics seemed to indicate "postal progress," the number of post offices merely reflected a growing population and, in a way, a certain lack of efficiency in getting the mail into the hands of the patrons. Of the nearly 76,000,000 people in the United States in 1890, more than half lived in rural areas. Free delivery service, though greatly improved since its introduction in 1863, remained available to only slightly more than 19,000,000 people. The rest of the people had to call at their local post office to send or receive their mail. The cross-roads post office, often part of a country store, remained the only source of contact for many people with the outside world. This relative isolation was just another facet of rural life for millions of farm dwellers.[195]

During his four years in office, Postmaster General John Wanamaker fought for parcel post, a postal savings system, for government ownership of the telegraph and telephone facilities, and for the delivery of mail to the farmer's door. While not the first to champion most of these reforms, he pursued practically everything he took up with great energy. Opposition to his proposals, however, was heavy.[196]

On his own, Wanamaker had the Department conduct a limited experimental rural free delivery (RFD) service in 1891. Although Wanamaker pronounced it feasible, the results were rather inconclusive. The newspapers supported the fight for rural free delivery—it was easy to visualize a newspaper in every farmer's mailbox each morning. The farmers, of course—especially those who gathered in the Grange Halls— were particularly enthusiastic.[197]

The first bill to establish rural free delivery failed, but pressure mounted. In 1893, however, Congress appropriated $10,000 to conduct an experimental service, but by this time William Bissell, a conservative, had been appointed Postmaster General and the Panic of 1893 had plunged the Nation into economic turmoil. Bissell refused to conduct the experiment; the farmers and their representatives insisted. The city free delivery system was costing about eleven million annually, and the farmers began to regard postage as a tax to provide a daily service to a rather select group of citizens —the "city folk." In 1895, Congress appropriated $20,000, but Bissell remained adament. Before the struggle could really be resolved, Bissell resigned and was succeeded by William L. Wilson, a man less violent in his opposition to rural mail delivery. Congress again appropriated funds, $40,000, and the experiment was carried out.[198]

In his comprehensive and colorful study, *RFD, The Changing Face of Rural America,* Wayne E. Fuller has commented about the beginning of rural mail service:[199]

> There were no Indians to fight along the rural routes and no Pony Express riders to race across the prairies. Mostly there were only muddy country roads and eager farmers, cranks, politicians, and fourth-class postmasters to provide what drama there was.
>
> And yet the establishment of the farmers' free delivery service was not without its epic proportions. More money was spent, more men employed, and more paperwork done to lay out the rural delivery system than to establish any single extension of the postal service.

On 1 October 1896, the experiment was launched in West Virginia with three carriers operating from the post offices of Charles Town, Halltown, and Uvilla. The *Annual Report* for 1897 was submitted by Postmaster General James A. Gary, who had succeeded Wilson, and contained a detailed and glowing account of the experiment. Gary reported that the farmers were enthusiastic in their approval of the new service and that it should be put on a permanent basis. Daily newspapers now reached the farmers to keep them informed about world events and the condition of the markets; delivery to roadside boxes had eliminated the often unpleasant necessity of taking a trip into town.[200]

Rural carriers at first received an annual pay of but $300 and furnished their own transportation. Perry S. Heath, First Assistant Postmaster General, described the actual service: "According to the varying conditions of the country traversed, the rural carriers perform their services on horseback, or riding in buckboards, buggies, two-wheeled carts, or on bicycles. In some States they have to cross farms and pull down bars and ride over fields to deliver and collect their mails."[201] Gary's report, dated 12 October 1897, stated that rural service was established in twenty-nine states over forty-four different routes. The experiment was purposely carried out under widely different local conditions—over the macadamized roads of California, on an island of Lake Champlain, "in the backwoods of Maine, and among the farmers and summer boarders of Massachusetts."[202]

Heath and August W. Machen, Superintendent of Free Delivery, fully realized that the administration would gain the political loyalty of rural areas that were given a successful delivery service. With a new appropriation of $150,000 to continue and expand rural delivery in 1898, Heath and Machen established new routes in areas served by adequate roads. This insured maximum success. The required support of the farmers was secured by a promise to establish new routes in response to petitions submitted by rural groups. The Department was flooded with petitions from the farmers. Many of these requests, however, were turned down because the areas lacked good roads.[203] Nevertheless, the Department's policy was very successful, as was reported in 1899:[204]

> It [Rural Free Delivery] is now in successful operation from 630 distributing points, scattered among 40 States and 1 Territory (the only States unrepresented in the list being Idaho, Mississippi, Montana, and Wyoming), giving service to 452,735 people, at an average annual cost of 66 cents per capita.
> The benefits . . . may be summarized as follows:
> Increased postal receipts. . . .
> Enhancement of the value of farm lands. . . .
> Improved means of travel, some hundreds of miles of country roads, especially in the Western States, having been graded specifically in order to obtain rural free delivery.
> Higher educational influences, broader circulation of the means of public intelligence, and closer daily contact with the great world of activity extended to the homes of heretofore isolated rural communities.

It was soon discovered that rural carrier routes radiating from the larger offices rendered some fourth-class post offices and the Star Routes which served them rather useless. The number of post offices continued to increase until 1901, the peak year, when 76,945 were reported. Thereafter, the number of U.S. post offices began a steady decline, dropping to 68,131 in 1905 and 52,641 in 1920.[205] Between 1902 and 1920, the number of rural routes increased from 8,298 to 43,445.[206]

The success of sorting mail aboard moving trains and the time gained by "working" these mails in transit inspired officials of the Department to apply the traveling post office system to virtually every basic type of vehicle used in the postal service. On 3 April 1899 the Department inaugurated a plan submitted by clerk Edwin W. Shriver utilizing a rather large and specially designed wagon to serve the rural district surrounding Westminster, Maryland. Mail was received, postmarked, sorted, and delivered en route by two clerks. In December 1899, when RFD was expanded throughout Carroll County, Maryland, three additional postal wagons were introduced, offering most services available at any post office. Postal Wagons also served one-man "feeder" routes at designated junctions on schedule. Distinctive postmarks were employed for the Postal Wagon service. In addition, wagon systems based on the "Carroll County Plan" were introduced elsewhere in Maryland, Pennsylvania, Missouri, and

Georgia, where local conditions made it difficult for certain counties to be served from central post offices. Although successful, Postal Wagon service was discontinued sometime before 30 June 1905, when one-man routes were able to serve all points more economically.[207]

The postmarking of mail on all rural lines was required after 1 August 1900. Compact hand-cancellers and ink pads were supplied to rural carriers. At first, each route in some counties had a separate number, indicated by the numeral appearing in the cancellation, but a revision of the numbering system about 1906, the use of automobiles by RFD carriers, and the consolidation of certain routes, nullified the purpose of many "numeral" cancellers. The Department ceased issuing the canceling devices after July 1903, but some clerks and postmasters purchased RFD cancelers privately to "advertise" the new service. As the horse-drawn wagon gave place to the automobile, the RFD postmarks began to disappear.[208]

There can be no doubt that RFD service provided a great incentive for the improvement of the nation's highways. In the early days of RFD the maintenance of roads was a local responsibility. The Department turned down many petitions for rural mail service because particular districts lacked good roads. Farmers generally made every effort to meet the standards set by the Department. Although any farmer might improve his road with the ingenious and home-made "King Road Drag," bridges, culverts, and major repairs required public expenditures. An estimated $72,000,000 had been spent by non-Federal agencies to improve roads between 1897 and 1908.[209] It was not until 1917 that a significant Federal Highway Act was passed.

An automobile was used experimentally for rural delivery as early as 1902 at Adrian, Michigan, and in 1906 the Department gave permission for rural carriers to use their automobiles.[210] The change from horse and wagon to the motor car paralleled improvements in highways and the development of more reliable automotive equipment and was further related to the increases in the salaries of the carriers and the decreases in the price of certain automobiles, notably the Model T Ford. By 1912 rural carriers received $1,100 annually and by 1920, $1,800.[211] At first, one-horse RFD wagons sold for only $45, complete with sliding doors, windows which could be opened and closed, pigeon-hole letter cases, a "desk" surface, and a cash-and-stamp drawer with lock and key.[212] In 1914 the price of a new Model T was $500.

Many miles could be served by the country mailman in his "flivver." Realizing this, officials of the Department in 1915 began an extensive program of consolidating and lengthening rural routes. Within a year, 939 routes were eliminated. Layoffs, difficulties in maintaining adequate service over the lengthened "motorized" routes in bad weather—most of the roads were dirt roads—and other problems created by the reorganized RFD system led Congress to pass an act in 1916 stipulating that horse routes were to be twenty-four miles in length and auto routes fifty miles. Extensions, where necessary, were strictly limited. Furthermore, new auto routes were to be established only on receipt of a petition signed by the majority of heads of families along the proposed motorized route.[213]

In 1915, to assist the rural carriers in servicing the roadside boxes which were produced in every shape or size imaginable, Postmaster General Burleson approved the now-familiar tunnel-shaped box with its flag and snap-latch door as the standard rural letter-box. The new design, executed by Roy J. Joroleman of the Department, was initially approved for boxes in two sizes.[214] Thus, the transition to the auto was made easier for the rural carriers.

VILLAGE DELIVERY SERVICE
1912

By 1911, when free city delivery had been established for nearly fifty years and when free rural delivery had been extended over the Nation, the Department turned its attention to the large number of patrons who were left without the advantages of house-to-house delivery. City delivery could only be established for communities with a population of 10,000 or with annual postal receipts of $10,000 or more. Postmaster General Frank H. Hitchcock pointed out that:[215]

> The carrier delivery system is now in operation in 1,541 cities, serving an urban population of about 45,000,000, while rural carriers deliver mail on 42,000 routes that reach about 20,000,000 people. This leaves about 25,000,000 people in the United States, most of whom live in small towns and villages, without any form of mail delivery.

Responding to Hitchcock's request, Congress appropriated $100,000 to inaugurate an experimental village delivery service in August 1912.

By 1 December 1912 carrier service had been established in twenty-nine small towns.[216] By October 1915 the experiment had been extended to included 133 offices with 180 carriers performing the service for annual salaries averaging $600.[217] The experiment was considered rather costly to both patron and the Department and new guidelines were put into effect in 1915 which restricted carrier service to offices with receipts of $5,000 per year and towns of more than 3,000 people.[218] Village delivery was thus essentially limited to third class offices, or those with annual receipts ranging from $5,000 to $8,000. By 1917 village delivery was in operation in 280 offices with about 400 carriers as compared with a city delivery system employing 34,592 carriers at 1,948 post offices of the first and second class.[219]

MAIL-PROCESSING PROBLEMS, CANCELLING MACHINES, AND POSTAL MECHANIZATION 1876-1920

While the Department was extending free delivery service to as many citizens as possible, the metropolitan areas were again requiring an increasing amount of attention from postal officials. As Wanamaker stated in 1890, every muscle and nerve was being strained to speed the movement of mail. But congestion in city post offices had become a problem that would haunt the Department for decades.

After the Civil War, the physical problems of the postal service could be grouped in four categories: (1) the collection of mail from the public; (2) the "working" of the mail, i.e., arranging letters address-side up ("facing"), postmarking and canceling, sorting, pouching, etc.; (3) the transporting of mail between post offices, whether within the same metropolitan area or between distant points; and (4) the delivery of mail to addressees. Although these four categories reduce the problem to its simplest terms, a variety of techniques and innovations were developed in an effort to maintain adequate communication for the United States which was becoming more industrialized, more urbanized, and more heavily populated each year.

The Railway Mail Service had reasonably solved the problem of rapidly moving mail between distant cities. The technique of sorting and pouching mail for terminals, way stations, and connecting routes while in transit was applied to partly alleviate congestion at large city post offices. A.N. Zevely, Third Assistant Postmaster General, had tested a plan whereby New York City clerks had sorted mail aboard city-bound trains as early as 1864, and Harrison Park had recommended that mail for the carrier routes of New York and Boston should be separated on Railway Post Office (R.P.O.) cars in 1867. A general system of R.P.O. city separation, however, was not inaugurated until 1883, after a successful experiment conducted in 1882.[220] At first, carrier route separations were made by city clerks riding the postal cars until either they were transferred to the Railway Mail Service or the R.P.O. clerks learned the new city schemes. The successful working of city mails in transit led many postmasters to request that this be applied to all cities, but the Department reiterated the basic objectives of city separation service in 1897:[221]

> The original idea of distributing city mail on the cars only contemplated that that should be done for the largest offices, where the amount of time consumed in preparing the mail for the carriers, after its arrival at the office, was so great as to cause it to miss one or more rounds of the carriers.

The results of the program for large offices were remarkable and, in addition to speeding delivery, prevented additional strains on the already overtaxed physical facilities of the postal service. City separation remained subordinate to the general distribution work performed on R.P.O. lines, but as early as 1884, more than 14,000,000 letters were presorted for New York City carriers alone.[222] City separation remained part of the regular R.P.O. service.[223]

Despite the success of the R.P.O. service, the clerk force in every metropolitan area continued to increase. Beginning in 1886, statistics indicated the amount of mail handled annually. A brief summary indicates the magnitude of this problem:[224] in fiscal year 1886, 3,747,000,000 pieces of mail of all kinds were handled; in 1895, 5,134,281,000; 1905, 10,187,506,000; and in 1913, 18,567,445,000. During this period, postal clerks worked long hours and performed some duties no longer required. For example, in 1879 it had become mandatory that letter mail (and postal cards) be "backstamped" to indicate transit time between the office of origin (shown by the place-date-time marking on the face of the letter) and the office of destination (where the second place-date-time marking was applied). The backstamping requirement was in force for first class mail until 8 May 1913 when backstamping was restricted essentially to special delivery and registered letters.[225]

The proper postmarking of mail had become a small but ever-present problem. In 1897 First Assistant Postmaster General Heath reported on a project to maintain a high standard for legible postmarks and set forth the reasons for doing so:[226]

> Legible postmarking is of the greatest importance to the public as evidence before the courts, in business transactions conducted through the mails, and in fixing the responsibility where mail has been improperly handled by postal officials.

The real problem in postmarking mail, however, was keeping pace with the ever-growing number of letters and cards which had to be processed.

Official interest in securing proper machines for postmarking letters and canceling stamps (the two operations were performed simultaneously) was expressed as early as 1862, but there is no record that any practical devices appeared. Inventors, however, had recognized the need for canceling machines and in 1868, 1870, 1871, 1874, and 1875 had received at least five patents for mechanical canceling devices.[227] These machines, nevertheless, remained experimental.

The first canceling machine to receive the serious consideration of postal officials was that invented by Thomas and Martin Leavitt of Boston and patented in 1876.[228] Thomas Leavitt arranged for trials of his machine in the Boston Post Office and in the next year, 1877, the Post Office Department placed an order for one hundred Leavitt machines of an improved design to be used at important offices in various cities.[229] Leavitt's machines, therefore, inaugurated the post-office mechanization program still in progress.

Leavitt's Number 3 machine was adopted by Congress in 1882 as the standard type to be used in post offices. The Number 1 and 2 models were primarily for postmarking postal cards which were, unlike letter mail, of uniform size and thickness. The Number 3 was improved in 1882 to process letter mail more effectively. These early models were operated by turning a handcrank, but in 1884 the American Postal Machines Company, which had taken over Leavitt's patents, brought out a belt-driven model.[230]

Although the first machines were less than perfect, they saved considerable in both time and labor. It was estimated that an experienced clerk could face and hand-stamp between 1,500 and 2,000 letters per hour whereas even the first Leavitt was reported to have canceled 25,000 postal cards in a speed trial.[231] The advertised claims of the manufacturers, however, were more modest. The Number 3 machine, for example, had a rated capacity of 15,000 pieces per hour and the power-driven Number 5 model of 1884 was rated for only between 4,000 and 8,000 pieces of mail per hour.[232]

In 1892, satisfactory machines were developed to operate on electric power and the Department began to accelerate the installation of canceling machines in as many offices as possible.[233] At this point, however, the postal officials were confronted with an increasing variety of makes and models and in 1891, perhaps wisely, had begun the policy of renting rapid canceling machines rather than purchasing this type of equipment. The new products were not always reliable. By 1898, 522 machines were rented, and Health requested that the program be expanded:[234]

> The satisfactory working of these machines and the enormous saving effected in clerk hire by their use at the larger offices call for a liberal increase in this appropriation [$25,000], that all first and second class offices having electrical current available at all hours may be provided with canceling machines at the beginning of the next fiscal year.

In 1899 the Department began to purchase machines which were deemed reliable, while continuing to rent an increasing number of them. More than fourteen different makes appeared before 1920 and, of these, most manufacturers offered several models. There were numerous consolidations, however, and some manufacturers produced only a limited number before going out of business.[235]

By 1910 the number of canceling machines used by the Department had increased to 2,172, including 1,751 on a rental basis, and had been installed in 1,767 post offices of the first and second class.[236] The rental policy was abandoned in 1914, purchasing the serviceable equipment as rental contracts expired. New equipment was also purchased and by 1920 some 2,873 canceling machines were in operation.[237]

While considerable information on canceling machines has been pre-served, other innovations have generally been ignored. Several significant experiments were made to mechanize mail processing at post offices before 1920. A photograph dated 28 September 1905 shows a clerk of the Chicago Post Office distributing "live mail" at a specially constructed sorting case with slots (rather than the customary pigeon holes) for twelve separations. Behind the slots, the letters were moved mechanically to twelve stacking trays. The machine, attributed to James Rehack of the Chicago office, apparently was intended to transport sorted mail to different locations in the post office, eliminating manual carriage of mail, relieving a certain amount of clerk congestion, and saving time by immediately moving each piece of mail after primary separation was completed.[238]

In 1907, a 24-position mechanical facing table was installed at the Main Post Office in Washington, D.C., by the United Store Service Company for testing. This machine was a simple table of considerable length which accommodated twelve clerks on either side. As the clerks faced the mail they dropped the cards and letters into slots at the sides of the table. The mail was carried by belts through the continuous slots to the end of the table and automatically fed into an International Postal Supply canceling machine for postmarking and stacking. Mr. Roy J. Joroleman, a mechanical engineer who spent fifty years with the Department, recalled that this machine was abandoned because letters jammed at the entrance to the canceling machine whenever the volume of letters became too heavy to pass into the feeder device. Basically useful during nonrush periods, the facing table lacked an automatic stacking device to meter the letters into the canceling machine at a controlled rate. Furthermore, the difference in elevation between the facing-table belt and the canceling machine prevented a smooth flow of mail, and nobody thought of reducing the height of the canceling machine base. Two photographs of this table are of considerable interest for, in addition to the machine, an overhead monorail conveyor system is clearly shown.[239]

In 1915, G. Bailey of the Boston post office developed a machine for distributing mail to carriers' desks. Twenty separations could be made. Bailey's machine moved cards and letters by a single belt, over which were twenty continuous slots or troughs forming guide-lanes. Clerks dropped the mail into the proper lane (each lane had a number), and the belt carried it until the letters were guided to the intended carrier's desk.[240]

A Gehring Mail Distributing Machine, developed and erected by the Mechanical Efficiency Company of Akron, Ohio, was tested by the Department in 1918. Five clerks worked at the machine simultaneously and sat at keyboards similar to those of typewriters. As each letter was carried past the clerk, he depressed keys which determined the route of the letter through the machine and automatically determined in which box the letter would be deposited. Canceling machines were also incorporated in the device. After testing and purchasing the Gehring machine, it was placed in storage and permanently abandoned.[241]

Early mail-handling equipment generally remained undeveloped. Although conveyor systems and canceling machines were regarded with considerable favor, conservative officials often left promising proposals—such as the pneumatic sorting machine proposed by Paul Burkert in 1922—at the drawing-board or mock-up stage.[242]

The problem of canceling stamps in a manner which would eliminate delays had been partly solved as early as 1847, when some stamps of the first issue of the United States were "precanceled," i.e., canceled before being affixed to mail. Thereafter, a number of postmasters permitted or utilized this expedient in handling U.S. stamps and mail. Nevertheless, precancels were unauthorized by the Department and remained quite limited in use until 1890. About that time, however, precancels were used to expedite the handling of large mailings of *Youth's Companion* magazine at Boston. Thereafter, many postmasters received Department approval for their use. By 1903, at least 113 firms were authorized to make certain bulk mailings with precanceled stamps at post offices in thirty cities. Uniform procedures for their use were established in 1911 when all but fourth class post offices were authorized to precancel stamps at local expense for use on package mail during the Christmas rush. Since that date, regulations governing the use of precancels have been liberalized and the saving in time to both the post office and authorized mailers is clearly recognized.[243]

In 1916, the Department ordered 40,000 precanceled stamps for three cities from the Bureau of Engraving and Printing as an experiment to reduce precanceling costs. In 1923, also for reasons of economy, the Bureau began the regular production of precanceled stamps for offices requiring the largest quantities.[244]

During the period 1898-1920, the postage stamp itself was reexamined as the most suitable means for indicating the prepayment of postage. Several devices were developed by private citizens. These machines imprinted postmark and postage data directly on envelopes or cards and were primarily intended for the use of business firms.

Although the early machines were not approved, they were tested by the Department in 1903 and 1904 and apparently inspired the passage of legislation on 28 April 1904 authorizing the Postmaster General to permit the mailing of certain matter without stamps affixed. Accordingly, the postal regulations were amended to allow 2,000 or more identical pieces of third or fourth class matter to be mailed without stamps but with a printed "permit marking" indicating the place of mailing, the number of the postal permit issued to the mailer, and the amount of postage "paid in money." "Permit mail" did not require cancellation at post offices and, therefore, represented another time-saving innovation of considerable importance.[245]

Rapid canceling machines, precanceled stamps, city separation on R.P.O.

lines, and related improvements gave the average clerk little comfort. In 1893 at Chicago, for example, about 400 employees were handling 125 million pieces of mail matter annually, including some 25 million pounds of newspapers and 10 million pounds of "miscellaneous matter,"[246] under the most unpleasant conditions. A New York City clerk complained that[247]

> The clerk is held strictly accountable for every moment of lost time. He has to work from ten to twelve hours per day and every holiday and Sunday without any extra compensation in an atmosphere laden with the most pestilential microbes brought by the sacks containing the mail matter, besides the most intolerable stenches which prevail for want of proper and scientific ventilation . . . . From the moment one enters until he emerges from the post office pest hole not a ray of God's luminary is seen, which is so necessary to the quickening of the natural functions.

The congested and inadequate post office buildings were a constant source of worry to officials. In 1898 there were 918 post offices of the first and second class, of which only 225 were located in Federal buildings. The remaining 603 were leased, as were an additional 241 stations and 23 third class offices, representing an annual expenditure of over $816,000 in rental.[248] Until 1898, leases were restricted to one-year terms and the Department was reluctant to improve property which it did not own.

New York City represented an especially difficult problem, the scope of which was outlined by Louis E. Van Norman in 1906:[249]

> The New York Post-Office is not only the center for the distribution of the vast amount of mail matter addressed to citizens in the metropolis and written by them to persons in the city and other portions of the country. It is also the gateway through which the tremendous amount of postal matter of all kinds from abroad is sent out to every portion of our own country, and the funnel through which almost all the letters, papers, and packages must pass from the United States to the rest of the world. . . .
>
> The city delivery department collected and delivered, in round numbers, a billion and a half pieces of mail matter. More than nine million dollars' worth of stamps and post-cards were sold . . . .
>
> The New York Post-Office, with its more than fifty-eight hundred employees, is not administered on the centralized plan . . . . It consists of a general office with . . . thirty-seven . . . branch stations . . . . Mail matter is assorted and bagged for these branch stations by clerks on incoming ships and trains as though they were separate cities . . . . Work is supplemented by two hundred and ten sub-stations,—located chiefly in drug stores,—at which regular post-office business is done, but which are not centers for the collection and delivery of mail. . . .
>
> Even after the postal clerks on incoming trains and steamers have done their best in the matter of assortment, there still remains a stupendous amount of labor in sorting. Besides the main tasks of separating the different classes of mail and then regrouping it for city, outside domestic, and foreign distribution,

there is the underpaid matter to be rated, the unmailable pieces to be weeded out, and the custom-house and Dead Letter Office to be remembered. The registry and money-order departments are, of course, practically separate offices . . . .

The bulk of the Canadian and foreign mail—incoming and outgoing—passes through New York . . . .

The best that can possibly be done with the present General Post-Office building and facilities is totally inadequate for the needs of New York locally and as a distributing center for the mails of the rest of the country. The present building is woefully inadequate in the matter of space and light. It is thirty years old, but it is fifty years behind the times . . . . In the working-rooms, every appliance and scheme that Yankee ingenuity could suggest has been adopted and is in use. But the devices and expedients only serve to emphasize the great needs. A general post-office needs unlimited free, light space . . . . The least possible amount of handling and the greatest possible amount of motion should be the watch-word of post-office administrators.

A new Post Office building, with space for Washington city post-office operations, was opened in 1898. Requests for new post offices in other major cities were repeatedly made; funds for labor-saving devices remained inadequate. By 1910, however, the situation seemed to be improving. Congress had appropriated $25,000 for plant and equipment improvement. Postal officials promptly ordered better facing tables and belt conveyor systems for three principal post offices. Conveyors had already proved satisfactory at Chicago and Washington and in the Hudson Terminal and Grand Central postal stations of New York City.[250]

A new policy for "constructing Federal buildings exclusively for post-office purposes in the large cities and of locating these buildings as near as possible to the principal railroad station" was under way in 1910, an improvement over the older method which often included other Federal agencies within the same building.[251] The new St. Louis post office, then under construction, was connected with the Union Railroad Station by tunnel. Mechanical conveyors moved mail within the new building, and belt conveyors carried mail from the receiving platform, the opening tables, and pouch racks to the tunnel entrance. A bucket conveyor was also employed from the tunnel to the distributing room on the main floor. Pneumatic tubes carried messages between the executive offices within the building. All these systems were installed for about $100,000. In Chicago, the Department contracted for 23,150 square feet of floor space in the new Chicago and Northwestern Railroad terminal at Canal and Madison Streets, with a conveyor belt to carry mail from the trains to the post office. The conveyor made it possible for the mail contained in the first sacks thrown off a car to be distributed before the car was emptied. Although the 400 employees in this subterranean office worked without benefit of daylight, they were at least given a "first-class ventilating system" while working the 100 tons of mail which were handled every day. At the same time, construction was under way on the long-awaited new post office for New York which, when completed in 1912, provided 361,000 square feet of useful floor surface. Portions were already in operation in 1910 before construction was completed. Chutes and conveyors were carrying mail from the railroad tracks to the basement and main-floor work areas where adequate natural light and ventilating systems made life more bearable for the clerks. In 1911 work was begun on a new central post office, located next to the main railroad station, in Washington, D.C., incorporating the best available mail handling equipment.[252]

The city post office clerks also received additional relief by 1911 with a reduction in the hours of service. The majority of employees had been given "a complete day of rest on Sunday and others granted compensatory time for Sunday work and service in excess of eight hours. Taking the average for the whole year for the entire number of first and second class offices," in 1911, "the hours of service daily do not exceed eight."[253]

MAIL TRANSPORTATION
IN
METROPOLITAN AREAS
1869-1920

During the period of great metropolitan growth, new and often unique problems in handling mail began to confront the Department. Railroad terminals in many cities were widely separated, although some urban areas such as St. Louis and Washington eventually benefited from "union" railroad terminals. At the same time, population growth meant ever-enlarging boundaries enclosing increased areas of cities. Even though cities and suburbs may have retained their separate identities in name, the gradual knitting together of cities and towns rendered some established transportation and distribution techniques inadequate. There was a strain on the free delivery service; carriers, besides delivering mail to addressees, gathered the mail deposited in street letter boxes and transported it to their post office. Carrier routes became quite lengthy or remote from the home office and in 1896, to cite one year as an example, $560,000 was requested to cover horse-hire, streetcar fare, and bicycle expense for the carrier service alone.[254] This problem was partly remedied by substantial increases in the number of stations and substations subsidiary to principal city post offices, growing from 424 subsidiary offices in 1893 to 857 in 1896. More efficiency and a saving in money were possible by establishing 151 urban stations and substations in lieu of second, third, and fourth class offices in 1895 and 1896.[255]

In 1896, the whole problem of postal wagon service in urban areas was reviewed. Two types of city service had been maintained over the years—"regulation wagon" and "screen wagon" service. All inland mail transportation was paid for out of a common fund, but in 1869 "mail-messenger" service was distinguished by name in an appropriation bill. This service had originally entailed the transportation of mail between depots or steamboat landings and the local post office. If these routes were less than a quarter of a mile, the transportation company was expected to furnish a messenger; if the route were longer, or if the company provided no service, the post office hired a messenger but not, it should be noted, under contract. In 1861, the rather informal employment of these messengers in New York City was considered inadequate and routes between the post office and stations were placed on a contract basis. In 1864 this contract service, provided with water-tight, one-horse wagons, was paid for with Star Route funds. After 1877, the construction of wagons for this service was standardized according to plans and specifications issued periodically by the Department. As implied, these vehicles became known formally as "regulation wagons."[256]

Meanwhile, a different type of wagon— the "screen wagon"—was introduced at Sherman, Texas, in 1886 as a feature of the mail-messenger service. Regulation and screen wagon service spread to other cities and towns, with regulation wagons being employed in thirty-seven of the largest cities in 1895. In that year, screen wagons were used in forty-eight cities under the mail-messenger system without contracts and in forty-three cities, also as part of the mail-messenger service, but under contracts.[257]

The whole system had become quite confusing, even to officials of the Department. In 1895, regulation wagon service was defined as the "service" performed in cities in wagons of uniform character prescribed by the Department. It is included in the estimate for star service, and is paid for out of the appropriation for that service."[258] In 1896, a comparable statement did little to clarify the screen wagon service. "Screen wagons are used for service similar to the regulation wagon in other cities and towns."[259] Fortunately, in 1896 all these services were combined in one appropriation and became easier to manage. Screen wagons were found to be more desirable vehicles for city service and by 1895 the Department predicted that regulation wagons would be supplanted by either the streetcar or "some improved device known as the horseless wagon."[260]

Although the auto-truck eventually made the prediction come true, it is of interest that horse-and-wagon postal service survived on the narrow streets of Philadelphia until 31 January 1955.[261]

Collection and Distribution Wagons

The management of the wagon service was concerned with the most rapid movement of mail through the congested city streets. Drivers were furnished schedules of incoming and outgoing trains and were expected to make all connections promptly.[262] The failure of wagon service could result in a delay of twenty-four hours in the ultimate delivery of a letter. In the effort to expedite delivery, the Department again adopted the R.P.O. technique and put the post office "on wheels," but in this instance behind a horse.

The Department announced in 1895 that an auto truck was under construction with a compartment for clerks to separate mail while being driven through city streets. At the same time, horse-drawn vehicles for a similar purpose were under construction and were apparently the only type to see service. Designated as Collection and Distribution Wagons, two were placed in service in Washington, D.C., and New York on 1 October 1896. Mail was collected from street letter boxes, postmarked, distributed, and pouched for railway mail lines at the depots, for post offices, and substations along the route. Officials believed that such wagons could be profitably introduced in critical metropolitan areas to alleviate the congestion in offices, keep the cost of clerk hire at a minimum, and reduce the cost of regulation wagon service. The cars were modeled after the R.P.O. cars. Unlike the service performed on R.P.O.s, however, the Collection and Distribution Wagons could only distribute the outbound mail and a limited amount of mail deposited or exchanged at intermediate points. This experimental service was tried for about three years and was extended to include Buffalo, but efforts were abandoned in favor of more productive mail-moving systems.[263]

Streetcar Railway Post Offices

A more practical and successful application of the traveling post office on city streets was the electric and cable-car railway system. The streetcar R.P.O. system had its origins in St. Louis in 1891, when Postmaster J.B. Harlowe arranged for a newly electrified line to collect mail from street letter boxes and substations for delivery to the main post office in addition to delivering mail to carriers on their routes. This first arrangement in St. Louis was unsatisfactory, but between December 1892 and February 1893, the experimental service was formalized by post office and streetcar officials. The service involved the pouching, canceling, and distribution of mail along the route. Carrier routes were serviced, as were the substations and post office. For its time, the service was not only practical but

A streetcar Railway Post Office in Pittsburgh. Such service operated in that city during the years 1898-1917. Notice the letter drop in the side of the car near the rear door.

reasonably rapid. In 1895, the new service became part of the Railway Mail Service[264] and by October, of that year, twelve streetcars were operating in six cities, with numerous advantages.[265]

Take for instance the Third avenue line in New York, upon which cars run from the post-office to One hundred and ninety-fourth street every thirty minutes; time in transit, one hour and forty-five minutes. This places the downtown and uptown stations in much quicker and more frequent communication than they have ever been before.

In Boston, by reason of the fact that the street-car lines are all under one management, we are able to move mails from one suburb to another, as, for instance, from North Cambridge and Cambridgeport to Brookline, by direct rapid transit, the mail not being compelled to pass through the main office . . . .

The railway post-offices centering at Boston can pouch to street-car lines all mails for suburban points reached by them, and the street-car lines in turn can gather up all the mail from suburban points and pouch it direct to the departing trains at various depots.

White postal streetcars rapidly became more numerous on city streets across the nation. By the end of October 1896, 26 lines were in operation, employing 75 clerks, and handling 505,481 pieces of mail daily. Most of the cars had a letter-drop in the side of the car for patrons to deposit letters at frequent stops. In addition, street letter boxes at important intersections were painted white to indicate to patrons that the mail picked up from such a box would be on its way with the next postal streetcar. Collections from boxes not on the streetcar line were deposited in the white boxes for expediting the mail, and the letter carriers on many routes undoubtedly were relieved of the task of carrying as much mail back to the post office as they had distributed.[266]

Although the streetcar distribution system was unquestionably successful, it was limited to only the largest cities. The extent of the service varied from year to year, as the lines were changed and routes were consolidated. The duration of the service within the various cities is shown in table 6.[267]

Table 6. Streetcar Railway Post Offices in the United States

Cities	Year Started	Year Ended
Baltimore	1897	1929
Boston	1895	1915
Brooklyn	1894	1914
Chicago	1895	1915
Cincinnati	1895	1915
Cleveland	1908	1920
New York	1895	1900
Omaha	1910	1921
Philadelphia	1895	1915
Pittsburgh	1898	1917
Rochester	1896	1908
St. Louis	1893	1915
San Francisco	1896	1905
Seattle	1905	1913
Washington	1895	1913

With the advent of the "horseless wagon," the Department was reluctant to establish the service after 1900 and few lines survived after 1915.

Wagons and streetcars operating between railroad depots, post offices, and substations were subject to delays in traffic jams and bad weather. In searching for a more rapid means of moving mail between city offices and eliminating as many interruptions as possible, the Department developed a practical underground system of transportation. Postal officials were impressed with the success of pneumatic postal tubes in Berlin, Paris, and other European cities and eventually were able to install a number of lines in some of the larger U.S. cities.[268] A major deterrent to the development of the U.S. pneumatic postal service, however, was that of leasing the tubes and related equipment from private companies rather than operating the system as a government-owned facility.

The first U.S. pneumatic tube line for postal purposes was installed in Philadelphia in 1893. On 1 March of that year service was inaugurated with a six-inch double-tube line between the central post office at Ninth and Market Streets and the Chestnut Street Station (the latter terminal was soon relocated in the Philadelphia Bourse Building [Substation 20] at the corner of 4th and Ranstead Streets). First, third, and fourth class matter was dispatched through the lines slightly more than a half mile in length in two minutes, compared with fifteen minutes by wagon between the same offices. After a year's experimental operation at no cost to the government, a four-year contract was concluded in 1894 at $3,450 per year.[269]

Although the first line was paid for from appropriations for mail-messenger service, Congress specifically allotted $35,000 for additional tube service in 1896. It was hoped that 24- or 36-inch tubes could be installed in Philadelphia, New York, and Boston. Existing city water and sewage lines, however, and the problem of water seepage in tidewater areas limited the maximum diameter of the new tubes to eight or ten inches. The carriers (mail-carrying cartridges) had an inside diameter of $6\frac{7}{8}$ inches.[270] Contracts were completed for the construction and operation of the new lines in 1896 and 1897. In Philadelphia the line connecting the central post office, the Pennsylvania Terminal (Broad Street Station), and the Reading Terminal was inaugurated 18 April 1898. Tube lines began operation in New York in October 1897, connecting the main post office and the Produce Exchange (Station P). By 1 August 1898, about six miles of New York tubes also linked the main post office with Station H (44th St. and Lexington Ave.) via Station D, Madison Square Station, and Station F, and the main post office in Brooklyn via the Brooklyn Bridge. The general post office in Boston was connected by tube with the Northern Union Station in December 1897.[271]

The pneumatic carriers moved great quantities of mail rapidly and efficiently, although there was always some controversy about justifying the high rental costs in relation to the results obtained. Each carrier was 21 inches long and had a capacity of 600 letters. During rush periods, carriers were dispatched at 6- to 15-second intervals and could move approximately 360,000 letters per hour in either direction. At certain offices pouches for out-of-town letters were kept open until five minutes before trains departed. Incoming mail reached letter carriers for earlier deliveries. Special delivery mail was expedited. Wagon service was reduced and, between certain offices, the tube lines were able to handle all first class mail.[272] In 1898 the importance of the tubes was obvious.[273]

> A carrier dispatched between [the New York] general post office and Station H arrives at its destination in seven minutes. The schedule time for wagons over the same route is from thirty-five to forty minutes, the latter time being the rule. The actual time by wagon varies on account of the congestion of the streets, weight of load, etc. . . .
> Inasmuch as the mail going by wagon has to be removed therefrom at the general post office, and the pouches opened and dumped, it is fully eight minutes before the distribution of the mail is begun . . . .

It was also noted that letters mailed in the general post office could be dispatched and placed on an outbound train sixty-five minutes after the last wagon from the post office to the depot had departed. In some instances, this could represent an ultimate advancement of twenty-four hours for letter delivery at certain destinations.

No extensions of the service were made between 1898 and 1902, because Congress believed that costs were excessive. In 1900, therefore, the cost of only 8.05 miles of double tubes then in operation in Boston, Brooklyn, New York, and Philadelphia, was $222,266 per year. When the contracts expired on 30 June 1901 there were no appropriated funds to cover new contracts and all tube service was suspended for a year.[274] During 1902-1903, however, Congress appropriated $500,000 for servicing and extending the pneumatic lines. Additional lines were placed in operation in Boston, Philadelphia, and New York, and new systems were constructed in Chicago and St. Louis. Before World War I, the system reached its maximum range (see table 7).[275]

The cost of the service was considered exceptionally high by some Members of Congress and in 1912 a joint commission of the Senate and House of Representatives began a study to determine the feasibility of Government purchase and operation of the tube systems. The majority report indicated that purchase was advisable but two members, Representatives Fred L. Blackmon and Victor Murdock, dissented. No action was taken, and in 1915 Postmaster General A.S. Burleson announced that existing contracts would expire on 30 June 1917, and that the Department would submit recommendations regarding the service.[276] Contracts were extended to 30 June 1918, and the Department, meanwhile, strongly urged that the service be discontinued in Chicago, Philadelphia, Boston, and St.

Table 7.   Pneumatic Tube Postal Mileage in United States Cities, 1910 and 1915

Metropolitan area	Miles (1910)	Miles (1915)
Boston	6.774	6.774
Brooklyn	1.35	1.35
New York	21.2763	26.421
Philadelphia	9.987	9.9999
Chicago	9.2058	10.0381
St. Louis	1.9465	1.988
Total miles	50.5396	56.571
Total annual Cost	$859,173.20	$961,707,00

Louis, with service to be maintained in New York if economical contracts could be negotiated.[277]

Opponents of the pneumatic service stated that certain mails were actually delayed and that the rental was "exorbitant, unjustified, and an extravagant waste of public funds."[278] Postmaster General Burleson concurred.[279]

> All . . . reports with one exception show an inevitable drift toward the abandonment of the tubes because of the advent of the automobile.
>
> While all other kinds of transportation facilities have been greatly improved during the past 15 years the pneumatic tubes have been at a standstill. The frequency of dispatch and the capacity of the container . . . are the same now as when the service was installed. . . .The tubes might have been of some use years ago when they carried all of the first-class mail, but their value decreased with the increase in the volume of mail and the . . . improvement of the auto truck until at this time, because of their limited capacity, it is necessary to parallel the tube lines with vehicle transportation to such extent that the mail carried by the tubes can be carried as expeditiously by the vehicles with but little additional cost.

These views undoubtedly tended to oversimplify the question of tube service. The statements that quantities of mail were actually delayed were open to question and the central issue in the controversy was that of cost. In order to conserve nearly a million dollars for the war effort, Burleson submitted no estimate for the cost of operating the pneumatic tubes and the entire service was suspended on 30 June 1918.[280]

There was considerable public agitation for the return of the tube service, however, and businessmen recommended that the government purchase the lines and make efforts to keep the vehicular service at a minimum on narrow city streets.[281] Finally, funds were made available for restoring service in New York, and on 2 October 1922 about twenty-seven miles of lines were placed in operation. Congested traffic conditions on city streets led Department officials to assume a more generous attitude toward the pneumatic lines and on 1 August 1926 service in Boston was restored.[282]

> The general post office and 23 of the larger postal stations in the city of New York and the general post office at Brooklyn are connected by pneumatic tubes, which provide an efficient facility for the expeditious movement of the mail between the hours of 4 a.m. and 11 p.m. . . .
> Boston has one of the most intensely congested business areas of any city in the country, and inasmuch as the general post office is located in the center of this area, about midway between the North and South railroad stations, which are on the northern and southern edges, respectively, of the congested section, the department recommended that these points be connected with pneumatic tubes.

The automobile increased in numbers during the twenties, but this phenomenon, which had been partly responsible for suspending a great portion of the tube lines in 1918, now made the pneumatic post more desirable in New York and Boston. While it was true that the capacity of the lines remained fixed, the basic value of the service became recognized and it is rather remarkable that lines in other cities were not restored to operation. In 1927, when the Nation was well into the auto age, Postmaster General Harry S. New observed that:[283]

> The increasing desire of the public for expedition in the transportation of business applies to the transportation of mail through the congested areas of the more important cities. The heavy traffic on the streets presents difficulties to ordinary transportation which become more serious in connection with the transportation of the mails which must move on prescribed schedules, otherwise train connections are missed and ultimate delivery is delayed.
> Pneumatic tubes operate underground where they are not affected by street congestion or weather conditions and therefore provide a means for the expeditious handling of first-class mail. The tubes can be used only to a limited degree in the transportation of other classes of mail. Conduits and carriers of larger capacities would be necessary for the efficient transportation of bulk mail by undersurface means. The subject requires further consideration . . . .

The tubes, therefore, could not entirely replace surface transportation unless a new system was installed. Nevertheless, 55 percent of New York City letter mail was handled by the pneumatic lines, and motor truck service in Boston was reduced.[284] The proposal to develop tube lines with increased capacity was apparently doomed when the Depression overtook the Department in 1931 and postal revenues fell sharply for four consecutive years.

Service in Boston and New York was maintained until well after World War II. As late as 1949 it was described as a "miraculous means of expediting the mail" by Albert Goldman, Postmaster of New York City.[285] Actual operation of the lines, however, did present some problems.[286]

> The carriers . . . hold about 15 pounds of mail and small packages. They average 35 miles an hour . . . . On a full day the lines carry over 8,000 carriers [6,000,000 letters daily] . . . .
>
> The rule is that anything marked fragile doesn't go into the carriers. But a good many of the citizens forget to mark their packages fragile, and the Postoffice boys have received carriers loaded with perfume, medicine, ball bearings, powder, nuts, bolts, and screws . . . .
>
> What with over 1,000 bends and turns in the lines jams are not infrequent.
>
> Joe [the unidentified traffic manager of the lines] has had as many as three or four [jams] in one day . . . Once he had to pick his way over the 12-inch catwalk alongside the cables of the Brooklyn Bridge hunting for a big block . . .
>
> It was caused by ice and we had to pour in denatured alcohol to thaw it out. That was sheer irony. The weather was below freezing. This was during prohibition and we couldn't get any stimulants ourselves.

On 28 April 1950 the tube line over the Brooklyn Bridge was discontinued during reconstruction work on the Bridge. The discontinuation was permanent.[287] The Boston lines were abandoned on 31 December 1950 upon the expiration of the rental contract of $24,000 per year for the 1.8-mile system connecting the North and South Stations and the main post office.[288] Shortly after entering into a new lease which would continue the remaining New York lines for ten years after 1951, the Department officials had second thoughts and proceeded to end the last of the tube service in 1953. Postmaster General Arthur E. Summerfield explained:[289]

> One of the things that we soon came upon was the apparent excessive cost of handling mail by the tube system . . . .The survey indicated rather clearly, we felt, that the cost of operation, which is something like a million dollars a year, could be practically eliminated . . . .
>
> So instead of canceling the contract, we notified the company that we were going to discontinue the service for an indefinite period, to determine if we could handle that volume of mail at much less cost. We put that so-called pilot operation in effect a week ago yesterday [December 2, 1953] . . . We are experiencing no difficulty in the handling of mail by other means. There is no delay in the service . . . .

On 31 December 1953 the tube service was formally suspended and mail was subsequently transported by motor vehicles.[290]

Automobile Service

The motor truck had triumphed over all other forms of city mail transportation by the mid-1950s—the horse and wagon, the streetcar, and the pneumatic tubes. In many respects, its adoption by the Post Office Department paralleled its use by commerce and industry. The officials in Washington followed its development with interest and were anxious to employ it at the earliest opportunity.

One of the earliest references to the automobile in Department literature is that of 1895 already cited.[291] Officials anticipated that the "horseless wagons" would be fitted out with a mail-sorting compartment so that a clerk could separate and pouch letters while the vehicle was in motion, but this plan apparently was unsuccessful until 1937, when mail was separated in a truck between the downtown Miami Florida, post office and the airport.[292] The highway post office vehicles of later years were essentially substitutes or extensions of the intercity railway mail service.

In December 1899, with snow on the ground, a Winton "motor wagon" labeled "U.S. Mail" appeared on the streets of Cleveland, Ohio. *The Horseless Age* for 20 December 1899 reported:[293]

> The Winton motor was subjected to an interesting test in Cleveland last week. Authority was granted by the postal authorities at Washington for the company to make a mail collection test in Cleveland. The weather was very "wintery." Snow was deep and in some place[s] badly drifted, and during the entire time of the run there was a big snow storm in progress. The [auto] wagon made a collection trip which covered over 22 miles of paved and unpaved streets from 101 letter boxes and 25 package boxes. The time required for this collection by horse and wagon (under favorable conditions of weather) is 6 hours and 1 minute. Before starting the local postmaster said that on account of the severe weather his report to the Washington authorities would be favorable if the wagon succeeded in pulling through on the regular schedule . . . .The first box was opened at 12:22 p.m. and the last one at 2:49 p.m., making a total time of 2 hours and 27 minutes and thereby reducing the scheduled time considerably over 50 percent.

Another experiment was carried out in Buffalo, New York, in 1899. Although the experiments showed favorable results, the Department was reluctant to expend money for automobile service until 1 October 1906 when two Columbia trucks were placed under contract to collect mail from street letter boxes in Baltimore. The favorable performance of these vehicles led Department officials to plan expanded auto service in other cities and to replace the horse carts.[294]

In 1907 postal trucks were introduced in Milwaukee, Detroit, and Washington, and in 1908-1909 in Indianapolis and Boston. By 1908 the service in Washington employed a tricycle Indian motor-van with a capacity of 250 pounds, five Brush package trucks, and two one-cylinder Cadillac vehicles. The decision to employ trucks followed successful tests of "a primitive machine capable of carrying about 300 pounds."[295] H.G. Ward, writing for *The Commercial Vehicle,* noted that conditions in Washington were quite favorable to motor trucks—there were few hills, and the streets were wide and well paved. The Milwaukee service was particularly

Two Columbia motor trucks share the driveway with horses and
wagons at the Baltimore Post Office, 1 October 1904, during the early
period of experimentation with motor vehicles.

successful and the Detroit service was extensive and economical. Ward also
noted that "the Department has frequently received proposals for furnishing
motor vehicle service in place of the usual screen wagon service, but except
in the cases of Detroit and Milwaukee the bids were not advantageous to the
government and were rejected.[296]

Certain aspects of the new service were troublesome in the early years.
Although automobiles were used in at least nine cities during 1909-1911,
their use was temporarily discontinued in Washington and Buffalo when
satisfactory bids for one-year contracts were not received. The Department
had reached a firm conclusion that efficient auto service was superior to
horse-drawn vehicles or service performed by carriers on foot. The idea of
sorting mail in transit was abandoned. The function of the auto in 1910 was
described as follows.[297]

Mail collections have been . . . expeditiously made by automobiles . . . .

With automobiles more frequent return trips can be made to the office, thus permitting earlier dispatches of the mail to its destination and a more even distribution of the work in the mailing division and preventing the congestion which occurs when a large amount of matter is brought in at about the same time from long trips.

In addition to the employment of automobiles in the collection service they have been advantageously used for making early morning deliveries of important mail in large quantities to mills and manufacturing plants, which are usually located in the outskirts of the cities, and also for carrying out heavy bundles of mail for delivery by foot carriers on routes remote from the office . . .

It is estimated that one automobile under contract manned by one carrier operating in residential and outlying districts will perform nearly as much service as three mounted carriers.

Increased burdens placed on the collection and delivery service by the new Parcel Post system, which was inaugurated on 1 January 1913, prompted the Department to purchase forty-one motor vehicles in 1914 for operation in several cities.[298] By 1915, a considerable number of streetcar postal routes were supplanted and, during 1914-1916, new contracts combined screen wagon and collection and distribution services, resulting in more economical and diversified use of auto trucks.[299] The cost of the service was not restricted to the purchase price of the vehicles, however, and the Department was forced to invest in garage facilities, replacement parts, and new mechanical services.[300]

The policy of purchasing vehicles received its greatest impetus when the Department discovered that some contractors had combined to submit "exorbitant" bids and that one company added many unnecessary trips to increase its compensation. The abandonment of contract service between 1914 and 1918 was pursued as fast as trucks could be purchased and by 1 July of the latter year government-owned mail trucks were operating in twelve of the larger cities. At that time, a total of 1,004 trucks were owned by the Department and required the services of about 1,200 mechanics, drivers, garagemen, clerks, and supervisory officials.[301] The change in traditional policy toward utilizing contract service and equipment was remarkable.

Wartime conditions also resulted in a substantial increase in the size of the government-owned mail truck fleet. Normal purchases had raised the total to 1,692 auto vehicles in 1919. By November of that year, the Department had begun to receive surplus vehicles transferred from the War Department under the Act of 2 July 1918. Under that authority, 5,778 trucks and 1,087 motorcycles were scheduled for transfer to the postal service.

It was found, however, that the Department could only absorb a limited quantity. Vehicles had to be stored and tires and tubes, which deteriorated in storage, were sent to various parts of the country as spare parts. Of the 2,606 trucks and motorcycles in service in 163 cities in July 1920, only 1,444 war surplus vehicles were included in the total. Over 700 motorcycles were in service. The war-surplus trucks required extensive modification and the construction of the costly screen bodies was a major problem. The War Department's twenty-eight different makes of trucks presented the problem of securing and stocking a multitude of parts, for combined with the Department's existing fleet, a total of thirty-five different makes were on the roster by July 1920, to say nothing of the motorcycles.[302] Despite the acceleration of the ownership policy, well over $4,000,000 was required for contract-vehicle service in the same year. In 1920 more than fifty percent of the vehicles in the postal service were of the auto type.[303]

Although the variety of vehicles was confusing, popular makes such as Overland, Riker, Selden, and Moreland were not heavily represented. There were 1,257 Fords of ⅜-ton capacity in service, and only a few cities contended with the headaches resulting from nonstandardization.[304] It did not take long, however, before the Department recognized the economy to be gained through standardization and in 1921, with the expenditure reaching more than $11,777,000 for government-owned vehicular service, the Department announced that it would retain only eight standard types of trucks.[305]

There is no question but what the automobile was the most important revolutionary means of urban transportation adopted during the 1890-1920 period. Unlike the Collection and Distribution Wagons, the streetcar Railway Post Offices, and the pneumatic tubes, automobiles were advantageously employed in large and small cities alike, and U.S. mail trucks were making their rounds in such cities as Augusta, Maine; Butte, Montana; and Santa Rosa, California, before the end of 1921. The growth of the Government-owned automobile service is as striking as any record of U.S. postal development, and there were indeed few postal innovations so enthusiastically embraced (table 8).[306]

Table 8. Government-owned Motor Vehicles in Postal Service

Year	Number
1914	41
1918	1,004
1920	2,606
1925	5,353
1931	8,087
1940	8,650
1951	15,755
1960	36,871

Under Postmaster General Wanamaker, the Department began a test of delivering and collecting mail from household letter boxes in 1891-1892. The boxes were originally considered for this combined dual function to eliminate the previous necessity of having the carrier ring a doorbell or knock at the door to deliver the mail and to permit the householder to conveniently deposit his mail in the same receptacle for pick-up by the carrier. So conceived, the plan required a specially designed box to provide adequate security against pilfering and the Department solicited models from inventors in order to determine a satisfactory type.

The Department was flooded with sample boxes and the experiment was put into operation in Washington and St. Louis with two approved box styles. As a result people wrote more letters and requested the carriers to sell postage stamps.[307] The experiment regarding the collections was not considered successful by later officials, but the value of household boxes to facilitate delivery was recognized.

The Department had suggested that patrons install household letter boxes for delivery as early as 1878. In 1909, city postmasters began a more intensive campaign to speed the adoption of household boxes. In that year it was estimated that a fifteen-second delay at each house deprived the letter carrier of an hour and a half in daily working time. This theoretical loss was considered quite serious since letter carriers were regarded as high-paid employees at $1000 per year.[308] In 1909 and subsequent years, the Department requested legislation making it compulsory for patrons to provide household letter boxes and by 1912 had instituted the policy of providing new or extended free city delivery only to patrons who provided household receptacles.[309] By 1920 the Department was requiring certain "civic improvements, such as good, continuous sidewalks, crosswalks, street lights and signs, house numbers, and receptables" before authorizing the establishment or extension of city delivery routes.[310]

Finally, after 1 March 1923 the Department implemented its new regulation of not delivering mail to homes which did not provide household boxes.[311]

Boxes for the deposit of mail in public places also received attention from officials over the years. Although letter drops were provided in the sides of streetcar R.P.O.s and the Collection and Distribution Wagons, some regular trolleys were utilized for carrying mail to post offices and were provided with letter deposit boxes in Des Moines, Iowa, in 1897-1898 and in Hartford and Grand Rapids in 1899.[312] Despite the four-pound limit for parcels, the need for improved "package boxes" with larger drops and capacity was noted as early as 1898.[313] In 1913, with the introduction of domestic parcel post service this need was even more apparent. In 1912 new styles of street letter boxes had been adopted with slanted and curved bottoms enabling letters to automatically slide into the collector's pouch when the boxes were opened, thereby saving a few valuable seconds of time at each stop along the route.[314]

One of the more interesting aspects of the collection box development is that of the mail chute installations in office buildings. The first mail chute-receiving box system was tested under Department supervision in Rochester, New York, in 1884. Following the successful tests, two chutes were installed in buildings in New York City. With widespread adoption of these chutes, certain legal problems arose and it was ruled in 1890 that the chutes were under the jurisdiction of the Postmaster General. When the ruling was questioned in 1893, Congress passed an act placing all chutes and mail matter deposited therein under the exclusive custody of the Department. By 1902 the construction of the chutes was closely regulated, requiring, for example, that an elastic cushion be provided in the bottom of the box if the chute was more than two stories high. By 1905, there were from 1,600 to 1,700 chutes in buildings throughout the country.[315]

The use of zone numbers as part of addresses is considered a recent development dating from 1943, but a similar innovation designed to facilitate the separation of mail for carrier routes was suggested by the Department as early as 1899. In that year, James E. White, General Superintendent of the Railway Mail Service, requested that postal officials follow the example of the postmaster of Chicago in urging patrons to include the carrier's number or the postal station letter or number in addresses which normally bore the addressee's name, street number, city, and state. White pointed out that, as a result of the circular letter sent to all Chicago patrons in 1895, thousands of people began to incorporate the helpful details in addresses.[316] The recommendation, however, was not widely adopted.

The Nationwide Improved Mail Service (NIMS) developed by the Department in 1961 was anticipated by William R. Willcox, Postmaster of New York City, as early as 1905. Willcox circulated a letter requesting that business mailings be made before the evening mail rush which occured between 4 and 9 p.m. The response to the request was so successful that Willcox achieved the elimination of most of the overtime work.[317] New York was also the scene of another innovation to expedite the distribution of incoming foreign mails for the city, the nation, and foreign countries. On 1 July 1897 a special "transfer service" was introduced employing a postal boat which met the incoming mail steamers at the quarantine station to receive and convey the mails to the railroad wharves, thus eliminating the time consumed by the steamers in docking and passing through customs. The actual transfer of the pouched mail took place in the harbor, with as many as two to three thousand sacks being dumped into the hold of the postal boat by means of a flexible canvas chute as the vessels were tied together. In 1905, it was stated that the sleek little harbor steamer, the

Postmaster General, saved from two to fifteen hours in the dispatch of certain letters. This was accomplished partly by sorting the mail aboard the harbor ship into three separate groups: one for Pennsylvania Railroad trains bound west, southwest and south; a group for Grand Central Station trains bound for the west, northwest, Canada, and transpacific points; and the last for New York City mail.[318] In 1914 a similar service was inaugurated in San Francisco.[319]

Another isolated but valuable service was the Postal Marine Service of Detroit, established during the Great Lakes shipping season of 1895. The idea apparently originated with Charles F. Swan, the superintendent of deliveries at Detroit and was at first considered an experimental service. The first season of operation was such a success that the Lake Carriers' Association urged the Department to continue the service. Essentially, it employed a postal boat which pulled alongside vessels passing through the Detroit River for the purpose of delivering mail to the crew and receiving mail from the ship. The actual exchange of mail took place from a rowboat dropped off by the postal boat. As the steamer overtook the rowboat, a line was dropped and secured by the oarsman, who exchanged the mail in a bucket at the end of a second line as the freighter towed the rowboat along "under full headway." During the shipping season of 1896, 175,850 pieces of mail were exchanged, and in 1900 the total reached 322,940. The round-the-clock service was performed in shifts. It was noted that each season's marine tonnage passing Detroit exceeded that of New York and Liverpool combined and that, since seven-tenths of the freighters did not stop at Detroit, it was considered a most important service to personnel who represented a population equivalent to a small city served by regular free-delivery.[320] The "carriers" who performed their duties on the Detroit River probably faced more hazards on each eight hour shift than the average pony express rider experienced during his entire career.

In 1905 a contract was executed to provide underground transportation of mail by electric powered trains running on tracks through tunnels in Chicago connecting several post offices and six railroad depots. The trains were to run at eight miles per hour while carrying ten tons of mail per trip and, if necessary, a postal employee. The contract also provided for the construction and operation of supplementary chutes, elevators, mechanical lifts and belts. By the summer of 1906, portions of the tunnel were in operation but the miniature subway system was not fully ready and accepted by the Department until 19 January 1907. Because the Department paid only for services rendered, the Illinois Tunnel Company received considerably less than the $172,600 per year authorized under the contract of 1905. Upon expiration of the contract, the Department refused to utilize the tunnel for postal service under terms of the tunnel company's bid requesting annual payments of $300,000. Instead, the Department contracted for screen wagon service for the same route at $145,400 per year, with the mail service being discontinued on 30 June 1908. However, an underground tunnel system employing electrically powered trains was adopted for the transportation of mail in London after a British postal investigating committee had toured the United States in 1911.[321]

PARCEL POST SERVICE
1913

The absence of a sound parcel post service before 1913 may seem surprising to present-day patrons of the U.S. Post Office. In many respects, reluctance on the part of many officials to support the establishment of such a service before 1913 is equally surprising. A number of elements are responsible for both the resistance to and the eventual acceptance of the idea.

Traditionally, parcel had been carried by colonial and early Federal post-riders "out of the mails" without the serious objections of most postal officials. The stagecoach companies and railroads had fallen legitimate heirs to the parcel transportation service because the Department had shown little interest in carrying "freight" until the latter part of the nineteenth century. The private expresses, whether individuals or international concerns, had developed a well organized and efficient group of services before the end of the century. In many respects, postal officials had quite enough to think about with regard to handling mail matter under the four-pound limit. Newspapers, books. magazines, free mail sent under official franks or penalty clauses, and advertising matter had posed serious problems in handling and transportation. When reformers such as Postmaster General Wanamaker and James I. Cowles proposed that a domestic parcel post be established, there arose a storm of protest.[322]

Unlike the United States, parcel post systems were in operation in many foreign countries before 1913, and the problem of exchanging parcels was one of the early major issues to come before the Universal Postal Union. With such an outside stimulus, the United States Post Office Department found itself involved with parcel post in connection with foreign mails long before a reasonable domestic service had been developed. The first parcel convention with a foreign country was negotiated with Jamaica, British West Indies, on 22 July 1887 (25 Stat. L. 1393). Gradually, parcel post arrangements were worked out with other countries, principally with Central American nations and British colonies in the West Indies. The service, however, did not represent a heavy burden on the Department, only 107,529 pounds of parcel mail being sent out of the United States in fiscal year 1899. Nevertheless, a convention with Germany was negotiated and placed in operation on 1 October 1899. Postmaster General Charles E. Smith noted that it was the first parcel post convention concluded with a European country and that it had excited a great deal of public interest, especially on the part of the business community. During the first year of U.S.-German service, 42,906 parcels were exchanged between the two countries. By 1910, U.S.-foreign parcel post service had grown to include exchange arrangements with forty foreign nations and colonies, accounting for the exchange of 827,131 packages with an aggregate weight of 2,937,075 pounds.[323]

Nevertheless, private express interests resisted the invasion of the Government in an effort to retain the domestic transportation of packages as a commercial monopoly. Cowles, a journalist who became the most vocal advocate of a parcel post reform, organized the Postal Progress League in 1902 and shortly thereafter secured the support of the National Grange in the fight for establishing the new system. The growth of the Rural Free Delivery system after 1900 also played a major role in popularizing the movement. RFD postmen were soon engaged in carrying packages of all descriptions "out of the mails." The old pattern of troubles arose again. As Surveyor Finlay had discovered on the eve of the Revolution that postmen engaged in carrying parcels often neglected the government's business, so the rural carriers of the early 1900s often neglected their primary duties of servicing United States mail. Their private express profits became more important than their annual allowance. Many rural patrons suffered and complained, and the Department, of course, received no revenues from the private transactions. Legislation soon remedied the abuses. The patrons who had benefitted from the rural postman's express, however, raised new complaints and the Department requested Congress to increase the four-pound limit on parcels delivered to rural addressees, a request which constituted a plea for "limited" domestic parcel post.[324]

The proposal for a rural parcel post was opposed by small town retailers who feared that their businesses would be wiped out by mail-order trade. The continued opposition of the express companies combined to defeat proposed legislation for five years. Political fortunes changed in 1911, however,and the express companies began to suffer under investigations which revealed that their rates and profits were exceedingly high. The companies naturally, did not offer service to millions of rural dwellers. When Wells Fargo declared a dividend of 300 percent to stockholders while the parcel post question was being debated, public opinion and political support crystallized in favor of a low cost parcel post.[325]

The Act of 24 August 1912 established a general domestic parcel post service which went into operation on 1 January 1913. The four-pound weight limit was at first increased to eleven pounds. Within a year, however, weight limits were increased to fifty pounds for short-haul packages and to twenty pounds for long-distance service. Weight and size limits have been increased over the years. Reasonable postage rates were established on a zone basis, with eight distance-zones governing the rates charged. The additional feature of a collect-on-delivery service was inaugurated on 1 July 1913 to accommodate shippers, who did not wish to extend credit, and buyers who did not wish to pay in advance. COD service, naturally, entailed additional fees for the necessary work rendered by the Department.[326]

The new service led to the issuance of a set of twelve special postage stamps bearing the legend "U.S. Parcel Post." These large stamps carried scenes which propagandized the postal service and suggested that certain segments of the population would benefit from the new parcel service, especially the rural population. The parcel post stamps, however, soon became a problem. Each of the twelve denominations was printed in the same color (a beautiful carmine). Clerks at stamp windows, who relied more on the color of stamps than on the numerals, were forced to slow their pace while selling the new issues. Shortly, it was decided that the special stamps (and the companion Parcel Post Due stamps) not only were a source of confusion but also created unnecessary supply problems and accounting work. On 1 July 1913 regular stamps became valid for parcel postage and related fees. The parcel post stamps were made valid for other mail matter and were sold until stocks on hand were exhausted.[327]

The anticipated benefit of moving farm products directly to the city household—thereby eliminating the middleman's profit and reducing the cost of living—failed to materialize. The COD service and increased weight limits did not solve the problem. When it was realized that city dwellers and farmers did not know each other, the Department experimented with a "farm-to-table" campaign. Names and addresses of farmers interested in participating were distributed by carriers in eight cities. After a successful beginning, the experiment was extended to include thirty-five cities, but the lists became complicated and patrons asked for more detailed lists also stating commodities available and the prices charged. While successful in some areas, the movement eventually failed. Too many letters had to be exchanged before agreements were reached between urban dwellers and farmers; some foodstuffs, such as eggs, were difficult to pack; the rural carriers did not favor the service; and farm prices were generally adequate in the traditional outlets. The war kept the plan alive for a short time and a heroic effort to establish cross-country parcel post truck service was suspended in 1920 after trials which had been begun in 1918.[328]

The mail order business, on the other hand, thrived on parcel post. While the express and freight service had stopped at the local depot, there was now little need for the farmer to worry about receiving his parcels from Montgomery Ward or Sears Roebuck. Instead of paying high express charges after an inconvenient trip to town, the RFD carrier became the dependable link between merchant and farmer at the lowest possible cost.[329]

The parcel post system placed an additional burden on city post offices, and by 1920 the problems were clearly recognized. Although facilities were heavily strained at times, the Department remained confident in its ability to meet any emergency.[330]

> The total number of pieces of parcel-post mail handled during the past fiscal year [ending 30 June 1920] is estimated to have exceeded 2,250,000,000 . . . . Parcels the size of an ordinary shoe box and not exceeding 4 pounds in weight are delivered by the regular foot carriers without appreciable additional cost, but those bulkier and heavier must be delivered by vehicle . . . . Horse-drawn vehicles are utilized almost exclusively in the strictly business districts where congested traffic conditions and frequency of stops preclude the economical use of automobiles. The latter have been found more efficient and economical in residential sections and the light business districts.
>
> The reliability of the service and public confidence in it were fully demonstrated in the past year during periods of railroad congestion and strikes of railway employees, expressmen, and teamsters, when an incalculable number of heavy packages of all kinds, running into the millions, were diverted from freight and express channels and thrust into the mails without notice . . .
>
> In many cities the post-office quarters available in Federal buildings, constructed years ago, have long since been outgrown, necessitating the leasing of large areas of space at high rental rates . . . . Facilities must be increased . . . .
>
> The number of parcels is becoming so great that in the large cities facilities should be had at the railroad depots or as convenient to the depots as possible for their handling

Although the service became firmly established and brought far-reaching changes to many facets of American life, the Government made no serious effort to extend the monopoly of carrying written communications to include the carriage of goods by mail. The parcel post has remained, as noted by Daniel C. Roper, First Assistant Postmaster-General (1913-1916), "with the money-order service and the postal savings system, a service incidental to the mail-service, called into existence at the will of the people, as a convenient facility which could be maintained at reasonable cost in connection with the postal establishment. It constitutes no assertion that the business done is necessarily a Government function."[331]

WORLD WAR I SERVICE

In addition to providing the Armed Forces with adequate postal facilities at training camps, at home, and the overseas theaters, several unusual developments changed the character of the postal service during the war years.

One of the first postal measures of consequence was the increase of postage rates under the War Revenue Act of 3 October 1917. First class letter postage was raised to three cents per ounce. The additional cent represented a war tax and the Postmaster General was directed to periodically deposit the extra money gained from the increase into the general fund of the Treasury. Some second class postage rates were also increased; fourth-class parcels were taxed, the amount being indicated by internal revenue stamps affixed to the wrappers. The two-cent domestic first class rate was restored in 1919, the Internal Revenue tax was discontinued on parcel mail on 1 January 1922, but certain second class rates remained high and were increased periodically until 1928. The privilege granted members of the Armed Forces to mail letters without prepayment of postage (under an Act of 3 March 1879) was modified under the Act of 3 October 1917 so that servicemen overseas could send their letters free of all postage.[332]

The increased volume of mail—reaching an unprecedented high in 1918 —and the wartime demands on the Bureau of Engraving and Printing led to the production of some postage stamps by the offset printing process rather than the traditional recessed engraved (intaglio) printing process. During the fiscal year 1917-1918, the sale of postage stamps and stamped postal stationery issues increased revenues from such sources twenty percent, reaching $353,969,861 for the twelve-month period.[333]

Mail exchanged with military personnel was censored in accordance with an Executive Order of the President on 12 October 1917. The work was carried out under the control of a censorship board composed of representatives of the Postmaster General, the Secretary of War, the Secretary of the Navy, the War Trade Board, and the chairman of the Committee on Public Information. Eleven censorship stations and additional substations along the Mexican border were manned by nearly 1,600 employees who, by 1918, were censoring about 125,000 pieces of mail per day at a cost of $509,742 (for October 1917-June 1918), paid out of the appropriations for foreign mails.[334]

The Military Post Office at Hoboken, New Jersey, which processed the majority of overseas military letters, grew from a one-room, two-man office in the summer of 1917 to a two-building (each with three floors and a basement), ninety-nine-employee affair at the height of the War. The canceling machine used at Hoboken—the distinctive International machine which carried a symbolic eagle in place of the place-date-time dial—canceled 6,801,924 pieces of soldiers' mail in 1918 alone. During the Christmas rush of 1917, some 250,000 packages were received at Hoboken. An emergency force of seventy-five officers and 1,500 enlisted men were required to open, inspect, repack, and relabel each package before being placed aboard vessels bound for Europe. Many packages had been damaged in transit and it was found that fried chicken, grapefruit, bottles of whiskey concealed in bread, and similar items had been mailed by the folks at home for their loved ones fighting in France. After the parcel problem had been straightened out, the weight limit of twenty pounds for overseas mail was reduced to a more manageable seven pounds. The Department and the military authorities were better prepared for the Christmas rush of 1918, and between 22 November and 8 December some 2,249,000 parcels were processed with little difficulty. After arrival overseas, however, the packages were often misdirected or not delivered at all, and the breakdown in processing resulted in many complaints.[335]

A United States postal agency was established at Bordeaux, France, and in September 1918 provision was made for mail service to and from the American Expeditionary Forces in Siberia. Domestic rates of postage were made applicable to mail addressed to servicemen stationed overseas.[336]

The war created unusual personnel problems for the Department, and although some were probably anticipated, the extent of the problem and the loss of trained postal workers reached serious proportions. During the first three months of the War, 2,278 postal clerks (5.45 percent of the force) were lost to the military service or war production work. During fiscal year 1917-1918, 4,898 clerks resigned and 399 were removed, reducing the force by 12.4 percent. Moreover, an additional 3,781 clerks entered the armed forces, making it necessary to replace 9,078 experienced men with inexperienced workers. In addition, the Railway Mail Service lost 3,722 trained men between April 1917 and September 1918, a reduction of 21 percent compared with a prewar annual average of 3.98 percent. The city delivery service also lost 3,618 carriers during 1918. Postal employees inducted directly into the Armed Forces were kept on the rolls of the Department and placed on leave without pay. Those entering work in plants manufacturing strategic materials resigned from the postal system.[337]

While personnel problems began to plague the Department, there was also a crisis in the national transportation system and it is remarkable that the postal service was carried on as well as it was. Under the voluntary Railroads' War Board, the numerous railroad companies failed to meet the demands of wartime traffic. In 1917-1918, the railroads represented the primary means of domestic transportation. Railway Post Offices operated over 231,501 miles of routes and closed-pouch mails were carried over 71,268 miles. Railroad traffic and schedules had suffered during the unusually severe winter weather of 1916-1917 and, when about to recover, were immediately faced with increased wartime traffic and labor shortages. Freight traffic in 1917 increased to forty-three percent over that of 1914-1915; the rail lines were glutted with trains heading eastward to the ports; eastern yards were jammed with 180,000 loaded cars during the fall of 1917; and railroad efficiency dropped again when the early and severe winter struck. On 28 December 1917 management of the railroads was taken over by the Federal government.[338]

Government management did not solve many problems for the Post Office Department. The movement of mail was not given top priority under the new system. Train schedules were changed without notice; trains were often ordered to depart from depots before the mail was loaded; some trains carried no mail; certain postal laws and regulations were not observed. During a seven-day period in January 1918, 28 million letters and 12 million parcels and newspapers were delayed at forty-nine important rail centers. Postmaster General A.S. Burleson requested remedial legislation. Without it, he said, "the splendid system of expeditious mail transportation built up in years past will rapidly crumble and fall to the level of express company service."[339] The following year, 1919, Burleson reported that circulars and catalogs were seldom processed in the Railway Post Offices, enabling the clerks to devote their primary attention to more important mail matter. The labor shortage was gradually remedied and safety to Railway Mail Service clerks and mail was improved through the acquisition of additional steel underframe and all-steel postal cars. After the Armistice, service was greatly restored and schedules were being improved, but, in many respects, immediate postwar postal service was not up to prewar standards.[340]

Under wartime pressures, telegraph and telephone service fell under the management of the Postmaster General. At the war's end Burleson made a strong plea for retaining these systems under Federal control and within the operations of the Department. Unfortunately, extraordinary wire traffic during wartime increased operating expenses, and the Wire Administration was compelled to increase rates. Burleson pointed out that the resulting criticism was unfair and that the temporary and brief period of Federal operation during abnormal conditions afforded an inadequate test upon which to base the conclusion that private industry could manage these systems better than the government. Nevertheless, operation reverted to private management and the Department lost its opportunity to demonstrate its ability to operate a Post-Telegraph-Telephone system (PTT) in the European manner.[341]

Before the War ended in 1918, the Department had already embarked on the great new adventure of airmail service. The War had witnessed the advent of the airplane as a reasonably reliable and efficient means of transportation and the Post Office Department stood ready to reap all possible benefits from this innovation.

THE AIRMAIL SERVICE

Several historical footnotes of early attempts at air transportation had been made in the century preceding World War I; and though they set no precedents for U.S. airmail service they amusingly preface the story of Man's first attempts to conquer the sky for transportation and communication.

In Europe, letters had been transported in balloons as early as 1784; but balloons were largely subject to the erratic course of the wind, and relatively few men devoted thought to overcoming this basic obstacle to practical transportation. John Wise in the United States, however, believed he could utilize the prevailing winds to his advantage, and in 1859 after a test flight from St. Louis to Henderson, New York, made arrangements to carry U.S. mail from Lafayette, Indiana, to either New York or Philadelphia. On 17 August 1859 Wise ascended in his balloon *Jupiter* with a pouch consisting of 123 letters and 23 circulars, received at the Lafayette post office in response to notices carried in the newspapers. He failed to find the currents he had hoped for and was forced to descend near Crawfordsville, Indiana, after a short flight of about thirty miles. The mail was forwarded by railroad to New York City and the first U.S. "airmail" flight faded into history.[342]

Balloons were successfully used to send messages on other occasions. The besieged cities of Paris and Metz during the Franco-Prussian War (1870-1871), maintained communications using sixty-six manned balloons. From 23 September 1870—the fifth day of the Siege of Paris—to 28 January 1871, 164 persons, several million letters, 384 pigeons, and 6 dogs were exchanged. The pigeons were used to fly messages into Paris after the balloons had landed. Altogether, fifty-four mail-carrying flights were made and were most successful in maintaining communications with the outside world.

Messages carried by the pigeons were transmitted in an ingenious manner. Copies of original messages were reproduced photographically, with a reduction in area through the camera lens. Introduced for the mails in December 1870, a new process termed microphotography was employed, whereby images (dispatches) were reduced to a ratio of about 9,000 to 4. About fifteen films were placed in a quill which was attached by a waxed silk thread to the carrier pigeon's tail. The average quill contained about 30,000 messages, but one quill, carried on 28 January 1871, contained 40,400. As many as thirty-five pigeons carried the same messages to insure delivery—winter weather and snipers' bullets took a heavy toll. When a pigeon arrived safely in Paris, the films were projected on a screen, copied by clerks, and mailed to the addressees within the city.[343]

In 1902 Augusto Severo, a Brazilian aeronaut, flew his "dirigible balloon" *PAX* over Paris and dropped some leaflets over the city before the gas bag exploded. At the first aviation meet in France, held at Betheny in August 1909, letters and special cards were carried by airplanes. Novel "aeroplane mail" became a feature of fairs and aviation meets. Calbraith P. "Cal" Rogers piloted the *Vin Fiz Flyer* from Sheepshead Bay, New York, to

Long Beach, California, in a series of "hops" requiring forty-nine days in 1911. To raise money en route, Rogers carried some mail bearing a special "Vin Fiz Flyer" stamp-like label. In India, the world's first official airmail by heavier-than-air craft had been carried from the fairgrounds at Allahabad to Naini Junction, a distance of about five miles, as early as 18 February 1911.

It was not until 3 September 1911, that the first serious thought was given to air mail transportation. On that date Postmaster General Frank H. Hitchcock granted approval to carry U.S. mail from the International Aviation Tournament at Garden City, New York, to Mineola, with Earl Ovington, as the first U.S. airmail pilot to take an oath. Thereafter, until World War I, numerous mail flights were made under authority of the Department, but no regular service was established. The first U.S. mail flight between cities—a flight of about ninety miles—was made on 10 April 1912. The experiment was impressive, with pilot George Mestach completing the trip from New Orleans to Baton Rouge in ninety-one minutes.[344]

In 1917, Postmaster General Burleson reported that $100,000 had been appropriated for the purchase and operation of airplanes for airmail service. Arrangements were made to procure suitable aircraft not needed by the military forces for the new postal operation. The airplanes for the first continuous intercity service on a scheduled basis were slightly modified Curtiss JN4H military training craft, affectionately known as "Jennies." The route selected linked New York City, Philadelphia, and Washington. An airmail rate of twenty-four cents per ounce was established, including the ten-cent special delivery fee, and distinctive stamps were printed depicting the Curtiss in flight. When the stamps were placed on sale at Washington on 13 May 1918, it was discovered that a sheet had been sold which had been produced with its blue center mistakenly inverted, giving the visual impression that the plane was flying upside down. Although it was not the first time that such a printing error had been made on U.S. stamps, the inverted center airmail became the most celebrated of U.S. issues. Happily, it was not taken as an omen and the new airmail service was inaugurated according to plan two days later.[345]

In Burleson's *Annual Report* for 1918, the inauguration of the new service was announced:[346]

> During the year there was created a new rapid medium of mail transportation through use of aeroplanes. This subject had been given considerable study and a number of spasmodic flights with mail had been undertaken by exhibition aviators, but it was not until the establishment of a regular and dependable aerial mail service between Washington and New York that transportation of mail by aeroplane became a permanent and practical feature of the Postal Service.

On 15 May 1918, U.S. Army pilots and planes were ready to start the new service from the three cities on the route, with service requiring simultaneous departures from New York and Washington. Belmont Park, the race track, served as the flying field in New York. Lt. Torrey Webb departed without trouble and headed for Philadelphia, where another pilot would fly to Washington. In Washington, the President and Mrs. Wilson were at Potomac Park to watch the departure of the Jenny flown by Lt. George L. Boyle. The engine refused to start and President Wilson grew impatient, ready to leave after twenty minutes of waiting. Finally, in comic-opera fashion, someone shouted "gasoline!" and the ground crew realized that the tanks had not been filled. After the tank was fueled, the engine started and Boyle was on his way. Once in the air, however, he turned south and headed toward Richmond instead of Philadelphia. Realizing he was off course, Boyle attempted to land on a country road twenty miles southeast of Washington to ask directions but wrecked the plane. Lt. James C. Edgerton relayed Webb's mail safely to Washington and Lt. H. Paul Culver departed from Philadelphia and arrived safely in New York after learning that Boyle was down.[347] The first day of airmail service was regarded as a success, therefore, despite Boyle's mishap.

During the first four and a half months of service, 66,555 pounds of mail were flown at an average speed of 72.56 miles per hour, advancing delivery time for New York mail by two and a half or three hours over train mail. On 12 August 1918 the Post Office Department took over the operation from the War Department with personnel and equipment of its own.[348]

The new airmail route became "a working laboratory," in the words of Burleson, and, while hostilities lasted in Europe, the New York-Philadelphia-Washington line remained the most ambitious airmail venture the Department could undertake. Aircraft production of (essentially American-produced De Havillands) advanced design was committed to the war effort.[349] Nevertheless, the time saved in the New York-Washington delivery was not significant in itself and postal officials were soon planning a more comprehensive application of air service which would justify expenditures and serve more impressive and practical purposes. Following the peace treaty with Germany a number of surplus military aircraft—principally DeHavilland-4 two-seat biplanes—were made available to the Department and the planned-for transcontinental airmail route was gradually put into operation.

The first segment of the New York-San Francisco route to receive attention was the New York-Chicago link. Experimental flights were made in September and December of 1918. On 15 May 1919 regular flights between Chicago and Cleveland began, including a service stop at Bryan, Ohio. In July the New York-Cleveland link was inaugurated over the hazardous Alleghenies, via Bellefonte, Pennsylvania.[350] In August 1920, a survey flight was made over the western route from Chicago to San Francisco and Los Angeles. Finally, on 8 September 1920 the transconti-

Thomas G. Patten, Postmaster of New York City, hands a pouch
of mail to pilot Torrey Webb at Belmont Park field, 15 May 1918, to
inaugurate the first regularly scheduled airmail service in the
United States. The mail was placed in the compartment ahead of the
cockpit of this modified Curtiss JN-4H.

nental service was put into operation between New York and San
Francisco, with the initial trip requiring a day and a half. Flying was done
in daylight only—in stages—and the second plane of the first trip developed
engine trouble and was delayed by bad weather.[351]

The Department soon learned that war surplus aircraft—as was the case
with the surplus motor vehicles—was not always suitable for carrying mail.
Although the DeHavilland biplanes were more plentiful and generally
satisfactory, there were some unfortunate accidents and the DH-4s had to
be rebuilt. The landing gear was repositioned, larger wheels were installed,
the fuselages were entirely covered with plywood, wing struts were more
securely attached, and the pilot's position was moved toward the rear (near
the former observer's cockpit) behind the fuel tank and mail compartment
(which had to be added). Each pilot eventually was assigned a plane for his
personal use. In August 1920 the Department began to secure radio
equipment to provide pilots with up-to-the-minute weather reports.[352]

With flying restricted to daylight hours, the mail was forwarded by train at night to achieve the best results. But the Department soon contemplated round-the-clock flying schedules to reduce delivery time. To demonstrate the value of "through" air service, a special flight involving four planes—two from the East and two from the West—was made 22-23 February 1921, over the 2,629-mile route between San Francisco and New York. Only one westbound plane reached Chicago before blizzard conditions made it impossible to continue. The future of the airmail service seemed to depend on the success of the eastbound flights, since appropriations had been reduced and Congress had remained unimpressed with the regular plane-and-train transcontinental operation. One eastbound plane crashed at Reno, killing the pilot, but the other continued on. Lights had not been installed on planes or at the fields. Darkness fell during the Cheyenne-North Platte relay, and the landing was made possible by field-side bonfires. At North Platte, Nebraska, pilot James H. ("Jack") Knight took over the mail and headed for Omaha. About midnight, near Kearny, Knight met with snow.

A DeHavilland mail plane and a Ford mail truck exchange mails at Chicago, circa 1923, when flying was limited to daylight hours.
The sun reflects brightly from the plywood fuselage of the "DH" plane.

Landing for fuel at Omaha by the light of burning gasoline drums set out along the runway, Knight found that there was no relief pilot to fly the next section to Chicago. The snow storm had become a blizzard. At 2 a.m., Knight took off from Omaha with a road map to guide him over a portion of the route he had never flown. With deep snow preventing a landing at Des Moines, Knight put down at the Iowa City emergency field, guided by the light of a railroad fussee set out by the night watchman, the only person at the field. Again refuelled, Knight took off and headed toward Lake Michigan which would serve as a "landmark" for him to find Chicago. When the snow stopped, Knight met with fog and had to fly to 1,000 feet before coming clear of it. With daybreak the fog cleared, Lake Michigan appeared, and Knight found Chicago's Checkerboard Field. News flashes had announced Knight's exploit. When he arrived at Chicago, he was met by people who had stayed up all night; he had become a celebrity. The mail was relayed on to Cleveland and New York, finally arriving thirty-three hours and twenty minutes after leaving San Francisco, a substantial reduction from the usual seventy-two hour plane-train relay service. The Department was assured that airmail service would continue.[353]

The actual conversion to night flying operations took considerable time. By 1923, some western portions of the route had been equipped with enough beacon and landing lights to permit some test flights at night. By the summer of 1924 the Transcontinental airway was lighted for 1,912 miles between Cleveland and Rock Springs, Wyoming and on 1 July 1924 regular schedules involving night flying were put into effect. At that time, the service had seventy-four planes in flying condition for the transcontinental route, the only line in operation that year. During 1923-1924, 1,853,251 miles were flown and an estimated 60,001,360 pieces of first class mail were carried. The lighted airway made it possible to reduce the schedule to thirty-four hours, twenty minutes westbound and twenty-nine hours, fifteen minutes eastbound. The now-reliable DeHavillands were equipped with landing and navigation lights, a lighted instrument panel, and two parachute flares for emergency landings. By 1925 there were ninety-six planes in service, with sixty-one equipped for night flying. On 1 July 1925, the airway was lighted between New York and Cleveland.[354]

In 1925 Congress authorized the Department to contract for airmail service on twelve routes, but the first two, the Detroit-Cleveland and Detroit-Chicago routes, were not placed in operation until 15 February 1926. Commercial aviation was greatly stimulated by the new program to carry airmail under contract. By 30 June 1926 nine contract routes were in operation. By September, 1927, the entire transcontinental route was being operated under contracts. The lighted airways and radio service were transferred to the Department of Commerce on 1 July 1927.[355] The airmail service which was developed and operated directly by the Post Office Department until 1927 stands as a landmark in the Department's long history. When direct operation was superseded by commercial operation, the new transcontinental contractors had at their disposal a well established, thoroughly developed, and costly system of flying fields, lighting installations, and communications systems.

Colonel Charles A. Lindbergh, undoubtedly the most famous airmail pilot of all time, was responsible for stimulating public interest in aviation and airmail service in particular after completing his historic flight from New York to Paris in 1927. Lindbergh, of course, made the flight as a private citizen and not as an airmail pilot. Postmaster General Harry S. New reported:[356]

> There was an increase of approximately 20 percent in the poundage carried on contract air mail routes during June [1927] over that carried during May. At least a part of this increase is attributable to the additional interest in the use of air mail service created by the accomplishment of Colonel Lindbergh and the publicity given air mail service and aviation in general on his return from Paris.

Upon Lindbergh's return, he was given full cooperation by the Department to carry the mail on special flights during two days in February 1928 over his old route between Springfield, Illinois, and St. Louis.[357]

The increased use of airmail became a permanent aspect of postal service. In 1928 it was reported that of 5,999,948 miles scheduled, 5,585,224 miles had been flown, an indication that technological improvements permitted considerable flying during bad weather. During the same year, 1,861,800 pounds of airmail were carried.[358]

With the Depression, airmail volume decreased from 8,845,968 pounds in 1932 to 6,741,788 pounds in 1933, being "due primarily to the general economic conditions."[359] Nevertheless, flights with mail in 1933 aggregated more than 35,900,000 miles.[360]

With the change in administration in 1933, the hearings of Senator Hugo L. Black's Special Committee on Investigation of Airmail and Ocean Mail Contracts received widespread attention. It was charged that previous airmail appropriations had been used to support a few favored corporations, that there had been no competitive bidding for new or extended contracts, that there had been collusion between rival aviation firms, that the transcontinental route had been placed under contract with the highest bidder, and that certain airlines had been overpaid. Consequently, existing contracts were declared illegal, and all domestic airmail contracts were annulled on 19 February 1934. Once again, after only ten days notice, the Department called upon the Army Air Corps to fly the mails. Of the 27,062 miles of contract service canceled, the Army could only take over 11,106 miles, using between 120 and 150 pursuit, observation, and bomber aircraft —many of which were obsolete or obsolescent. Disaster followed disaster from the very beginning.

On 16 February three days before Army service began, three Army pilots en route to their new mail assignments died in a crash at Weber Canyon, Utah; another Army pilot was killed in a crash near Jerome, Idaho; and yet another, barely escaping death, crashed near Linden, New Jersey—all on the same day. During the first week of Army operation, five more pilots were killed. Again on 22 February two Army pilots were killed and another was injured. In March, schedules were reduced and the Department began to advertise for new commercial contracts. Before contract service could be restored, night flights were eliminated but on 9 March four more Army pilots were killed. On 10 March the entire service was abandoned for eight days to procure better equipment. On 8 May the first route under the new commercial service was placed in operation after the Army had endured sixty-six forced landings and twelve deaths. By 31 May the airmail was once again in the hands of commercial operators over a new system of routes totaling 28,924 miles. Until 1938, however, commercial airmail contracts were greatly restrictive, and commercial aviation did not develop as rapidly as it might have. The Army's difficulties with poor equipment, on the other hand, focused attention on this deficiency and resulted in greater support for developing that branch of service.[361]

In 1941, Commissioner Richard H. Akers of the U.S. Court of Claims absolved the former Postmaster General and airline operators of the fraud and collusion charges brought against them in 1934.

In 1939 the Department engaged in a number of experimental types of airmail service, one being an autogiro route which connected the Camden Airport with downtown Philadelphia. The roof of the Philadelphia Post Office was used for a landing field. During the year this service was tried, one autogiro fell off the roof to 30th Street below. Elsewhere in Pennsylvania, mail was picked up and delivered "on the fly" as was the practice on railroad lines. This service, operated at first as an experiment in 1939, was placed on a regular basis under contract with All American Aviation, Inc. Routes eventually zig-zagged between Pittsburgh and Cincinnati; Huntington, West Virginia, and Pittsburgh; Jamestown, New York, and Pittsburgh; and Pittsburgh and Philadelphia, with a southern extension to Washington, D.C., when the Philadelphia airport was closed in 1944. Pickup stations consisted of two poles with a mail bag suspended from a rope, which hung between the poles like a clothesline. As the plane approached at low altitude, a grapple was lowered at the end of a line from the plane. When the grapple caught, the mail pouch at the end of plane's cable was brought into the fuselage with a winch. Mail was tossed out of the plane in a large rubberized cylinder. In 1948, All American began carrying passengers and abandoned the pickup service.[362]

In 1941 there were 43,411 miles of domestic airmail routes in operation. Of the scheduled 78,750,326 miles of service for the year, more than 74,297,000 miles were flown at a cost of 27.4 cents per mile.[363]

Generally speaking, the cost of sending an airmail letter has been higher than under first class or surface rates. The first airmail rate of twenty-four cents in 1918 included the ten-cent fee for special delivery service, which was dropped in December of that year. Between 18 July 1919 and 1 July 1924 airmail was carried at the regular first class rate of two cents per ounce. Since the latter date, domestic airmail rates have undergone numerous revisions and even in tabular form seem quite complex (see table 9).[364]

Table 9.   United States Domestic Airmail Rates, 1918-1949

Date	Rate per first ounce	Comments
	cents	
15 May 1918	24	incl. 10 cents special delivery fee
15 July 1918	16	incl. 10 cents special delivery fee
15 Dec. 1918	6	without special delivery
18 July 1919	2	same as first class mail
1 July 1924	8	per each of 3 zones
1 July 1925	10	for overnight New York-Chicago service
	8	for daytime service
15 Feb. 1926	10	under 1000 miles for routes under contracts
	15	1000 to 1500 miles for routes under contracts
	20	over 1500 miles for routes under contracts
		Rates of 1 July 1925, continued for Government-operated service
1 Feb. 1927	10	for both Government and contract service; flat rate regardless of distance
1 Aug. 1928	5	
6 July 1932	8	
1 July 1934	6	
26 Mar. 1944	8	
1 Oct. 1946	5	
1 Sept. 1948		Air parcel post introduced
1 Jan. 1949	6	Airmail postal and post cards at 4 cents each became mailable.

The first U.S.-foreign airmail contract was made for service between Seattle, Washington, and Victoria, British Columbia, in 1920. The 74-mile route, flown by Edward Hubbard, functioned until 1937. Its purpose was to fly mail arriving at Seattle after the departure of orient-bound steamships for British Columbia, so that the mail could be placed aboard at Victoria. Mail for the U.S. arriving on incoming steamers at Victoria was flown into Seattle on the return trips to advance delivery. A similar service was performed by hydroplane between New Orleans and Pilottown, Louisiana, in 1923, to service late mail to Central and South America. Although the route was within the United States, the contract was designated as foreign airmail service. Between 1920 and 1923, mail was flown under contract between Key West, Florida, and Havana, Cuba.[365]

The Cuban airmail route was reestablished in 1927, and in 1929, as technical advisor for establishing Latin American routes, Colonel Charles Lindbergh piloted the first mail-carrying plane from Miami to Cristobal, Canal Zone.

In 1935, regular transpacific airmail service was inaugurated between San Francisco, Hawaii, Wake, Guam, and Manila, Philippine Islands. Two years later, the route was extended to Hong Kong, and in 1941 to Singapore. Transatlantic airmail service began in 1939 between New York, Bermuda, Portugal, and France. Later in the same year, New York-South-hampton airmail was also begun.[366]

No account of pre-World War II airmail service would be complete without some mention of the dirigible flights that commanded so much attention between the wars. The giant lighter-than-air craft was carrying mail in Germany as early as 1909. In July 1919 the British dirigible R-34 made the first successful transatlantic round trip between East Fortune, Scotland, and Roosevelt Field, New York. Italian airships also made a number of mail-carrying flights in the 1920s, and dirigibles of the United States occasionally carried mail on special flights. The airships of Germany, however, provided the most dramatic and dependable international mail and passenger service. The *Graf Zeppelin* made its first flight from Friedrichshafen to Lakehurst, New Jersey, in October 1928, returning to Germany the following month. In 1929 the *Graf Zeppelin* returned to Lakehurst and, after reaching Friedrichshafen, continued on to Tokyo, Los Angeles, and Lakehurst again before returning home. In 1930, the *Graf Zeppelin* flew from Germany to Brazil and the United States, and in 1932 began regular seasonal service to South America, lasting through 1936. The *Hindenburg*, which was ready for service in 1936, made ten flights to North America and seven to South America that year. On the first North American flight of 1937, on 3 May, the *Hindenburg* tragically burned at Lakehurst while attempting to land. Before the Lakehurst accident, German Zeppelins had carried mail on 172 transatlantic crossings. The new Zeppelin, the LZ-130, although flown in Germany in 1938 and 1939, was never put into scheduled operation for international passenger or mail service.[367]

MECHANIZATION OF
COMMERCIAL MAIL

United States postal officials have characteristically been concerned with the expeditious handling of commercial mail matter. The prompt dispatch of business mail was an important reason for improving mail service between cities, and such features as overnight mail flights between New York and Chicago in the 1920s were implemented for the convenience of businessmen.

Certain innovations—canceling machines, precanceled stamps, and the permit system—have already been reviewed in relation to efforts to expedite the processing of mail in post offices and to eliminate or alter the nature and use of adhesive postage stamps which required cancellation. The mechanical device which eventually became acceptable to postal authorities and which held the most promise for solving the "stamp and cancellation" problem was the postage meter machine, an ingenious device which imprinted a combined stamp and postmark in a single operation while performing other functions necessary in preparing mail for dispatch. The user of the meter machine, of course, benefited, but the post office also gains substantially in time and saves a considerable amount of money in processing metered mail.

The first devices to assist the work of commercial mailers were stamp affixing machines. One of the earliest machines was patented by George K. Snow on 18 May 1858.[368] Snow's hand-operated device was intended to automatically separate, moisten, and affix stamps to envelopes. A sheet of stamps was torn into strips which were fed through a head, at which point each stamp was cut before being affixed. Snow claimed that the "machine is very efficient in operation and calculated for use in post offices, or in merchants' counting rooms, as well as elsewhere, particularly where it may be desirable to post-stamp letters with expedition."[369] In 1875, Eddy Taylor Thomas of Boston patented a rather simple hand-plunger for attaching stamps and sealing envelopes in one operation, the stamps being stacked as singles into the machine before use.[370] Snow's method of using a strip of stamps was not used by Thomas. It is not known if these or similar machines were used successfully. Two other hand-plunger stamp affixers may be noted because of their general acceptance by commercial mailers. Victoria I. H. Bundsen of London, England, patented a hand-plunger machine in England in 1884 and in the United States in 1885.[371] In 1886, a patent for a similar device was taken out by John L. Shaw.[372] Both machines were operated by hand and utilized stamps piled in a box.

By 1887, inventors were returning to the use of strips of stamps in these devices and in 1899 the Hewitt Sealer & Stamper Company of

Chicago developed another, and probably more practical, combination stamper and sealer. A host of mechanical stamp affixers had appeared by 1905.[373]

After 1887, inventors began to turn their attention to vending machines and by 1906, some fifteen stamp vending devices had been patented. Some of these devices used strips of stamps, generally coiled and stored within the machine until used. The Hewitt Company also marketed a vending device.[374]

Finally, affixing-sealing machines were powered by electric motors and the commercial mailers were able to save considerable time in getting business correspondence ready for deposit at the post office. Electrical affixing machines and coin-operated vending devices operated at maximum efficiency with coiled postage stamps. The manufacturers of both types found that strips of perforated stamps were generally unsatisfactory. The fine perforations caused the strips to tear and jam the mechanisms. In October 1906, the Department issued imperforate sheets of 400 stamps for use in these devices, and the various vending and affixing machine manufacturers began to prepare their own coiled stamps. The privately produced coils generally consisted of strips cut from the sheets and pasted together, with coarser perforations between the individual stamps. The coarser perforations permitted the fingers of the machines to feed the stamps through the devices without tearing the web of paper. While not all of the privately coiled stamps were of a coarse gauge, the smooth knife-cut edges of the strips helped to eliminate some mechanical difficulties. In 1908, the Department brought out its own coiled stamps, but the gauge of perforations was still too fine for many machines; in 1910, therefore, the government issued coils in a coarser gauge.[375] After the Department issued coils of 3,000 stamps wound gum-side-out in December 1927, the issuance of imperforate sheets for privately manufactured coils was discontinued.[376]

Joseph J. Schermack is perhaps the most widely known person associated with stamp machines. After working on mailing devices as early as 1902, he developed an electrical envelope sealing and stamping machine in 1909 which reportedly processed 10,000 pieces of mail per hour. Stamps used in some of Schermack's devices bore distinctive rectangular holes (perforations), occasionally seen in strips of U.S. stamps of the 1908-1928 period.

Products of the Schermack Mailing Machine Company soon became popular with many business firms. When Schermack began to prepare his "hyphen-holed" coiled stamps in one plant for distribution across the country, he met with opposition from the Department. Regulations prohibited the preparation of coils in one city for use in another because local city postmasters received credit for stamps sold at their post offices. Schermack left the company about 1909 to devote his attention to vending machines, but the basic sealing and stamping machine, utilizing the hyphen-hole coils, was continued by the firm after reorganization as the

Mailometer Company. The company also manufactured a hand-plunger affixer. By 1915 or 1916 owners of certain Mailometer machines found that the 10-gauge government coils could be used after they had been rewound gum-side out, and orders for the privately-perforated stamps—which were prepared in coils of 3,000 at fifty cents more than face value—began to decline. The National Mailing Machine, similar to the Schermack product, was marketed in 1909. It used government-prepared coils and sealed, stamped, and counted 4,500 letters per hour.[377]

The first machine developed to eliminate the adhesive postage stamp entirely was the invention of Elmer E. Wolf. The hand-cranked device was conceived in 1898 and patented the following year. It was designed to print nine postage rates and automatically lock when the amount of postage purchased by the user had been used. The imprint included the time, date, and place of use, together with the name of firm, the amount of postage for the letter, and the amount of postage still credited to the meter. Wolf's device was not accepted for actual use and was probably not postally tested.[378]

In 1901 a second meter machine was developed, the invention of Arthur H. Pitney who was to lend his name to the most successful mailing machine company in the industry. Pitney's first model was patented in 1902 and, like the Wolf machine, was a hand cranked device which imprinted the postage denomination, a license number, a serial number, and the legend, "United States Postage."[379] In 1902, an improved model, using a revolving cylinder for imprinting the "stamp," was demonstrated at the Department but never used for actual mailings. In 1903, however, a third Pitney machine favorably impressed Department officials and between November 1903 and March 1904 a machine was used to imprint official mail matter originating in the Office of the Third Assistant Postmaster General in Washington, D.C. The printing die of this machine impressed the familiar "penalty" clause on the envelopes, together with a serial number for control purposes. As already noted, the first regular third and fourth class mailings of matter without adhesive stamps were the result of this relatively satisfactory test. Nevertheless, authority was not granted for mailing first class matter with metered imprints. Pitney's machines were given additional trials in Washington in 1912 for third class mail originating from the offices of the National Tribune, and in 1914 more extensive tests utilizing two machines were run with Department approval in Chicago. The imprinted indicia ("stamps") of the 1912 and 1914 tests included the postage denominations, the place of mailing, a serial number, and the number of the local permit (no. 1041) assigned by the post office. The Chicago tests were made between 28 January and mid-May 1914.[380]

The practical machines developed by Pitney were electrically powered and were similar to the stamp affixing and sealing machines already in use. The machines of 1912 and 1914 sealed the envelopes and imprinted a

The meter unit of the first postage meter
machine to be placed in service in the United States
under the general authorization of 1920.

postal indicia and postmark data in place of adhesive stamps. In 1918,
Walter H. Bowes, president of the Universal Stamping Machine Company
—a producer of canceling machines—proposed that the "Bowes Mailing
System" be adopted by the Post Office Department. In 1920 Pitney's
American Postage Meter Company and Bowes' Universal Stamping
Machine Company merged to form the Postage Meter Company (later
Pitney-Bowes) to manufacture metered mail machines and Universal
canceling machines.[381]

The improved product of the new firm, the Pitney-Bowes Model A
machine, was approved by the Department after Congress had authorized
mailings of first class matter without postage stamps in 1920. Approval for
the Model A was granted in September 1920, and the initial mailing of first
class mail by metered postage was made in December of the same year at
Stamford, Connecticut.[382]

Postage meter machines, it should be stressed, were not primarily developed for use in post offices. Although the mechanism imprinted the postage, date, and place of mailing—elements which had been the exclusive concern of the post office—the devices were (and are) leased to private mailers who used the machines on their own premises. It is apparent that the meters must be constructed so that tampering is virtually impossible or easily detected. Adequate security features had been developed by 1920, and, therefore, the Department approved the new devices. Those who leased the machines from the manufacturers took the detachable meter "unit" to the local post office, paid for the postage in advance, and had the amount of postage purchased registered on the meter by a postal employee, who then locked the unit and returned it to the leaser. The officially registered and locked unit was then inserted in the mailing machine, ready to imprint postage on each envelope which was fed through the sealer. Small, hand-operated desk models, which did not seal the envelopes, were also developed. Each machine and imprinting die had a control number. When the prepaid postage was used (or "metered out"), the unit automatically shut off and could not be used to imprint more impressions until reset at the post office.[383]

One of the first ideas emphasized by Pitney-Bowes after their machines were approved was that large business houses could avoid the danger of having postage stamps stolen by employees. The practice of perforating stamps with firms' initials or some other identifiable symbol—such stamps were termed "perfins"—had been widely adopted to discourage theft; however, the meter manufacturers advertised the product as nearly fool-proof. Essentially, the claim was correct, although some metered postage has been occasionally used without the approval of the leasers. Nevertheless, the registers, which indicate the amount of postage which has been or remains to be used, serve as positive records. Pitney-Bowes also emphasized the idea that metered postage safeguarded the government's interests by preventing the use of forged stamps to defraud the Department. Unlike postage stamps and stamped envelopes, metered impressions bear the serial number of the meter (actually a die number). Forged stamps of lower denominations have been manufactured, though infrequently, in large enough quantities to represent a considerable revenue loss to the Department. While many forged stamps have filtered into philatelic circles, the lower denominations, if reasonably accurate in appearance, have passed through the mails and escaped immediate detection. The serial numbers of meter machines, however, are recorded at post offices and, naturally, would enable officials to easily detect forged meter dies.[384]

The positive control of large amounts of postage seemed to be a feature which many patrons appreciated. Furthermore, the new machines were versatile and quite convenient. In addition to the utilitarian aspect of the devices, "Postmark Ads," or "Meter Slogans" (as they are generally known to collectors) became another attractive feature introduced by Pitney-Bowes in 1929. A simple die bearing an advertisement, symbol, or slogan was inserted next to the mail-imprinting dies. Every time the postage indicia was imprinted on the envelope the advertisement was imprinted alongside. The idea caught on after the N.R.A. slogan of the 1933-1935 period enjoyed wide circulation.[385]

In 1929 the additional refinement of imprinting the metered indicia on gummed tape was introduced, permitting meters to be used for larger pieces of mail which could not be inserted in the machines. The National Cash Register Company produced a machine which metered postage according to the amounts punched on the traditional cash-register keyboard. This product was exclusively a tape-shooting machine, originally brought out in 1931.[386]

Pitney-Bowes became the largest but not the only manufacturer of metered mail equipment. The Mailometer Company, which had produced affixing and sealing machines, introduced a combination metering-sealing machine in 1922. International Postal Supply Company, Whitlock Metered Mail Company, Multipost Company, Continental Postage Meter Corporation, and National Postal Meter Company were among other manufacturers of meter equipment. After 1944, the various companies merged, were purchased by larger organizations, or left the field, leaving Pitney-Bowes and the Commercial Controls Corporation quite alone in the industry.[387]

Over the years, the basic function of the meter machine has remained the same. Numerous mechanical refinements, however, have been introduced. In 1956, for example, a formidable but very successful machine was being sold which assembled and nested enclosures; opened and stuffed the collated enclosures into envelopes; counted, sealed, and stacked the stuffed envelopes; and imprinted metered postage, all in one continuous operation at the rate of 6,000 completed envelopes per hour.[388]

The Post Office Department, which had installed stamp vending machines in post offices of five cities in 1908, sanctioned the testing of the first coin-operated U.S. postage meter machine in 1936 in the Stamford post office. By 1939 the Department regarded the coin operated machines ready for installation in public places, and the first Mailomat was placed in operation in the main New York post office lobby. Users placed the letter in the proper slot, selected the postage required by adjusting a dial, deposited a coin, and watched the letter as it was "swallowed" by the machine, inside of which the letter received an imprinted indicia and dropped into the built-in mail box. Mailomats never became too numerous, but one model still operated in the lobby of the Benjamin Franklin (post office) Station in Washington as late as 1969. Development of coin-operated meter machines has progressed and generally is a feature of plans recently advanced by the Department in connection with its current mechanization program.[389]

Government use of tape-shooting meter machines dates from 1934. After rather extended trials, the Department gradually adopted tape equipment for use at parcel post windows in the larger offices. Post Office meter tapes bearing the words "Postage Due" were also employed, dating from the first trials in 1941.[390]

The volume of mail carried under metered impressions is difficult to visualize. By 1957, postal revenues from metered postage began to exceed revenues derived from the sale of stamps and postal stationery.[391] In 1966 four meter companies were active in the United States: the pioneer company, Pitney-Bowes; the old Commercial Controls, which had become a subsidiary of Friden Calculating Machine Company; National Cash Register Company; and Postalia. As William K. Thomas, an historian of the industry, has observed, yet another revolution (more quiet, perhaps, than that of airmail) had occurred in postal history.[392]

PROSPERITY, DEPRESSION, AND WAR

In reviewing the history of the Post Office Department's service, it is all too easy to touch upon the accomplishments and to reflect on statistics which generally indicate growth and development. The danger, of course, is to pass over the mistakes and frustrations and to imply that all aspects of the system developed in an orderly and perfect manner. The implication, perhaps, is a bit unavoidable because the essential story is one of genuine accomplishment and great growth. The United States postal system, which handles about half of the world's total volume of mail, has performed remarkably well. However, within the twentieth century, the Department has been called upon to deal with problems which in many respects remain inadequately solved.

The immediate post-World War I period seemed to promise great advances in the postal service. Certain developments with lasting benefits —the airmail service and the introduction of postage meter machines, to name but two—were actually established on a firm basis. The plans to redevelop the pneumatic tube system have already been reviewed. The nation and government appeared to be financially healthy. In 1919 the Department showed one of its rare surpluses of modern times, with revenues of $436,239,126 and expenditures of $362,497,636.[393] Although that year was the last showing such a surplus for a long time to come, revenues and expenditures seemed to keep a reasonable balance for the next eleven years (see table 10).[394]

Table 10. United States Post Office Revenues and Expenditures, 1920-1930

Year	Revenues	Expenditures
1920	$437,150,212	$454,322,609
1922	484,853,541	545,644,209
1924	572,948,778	587,376,916
1926	659,819,801	679,704,053
1928	693,633,921	725,699,766
1930	705,484,098	803,667,219

The greatest gap, in 1930, reflects the early effects of the Depression, but the revenue for the fiscal year still represented an advance over the previous year.

In 1919 the first class letter rate was restored to the pre-war level of two cents per ounce. Postal and post card rates were also restored to one cent. Post card rates were raised to two cents in 1925 but were lowered to one cent in 1928. Airmail rates during the 1920s were reasonable for the service rendered over the pioneer air routes, and registry fees remained at prewar levels until 1925. Even then, the adjustment was slight, with five fees being raised and five lowered. Post-war rates, therefore, remained quite stable, with a half-cent increase in third class rates being made in 1925. The slight increases in parcel post rates of 1925 were offset by downward adjustments in 1928.[395] International letter postage remained at the five-cent level.

The railroads still transported the greatest volume of mail between cities and in 1924 reached their peak in carrying mail more than 586 million miles.[396] The rural free delivery service was still undergoing orderly development and extension. In 1925 RFD service operated on 45,189 routes and reached an estimated 30,348,900 individuals. In the same year, Village Delivery Service for towns of 2,500 or more in population or annual gross postal receipts of $5,000 was in operation in 817 villages. City Delivery Service was performed in 2,401 cities. These services were being expanded, with an additional 140,000 city and village residents being served in 1925 alone.[397]

Interest in improved mail-handling equipment remained uneven. Between 1919 and 1922, Roy Joroleman developed the "DJS" rotary facing table unto which mail was metered from an overhead hopper. This permitted the first letters deposited at the machine to be worked ahead of subsequent batches. After being faced, the regular letters and cards were automatically carried through two lanes to a double-headed canceling

A Model T brings the mail to a patron on a Rural Free Delivery
route in Maine. The year is 1930.

machine which was adjusted to cancel the short and long pieces at two
positions. Flexible feeding arms controlled mail flow and prevented
jamming at the canceling heads, correcting the problem which plagued the
earlier automatic devices. In working at this machine, clerks put special
delivery mail in a special "rotary sweep-off" track for immediate handling.
In later years, a simplified rotary facing machine of aluminum construction
was produced. The later version was portable and could be moved aside
when not in use, an important innovation especially useful in small or
congested offices. Each machine cost about $1,000, and 130 were
eventually placed in service in large and small offices around the country,
with some remaining in use as late as 1967.[398]

The salaries of most postal employees were increased in 1925, the slight
increases for rates already noted being designed to offset the additional
expenses. Post office clerks at first and second class post offices received an
average increase of $300 per year, placing their total annual salaries at
between $1,700 and $2,100, with duplicate salaries being provided for city
letter carriers. The salaries and equipment allowances for rural carrier
service were established at a level providing an annual compensation of
$1,263 for a 15-mile route and $2,600 for a 36-mile route. Overtime was
calculated at the annual rate on a 306-working-day-year basis. The salaries
of postmasters of First Class offices were not increased, remaining at $3,200
to $8,000 per annum.[399]

In 1931, after an unbroken rise in annual revenues since 1916, the Great Depression caught up with the Department. Revenues began to plunge and the deficits seemed more serious (see table 11).[400]

Table 11.   United States Post Office Revenues and Expenditures, 1931-1936

Year	Revenues	Expenditures
1931	$656,463,383	$802,484,840
1932	588,171,923	793,684,323
1933	587,631,364	699,887,186
1934	586,733,166	630,732,934
1935	630,795,302	696,503,235
1936	665,343,356	753,616,212

The startling drop of nearly 119 million dollars in revenues between 1930 and 1934 was, of course, unprecedented in the annals of the Department. For that matter, the nation had not suffered an economic depression on such a scale either. Between 1929 and 1933, compensation to all employees in the United States dropped from $50.8 billion to $29.3 billion; unincorporated business income dropped from $8.1 billion to $2.9 billion between 1929 and 1932; farm proprietors' income dropped from $5.7 billion to $1.7 billion during the same period; and corporations registered a net loss of $2 billion in 1932, compared with aggregate profits of $10.3 billion in 1929.[401] Furthermore, as David A. Shannon has observed, "The most disheartening aspect of the early depression was that there was no sign of recovery."[402]

Although the operating efficiency of railroads had reached new levels prior to the Depression, the general health of the industry was in serious danger. In every year since 1929, with the exception of the war years, 1942-1945, the railroads have claimed annual deficits in passenger train operation. Railroad mileage had reached its peak in 1916 with 254,000 miles of line in operation.[403] With the decline in mileage and first class service due to the growing popularity of other forms of transportation, the mail service began to meet with difficulties. At first, the Department took the reduced service in stride, as in 1931:[404]

> Railroad companies have continued their policy of curtailing train serv-
> ice and many important mail trains have been withdrawn during the year.
> This has necessitated other provision for transporting mails. In most cases
> satisfactory star-route service has been provided without increase in cost.

In 1932, the same statement was repeated. As had been stated the year before, a reduction in traffic over the lines permitted the remaining trains to operate at faster schedules. But it was also observed that "under existing conditions some railroad companies are experiencing difficulty in providing labor and equipment for handling mails."[405] The reduced rail service represented one bright spot of dubious nature in 1933: "The withdrawal of trains which carried mail has permitted the Department to effect a substantial saving in cost of mail transportation."[406] In 1932, 1933, and 1934 Railway Post Office personnel-force reductions were announced.[407] In 1929 mails had been carried on 4,651 Railway Post Office trains over 206,692 miles of routes; in 1932 mails were carried on 3,988 R.P.O. trains over 192,284 miles.[408]

The status of Railway Mail Service merely indicates the nature of the problem facing the entire postal service. In 1932, the first class letter rate was increased to three cents per ounce. Postmaster General James A. Farley observed in 1933:[409]

> The Post Office Department is now confronted with the problem of maintaining its revenues at the highest possible level so that it may continue to provide the service which the public properly expects of it . . . .
>
> During the fiscal year 1933 the first attack was made upon the deficit, not only by the increase of certain postal rates but also by a sharp reduction of expenditures.

No new motor vehicles were purchased in 1933. Between 1932 and 1933, expenditures for salaries and wages were reduced by $80,611,749; for transportation of the mails by $10,070,141; and for rent, supplies, and miscellaneous items by $9,749,942. Subsidies to steamship companies and airlines were also reduced.[410]

Notwithstanding the grim conditions of the times, the public works program of the depression years found some fertile soil in new post office construction projects. In 1933 the Department announced that it had participated in the planning of 201 new federal buildings.[411] The following year, 302 construction projects were selected and "distributed throughout the country; . . . the necessary preliminary steps have already been taken to assure a speedy compliance with that part of the act [of 20 June 1934] which will provide for countrywide relief of unemployment."[412] While the Department carried on some major projects such as the installation of conveyor systems in the larger post offices, it was often looking for ways to save a few dollars on expenditures (such as the cost of electricity) which had received but scant attention in more prosperous years.[413]

Slowly, after 1934, there was a general recovery. In 1939, Postmaster General Farley summed up the condition of the Department:[414]

> Postal revenue has increased in each of the past five years because of the greater hire of postal facilities. From the low point in 1934 there has been a

total gain in revenue of $159,221,909.44, or 27 percent. In the same period, each year has brought an increase in postal expense from the rising costs of increased mail volume and statutory enactments for the benefit of postal employees . . . . I take this to be a true measure of our progress, for while our earnings in fiscal 1939 are again an all-time high in postal history, 1939 expense is nineteen millions less than the all-time high of 1930

The operation of the Postal Savings System was one of the more encouraging successes of the Department during hard times. The system had gone into operation in 1911 to "establish postal savings depositories for depositing savings at interest with the security of the Government for repayment thereof."[415] The original reasons for the establishment of the system had been summarized by Postmaster General Hitchcock in 1909.[416]

All agree that whatever induces in the mass of the people habits of saving makes for the public good. The betterment resulting from such a cause is not limited to pecuniary advantage, but includes improved standards of living, character, and morals . . . .

Our private savings banks neither are nor can be sufficiently numerous and accessible to meet this growing need . . . .

The occasional failure of a bank is sufficient to transform . . . natural caution into a kind of distrust that restrains . . . people from depositing at any time in a bank . . . .

On the other hand, all classes have unshakable confidence in the Government and its guaranty . . . .

Evidence of the universal confidence in the Government's reliability is found in the constantly increasing practice by which individuals buy postal money orders payable to themselves, merely as a method of safely keeping their earnings, for which safety they are willing to pay the fees and lose the interest their money might otherwise earn.

The acid test arrived during the Depression. Since 1918, the maximum allowable interest-bearing deposit had remained at $2,500. Interest was a low two percent. Between 1917 and 1929 the number of depositors had varied between 399,305 and 674,728 with total deposits ranging between $131 million and $167 million. With the investment and banking troubles characteristic of the Depression, however, the number of postal savings depositors sharply rose in 1931 to 770,859, and by 1935 the number of depositors reached an unprecedented 2,598,391, with total savings amounting to more than $1,204,800,000. The increase remained steady until 1947, when more than four million depositors had placed well over $3 billion in postal savings accounts. After that year, the number of depositors and funds began to decrease and, by the 1960s, with other forms of government savings and Federally insured bank accounts offering more interest, the system became superfluous.[417]

No sooner had the Department weathered the storm of the Depression than it was faced with the new problems created by national defense and, after December 1941, actual war. On the eve of World War II, the Department had established a new service for carrying cross-country mails: the Highway Post Office (H.P.O.) system. An experimental 146-mile route was opened on 10 February 1941, between Washington, D.C., and Harrisonburg, Virginia. The new system was operated under the Division of Railway Mail Service and was succinctly described in that year's *Annual Report*.[418]

> Specially-constructed motor vehicles operating over highways are used in this service. Railway mail clerks are employed in the vehicles and make distribution of mail in a manner similar to that performed in Railway Post Office cars. The purpose of this service is not to compete in any way with existing railway transportation. Rather, it is to supersede discontinued train service or supplement that which does not adequately supply postal patrons in a given area.

New wartime conditions, already evident in 1941, required that adequate mail facilities and services be provided for servicemen and defense workers. Shifts in population were apparent to the postal officials before hostilities began on 7 December of that year.[419]

As in previous wars, the volume of mail increased greatly. In 1942 it was reported that "during the fiscal year . . . there were received, transported, and delivered 30,117,633,460 pieces [of mail] weighing 3,244,719 tons, representing an increase over the previous fiscal year of 881,842,132 pieces of mail or 120,492 tons."[420] In addition to this heavy burden, the Department found itself increasingly involved with nonpostal matters. The Department sold War Savings Bonds and Stamps, migratory-bird hunting stamps, internal revenue and motor vehicle tax stamps, took the census of certain types of livestock, aided in the censorship activities reinstituted during wartime, assisted in the apprehension of criminals, assisted the Civil Service Commission by supplying secretarial help and holding examinations, conducting alien registration, and taking a census of women eligible for employment. These responsibilities had not been taken on at once or even, for that matter, within the year; but the responsibilities assumed greater proportions as the war went on. Good wages in defense industry caused dissatisfaction in the ranks of the postal workers who, although not on the fighting lines, had suffered through the long Depression and requested a share of new prosperity. The Department seemed willing to listen to complaints but pointed to its inability to increase compensation.[421]

In 1942 it was claimed that postal service was being performed more efficiently than ever before, despite dislocations in business, social, and government life. The most important task which confronted the Department was providing mail facilities for the Armed Forces scattered over much wider areas than in previous wars. The War and Navy Departments were responsible for delivering the mail to forces overseas. It was noted that "frequent and rapid communication with parents, associates, and other loved ones strengthens fortitude, enlivens patriotism, makes loneliness endurable, and inspires to even greater devotion the men and women who are carrying on our fight far from home and friends."[422] The statement touched upon the same truths expressed by Department officials in prior wars but was perhaps more neatly phrased in the sophisticated jargon of mid-twentieth century governments more attuned to psychological aspects of human nature. On 7 December 1941, there were 517 Army camps receiving postal service. On 1 July 1941 there were three Army Post Offices (A.P.O.s) located outside the continental United States, but by 30 June 1942 this number had increased to 202, spread over virtually every part of the world. By 30 June 1942 the Navy had 1,326 postal facilities. The Department was operating more efficiently than in World War I, despite the loss of some 10,500 postal workers on duty with the Armed Forces.[423]

On 15 June 1942 the Department introduced a "new" method of transmitting mail between servicemen and their correspondents which was reminiscent of the microphotographic communications of the Siege of Paris some seventy years before. The new system was dubbed "V-mail" ("V" was for victory, the most widely employed symbol of the Allied propaganda). Special letter sheets were utilized for writing the original letter. After deposit in the postal facility, the letters were opened, censored, and photographed in reduced proportions on film. The original letter sheets were not transported but the films were:[424]

> The purpose was to conserve cargo space for war material and supplies. As an example of the saving of weight and space, a dispatch of 150,000 1-sheet letters requires 37 mail sacks and weighs 2,575 pounds. When these letters are micro-filmed the 2,575 pounds are reduced to 45 pounds and the 37 mail sacks are reduced to 1, leaving the saved space available for other vital military needs. The regular domestic postage rates apply to V-mail.

After arriving at the destination post office, the filmed letters were enlarged on photographic paper, placed in small window-envelopes to allow the address to be read, and delivered to the addressee.

Overseas airmail rates, ranging from ten to seventy cents, presented a problem. Since the locations of certain troops were considered secret, the variable rates could easily reveal key installations. Therefore, the new uniform overseas airmail rate of six cents per half ounce not only insured secrecy of troop locations but also seemed more fair to those who were sent to the far corners of the world. Volume under the new airmail rate greatly increased. On 27 March 1942 letters sent by ordinary mail (surface) by servicemen were carried free of postage.[425] Unlike World War I, there was no increase in first class letter rates except the one-cent raise for local delivery.

Mail service by railroad actually decreased, despite the comparatively smooth operation of the rail network during the Second World War. Although the Armed Forces requisitioned commercial aircraft, three new airmail routes were established in 1942. In 1944, the transportation problem seemed to be the principal concern of postal authorities. Rail, air, water, and highway facilities, while handling the greatest volume of mail in history, primarily served the military establishment. No priority for moving mail was recognized; mail was often delayed while troops, food, munitions, and medicine (in that order) were given precedence over the transportation lines. A study of the transportation systems, meanwhile, had been undertaken to plan for possible postwar improvements, but in 1944 the Department did not anticipate any "revolutionary" changes.[426]

By April 1945, the Department estimated that it was serving an approximate eleven and a half million men in the Armed Forces through 705 domestic military post offices, 806 overseas A.P.O.s, and 4,869 Navy post offices.[427] It was pointed out that "during 1918, in World War I, there were sent to the American Expeditionary Forces in France 35 million letters and 15 million parcels and papers. During the month of October 1944 alone there were mailed overseas to our forces more than 65 million letters, exclusive of air mail and V-mail".[428]

World War II made everyone more aware of and involved with numbers; and the new concern with numbers lingered on after the end of hostilities. With many millions of men under arms, their service serial number had appeared as part of the address. A.P.O.s were not given names, they had been given numbers. The passion for numbers was soon reflected in civilian addresses. The postal zone number became an integral part of the address by 1943 until it was transformed into the Zip Code (see p. 181) which is applicable to every address in the United States system. With the full weight of the Department behind the campaign, a nation-wide zone system, originally tried in Chicago in 1899, (see p. 141) arrived to stay.[429]

On May 1, 1943, there was inaugurated at 124 of the larger post offices a system through which each carrier delivery district in the city would be given a unit number corresponding to the post-office station from which the carriers emanated . . . . An intensive campaign was conducted to induce mailers to add the unit number to addresses on mail matter, thus making it possible for inexperienced clerks [hired under wartime pressures] to distribute mail [more rapidly] to delivery units. The plan expedites deliveries and promotes accuracy and economy. Excellent cooperation was had from large mailers and the public, and the plan already has shown pleasing results.

Perhaps the best measure of the work performed by the postal service is a review of statistics indicating the number of pieces of mail (of all kinds) processed during the war years. Unfortunately, the Department did not compile such statistics during World War I, but several typical early years are included for comparison purposes (see table 12).[430]

As in World War I, the Department faced personnel problems. Temporary workers—some of whom were women—assumed the duties of those in the

Table 12. United States Post Office Mail Volume, 1900-1946

Year	Number of pieces handled
1900	7,129,990,000
1913	18,567,445,000
1929	27,951,548,000
1940	27,749,467,000
1941	29,235,791,000
1942	30,117,633,000
1943	32,818,262,000
1944	34,930,685,000
1945	37,912,067,000
1946	36,318,158,000

Armed Forces. Special training programs were set up to familiarize the new employees with postal duties. Between 1942 and 1945, the New York City postal establishment alone had its force of regular employees reduced from 22,061 to 18,319. During the Christmas rush of 1943, 700 soldiers and 600 sailors assisted the New York office in handling the mail. The turnover in temporary personnel at New York required that some 40,000 workers were hired in 1944 to maintain the required 20,000 temporary positions.[431] Other cities were faced with similar problems.

The wartime record is all the more impressive if it is recalled that postal workers carried on without the incentive of salary increases. Although promotions were given to veteran postal employees, the basic salary rates had remained unchanged since 1925. Finally, on 1 July 1945 salary increases became effective, and during the next six years, up to mid-1951, three additional increases were made.[432] Postal workers had endured a long, dry season.

POSTWAR PROBLEMS
AND
DEVELOPMENTS

The postwar operations of the Department may have more significance if viewed in relation to certain statistics (see table 13).

Railway Post Office service was greatly reduced after World War II.

Table 13. Growth of United States Postal Service, 1945-1965

Year	Number of Postal Employees (Including part-time)	Number of Pieces of Mail Handled	Revenues	Expenditures	RAILWAY MAIL			POWERBOAT MAIL	
					Number of Post Offices	Number of Routes	Miles of Service	Number of Routes	Miles of Service
1945	435,955	37,912,067,000	$1,314,240,132	$1,145,002,246	41,792	528	260,140,016	146	1,505,178
1950	500,578	45,063,737,000	1,677,486,967	2,222,949,000	41,464	415	341,084,566	125	1,262,042
1955	511,613	55,233,564,000	2,349,476,528	2,712,150,214	38,316	266	150,527,707	108	989,169
1960	562,868	63,674,604,000	3,276,818,433	3,873,952,908	35,238	239	117,544,960	80	685,653
1965	595,512	71,873,166,000	4,483,389,834	5,274,828,260	33,624	190	77,456,000	76	422,208

Year	POST OFFICES CONTRACT HWY		AIRMAIL SERVICE	STAR ROUTE SERVICE		CITY DELIVERY		RURAL DELIVERY	
	Number of Routes	Miles of Service	Ton-miles Flown	Number of Routes	Annual scheduled Miles	Number of Cities	Number of Carriers	Number of Routes	Total Mileage
1945	-	-	61,454,481	11,260	204,596,838	3,884	57,993	32,106	1,435,059
1950	16	1,838,750	42,175,437	11,597	229,108,419	4,632	90,189	32,619	1,486,775
1955	126	13,474,700	87,428,001	11,306	244,789,541	5,032	91,418	32,076	1,544,704
1960	170	18,660,385	111,453,000 (airmail) 19,984,274 (1st class)	10,291	312,717,582	5,652	109,749	31,379	1,768,476
1965	147	19,025,987	188,103,000 (airmail) 34,344,000 (1st class)	11,877	457,953,389	6,091	132,522	31,135	1,890,253

Within ten years, R.P.O. service had fallen to nearly half the wartime level. By 1 January 1968 only forty-six R.P.O. routes remained in operation. Abandonment of the mobile post office system is further evident in the reduction of Highway Post Office service after 1960. The decline of the enroute distribution system was essentially beyond the control of the Department. On 30 June 1925 there had been 1,550 R.P.O. routes which performed service exceeding 579 million miles during a twelve-month period. By 1965, the service had dwindled to 190 routes and a total of less than 78 million annual miles. In 1959 Postmaster General Arthur Summerfield summarized the problem:[433]

> Today, less than 2,300 passenger trains with usable mail schedules are in operation. Only about 31 percent of the Nation's post offices are now served by passenger trains compared with 60 percent in 1925. Following the Second World War, railway passenger service began to decline rapidly. Since January 1958, these trains have been withdrawn from service at the rate of about one each business day.

Although Highway Post Offices increased in number for fifteen years after World War II, the trend toward abandonment of all forms of in-transit mail processing over the railroads rendered the distribution system inaugurated in 1864 meaningless. Virtually all processing was once again being performed in stationary offices. By 1965, H.P.O.s were being discontinued as rapidly as possible.

Thus, closed-pouch mail transportation gradually returned. In September 1953 the Department had started an experiment to move closed-pouch mail in highway trailers carried by railroad flat cars ("piggy-back") on the Boston-New York City route.[434] This eliminated a great deal of mail re-handling at terminals, but the service was discontinued within a year because facilities to load and unload the trailers at Boston were inadequate. Rail-van or "piggy-back" experiments were again conducted in fiscal 1958 over several routes. During the next decade, successful rail-van service became a new and economical feature of the mail transportation system.[435] Railroads continued to transport large quantities of closed-pouch and bulk mail, but the problems resulting from poor routing procedures and inadequate terminal facilities and handling techniques continued to plague the Department.[436]

The trend toward a more diverse mail transportation service had become apparent as early as 1951, when short-haul truck routes were established at lower costs than rail service.[437] In 1955 eighty-one new routes were inaugurated for the carriage of first class mail by passenger buses.[438] Highway truck routes grew from 270 in number in 1952 to 673 by 30 June 1957. In addition, about 300 truck routes were being operated by the railroad companies and some 21,000 highway routes classified under the Star Route and mail-messenger systems supplemented the principal rail, highway, and airmail services.[439] Truck routes, at first operating over relatively short distances, rapidly assumed more importance. In 1951, trucks provided parcel post service between Chicago and Cincinnati, and, by 1957, one highway contractor was moving all mail between Pittsburgh and Cleveland.[440] Long-haul truck service was established in 1966 between the North Jersey Truck Terminal and Jacksonville, Florida, and between Memphis, Tennessee, and Fort Worth, Texas. In the same year, passenger buses moved about one million pouches of letter mail and newspapers. Bulk mailers, in 1966, were sending ZIP coded shipments directly from plants to distant points by motor trucks or piggy-back rail-highway vans.[441]

Existing facilities, most of which had been constructed before World War II, were subjected to unusual pressures. In 1953, the long-range nature of a rebuilding program was acknowledged, and the problems associated with changing from rail service to a far-flung highway-oriented system were summarized:[442]

> The program is far from complete, and the potential economies are only partly accomplished. The major obstacle to expansion of this operation is the shortage of dock or terminal facilities for loading and unloading the trucks. Geared principally to railroad transportation and located conveniently to the tracks, the post offices and railway post office terminals are limited in space to accommodate the trucking operation. In some cities the post office platforms are used [by cross-country trucks] during hours when they are not needed for local postal traffic.

In 1966 the Department was still handicapped by lack of adequate facilities. The growth of highway mail transportation "created an acute shortage of truck docking space,"[443] and truck terminals had to be operated under contract, built, or enlarged at a number of major cities. To illustrate the dimension of the problem, it was reported that the contract truck terminal at Dallas, Texas, had been enlarged by fifty percent to handle some five million pieces of mail annually.[444]

Cross-country motor vehicle traffic was only part of the problem. The "local" mail truck traffic was not only created by the growing metropolitan collection and delivery services, but also resulted from shuttle service between airports and city post offices. Postwar airmail service had steadily expanded. In October 1953 regular first-class mail (non-airmail) was sent by air whenever space was available. This "space-available" service, originally limited to mainline routes, was extended to include the shorter local ("feeder") lines in 1954. While there was at first no guarantee that first-class mail would be flown, the premium-rated airmail letters were always carried on a "must-go" basis.[445] Gradually, the Department strove to improve service so that letter mail could be delivered anywhere in the country the day after being deposited in a letter box. Jet service seemed to bring this goal within reach. In 1960 it was pointed out that mail carried by jets could leave New York City at 1:00 a.m. and arrive in Los Angeles at 5:00 a.m. and at San Francisco at 5:15 a.m. of the same day.[446] The airlifting of first-class mail was carried out as quickly as arrangements could be concluded so that an ever-increasing area of the country could receive the advantages of rapid transportation in the jet age.[447]

But the gain in intercity transit time was often lost in ways which were uncommon during the period when most of the first-class mail had traveled by Railway Post Office. The most obvious change, of course, was that virtually all significant distribution work had to be performed in stationary offices. In the thirty- to twenty-year period before World War I, a number of developments in transportation had enabled the Department to perfect the mobile distribution system by adopting innovations concerned with in-transit sorting methods. When in-transit sorting disappeared with passenger train traffic, the postal planners had to make innovations within the post offices. Not only was in-transit time lost for distribution work, available time was further reduced when trucks were required to carry increasing amounts of important mail between outlying airport facilities and post offices which had been erected in the downtown areas of cities.

The pneumatic tube installation in a lower-Manhattan post office.
The operator is ready to send a cartridge of mail over the Brooklyn
Bridge line in 1946. New York City pneumatic tubes carried
mail underground from 1897 until 1953.

Although postwar airport construction gradually alleviated the problem of handling mail at inadequate airmail field installations and at some points lacking sufficient truck docking space, mail still had to be trucked into town over traffic-clogged streets for carrier delivery. Therefore, the development of new highspeed mail-handling equipment seemed the only answer to making up the lost in-transit time and keeping the facilities from choking under the incredible load of mail. From an already startling total of 38 billion pieces of mail per year in 1945, mail volume surpassed 55 billion pieces in 1955 and 70 billion by 1965.

The installation of improved and more extensive conveyor systems was speeded up. Since 1921, canceling machines had remained rather standardized, with little improvement in capacity. In 1958, after about four years of development, equipment was introduced to automatically "face" (arrange letters and cards address-side up) *and* postmark mail at the rate of seven or eight pieces per second.[448] In the same year, 1958, a new postal Research and Engineering Laboratory was established in Washington, D.C., to develop and test new mail-handling equipment. Keyboard controlled semi-automatic letter sorters, automatic address-readers, semi-automatic parcel sorting machines, semi-automatic sacked-mail sorters, and some electro-mechanical stamp, envelope, card, and stationery vending machines were all under study. Customer self-service post offices and presorting schemes were seriously pursued. In the field of transportation, where a number of significant developments had once been pioneered by the Department, postal innovation seemed less vigorous. It was admitted that "the Department must follow largely what the transportation companies develop."[449] Efforts were essentially devoted to developing improved containers which could move more mail between points of origin and destination than was possible in small sacks. The mail pouch, though no longer made of leather, had remained virtually unchanged in design or capacity for more than a century. When manual handling could be reduced by new conveyor systems at main terminals, the development of new mail containers became an important area of concern for postal engineers.

"Mechanization" became a term frequently encountered in Department publications during the 1950s and 1960s. Manual handling of mail was reduced to a minimum with the installation of a "Mail-Flo" system in the Detroit office in 1956.[450] In March 1959 and September 1960, the main post offices in Washington and Detroit became the most thoroughly mechanized postal facilities in the nation. The features of the Detroit office were significant:[451]

1. 28 letter sorting machines, each with 12 keyboards— sorting to approximately 2,000 cities.

2. Thousands of feet of tray conveyor systems moving mail quickly and efficiently between sorting areas.

3. Five "facer-canceller" machines canceling 30,000 letters each hourly—faster than the eye can follow—and "facing" them in a proper position for sorting by machine operators.

4. Eight giant parcel post sorting machines, 6 feet wide and 300 feet long, that can sort more than 20,000 parcels per hour to as many as 49 destinations, areas, or city zones.

5. Two sack sorting machines each 225 feet long that sort up to 6,000 mail sacks per hour to fifty major truck or rail dispatch areas.

6. Twenty miles of conveyors moving hundreds of thousands of pieces per hour between all floors. Conveyor belts are up to 5 feet wide, and individual conveyors within this system range up to 575 feet in length.

7. Three unique machines to "cull" letter mail from other mail collected from street letter boxes.

These are the newest postal machines developed in automation and engineering programs starting "from scratch" in 1953 . . . .

As a direct step to reinforce the automatic handling systems under development, ZIP Codes (Zoning Improvement Plan), consisting of five-digit numbers, were introduced on 1 July 1963. Electronic address-reading equipment was to be utilized to sort mail through recognizing the code number assigned to any postal district in the country, whether the address indicated a metropolitan or rural location. Development of such equipment was begun in November 1963. An advertising campaign to induce patrons to use the new five-digit codes included the use of posters, magazine ads, television spot announcements, postmark slogans, and the cartoon figure of "Mr. ZIP" on the selvage of postage stamp sheets. In 1965 the program was strengthened by the publication of a National ZIP Code Directory, the incorporation of ZIP numbers in postmarks of more than 30,000 offices serving single-code areas, and the conversion of military mail facilities (A.P.O.s) to the ZIP system.[452] Addresses incorporating ZIP numbers for second and third class volume mail became mandatory on 1 January 1967.[453] By the end of that year, more than one hundred semi-automatic letter sorting machines were scheduled for service in thirty-six post offices.

The Nationwide Improved Mail Service (NIMS), introduced in 1961 and, as already mentioned, reminiscent of the New York City plan of 1905, encouraged businessmen to make large mailings during non-rush hours. In 1963, a similar ABCD Service (Accelerated Business Collection Delivery) assured four-hour delivery of mail within a community's business district.[454] The peculiar problem of providing adequate mail service for large office and apartment buildings in metropolitan areas was given special attention in 1962, when the initial steps were taken in the VIM program (Vertical Improved Mail service). About the only realistic step taken by industry to improve mail service in high-rise structures had been the development of the mail chute eighty years before. Architects, engineers, those involved in other aspects of the construction industry, and the Post Office Department itself seemed to neglect this area of urban postal service. With the VIM program, however, locked box space, self-service facilities in lobbies, mail rooms, and mail truck dock space was being provided in some existing buildings. Similar facilities and vertical conveyor systems were developed for other important new structures. In 1967 it was observed that 645 buildings in sixty cities required the services of more than 1,400 carriers, an expensive and rather inefficient method of collecting and delivering mail at such structures. In the same year only 75 buildings had call windows under the VIM program. But the concept was being widely accepted by planners to reduce delivery costs by thirty percent and to improve urban service. The 700-foot high Houston office building, One Shell Plaza, was being constructed with a vertical mail conveyor which would provide the best possible service for 160 to 200 firms.[455]

Other postwar innovations, some of a rather controversial nature, were also introduced:[456]

> On April 17, 1950, an order was issued to postmasters readjusting the number of deliveries in residential sections from two to one trip each day. No change was made in the [carrier] deliveries accorded business sections except that on Saturdays the business section would get one delivery less than on other days of the week.

The prewar generation of patrons did not welcome this change with enthusiasm. Further changes related to the nearly universal motorized aspect of life.

Although curbside mail boxes had been tested in Cleveland and Salt Lake City in 1939, they were installed in additional cities in greater numbers in 1953 for the convenience of patrons who were becoming more enmeshed in the new "drive-in" or "drive-up" world.[457]

The motor vehicle service of the Department underwent extensive changes in the postwar years. The old color scheme of black chassis, olive drab body, and cream colored body stripe gave way to a new red, white, and blue scheme in 1954 to provide a more conspicuous appearance in the interest of safety and to enliven the streets and highways with "more attractive colors."[458] By 1960, two-way radios were being installed in some of the motor vehicles to maintain better and more flexible collection and delivery services.[459] Many different types of vehicles were employed in an attempt to suit the equipment to the job, and in 1960 a total of 36,871 motor vehicles—trucks, tractors, trailers, "very light" vehicles, and three-wheeled "Mailsters"—were inventoried by the Department. Bicycles,

Loading mail sacks by mechanical conveyor into a four-engine
Douglas DC-7 during the mid-1950s.

totaling 4,273 in 1960, had been reintroduced in 1952.[460] The motor
vehicle fleet operating between urban post offices and postal stations
reached proportions nearly as incredible as the volume of mail. In fiscal
1967 it was reported that the Department owned 58,666 vehicles and
employed 4,777 people to maintain the fleet. In addition to the trucks
owned by the Department, some 20,000 hired vehicles were needed to
supplement the urban collection and delivery work.[461] In this area, as in
others, the Department seemed to rely primarily on developments in private
industry; and if the automobile seemed to be the primary method of moving
things within the congested urban centers, the Department was powerless to
innovate or develop other forms of urban transportation.

Looking to the future—to the far-distant future—several government
missiles carried mail on an experimental basis in 1949, 1957, and 1959.

Actually, private experimenters in rocketry had placed letters in rockets, selling "stamps" or labels to help pay for the experimental flights some years before World War II. But such mail-carrying flights were not utilized to any extensive or practical degree. In 1959, 1960, and 1961, however, "Speed Mail" experiments were planned and conducted to transmit facsimile letters electronically between distant points. These tests were, of course, a postal adaptation of telegraphic facsimile transmission systems previously developed by private industry. It was, nevertheless, the most dramatic effort to revolutionize the mail service and the most forward-looking step taken in the postwar years. There were problems, of course. The tests were strictly experimental. The old question of government vs. private control of telegraphic facilities and services seemed ready for resurrection but, after investing between four and five million dollars in the project up to January 1961, it was abandoned.[462]

The century had opened with first class postage rates of two cents per one-ounce letter. First class rates had been raised to three cents during the Depression. After World War II, postage rates were increased to four cents (1958), five cents (1963), and six cents (1968). Rising labor costs, increased transportation costs, and slow but steady inflation were cited as good reasons for calling for rate increases. Although the economy had been anything but stable during the period of low first-class postage after the reforms of the 1840s and 1850s, the postage rates for letters had seemed stable enough. After World War II, the "penny postal card" had become as obsolete as the steam whistle.

Thus, slowly after the Second World War, changes in the postal service were introduced which were unanticipated by those who had lived through Prohibition and the Depression. Despite the untiring efforts of those laboring in the postal system, the problem of moving the mail from one person to another seemed as challenging as ever.

SUMMARY

Developments of the last hundred years have been presented here essentially in the limited terms of the United States postal system, but it should be pointed out, perhaps, that efficient postal systems have served all highly industrialized areas of the world since the middle of the last century. Indeed, many postal innovations were first introduced abroad, and there has been no attempt to imply here that the United States Post Office Department has provided either the "best" or the "worst" service. In addition to similarities in systems, each modern postal establishment presents features which set it apart from others. While many nations incorporated telephonic and telegraphic systems within the postal organization, the United States did not. Furthermore, few industrialized nations faced the problem of or had to consider the necessity of providing mail deliveries to millions of citizens scattered over such a vast area as that of the United States. Generally speaking, if one were to evaluate the matter in one phrase, the United States postal system successfully has kept pace with the requirements of its people for the last century and a half.

When the important developments in postal communications are presented in rough chronological order, there is a natural tendency to view the total development as one which demonstrates some sort of "progress." Since 1800 the mails have been carried by sailboats and couriers on horse, in coaches, by steamboats and steamships, railroads, pneumatic tubes, automobiles, and by aircraft. The shift from one form of transportation to another, representing as a rule significant increases in speed is, undeniably, progress. Furthermore, the United States Post Office Department has generally—and with but few exceptions—utilized the fastest methods available to tansport mail at little or no extra charge to the patron. This was done largely in response to public (and business) demand and partly as a result of the vision of leaders and innovators. Men such as George Armstrong and John Wanamaker come to mind. Moreover, the public service philosophy dominated the U.S. postal organization until the 1930s. In certain respects the public-service philosophy survives until the present time.

The character of the postal service in the United States was also molded by several innovations in mail transportation. Perhaps the most revolutionary was the Railway Mail Service, with its traveling post offices, which permitted the Department to decentralize operations and utilize in-transit time for the task of sorting and processing the mail. The system became highly developed at a critical period. The nation's industry, commerce, and population were growing and, moreover, were rapidly concentrating in metropolitan centers. As long as the railroads provided adequate first class service, the postal system seemed to function very well indeed. The cost of service had been reduced: from three cents per half ounce in 1863 to two cents per half ounce in 1883 and to two cents per ounce in 1885.

During the eighty-year period, 1861-1940, low cost postal service was provided while the Post Office Department "lost" money every year except eight—and two of those years, 1918 and 1919, showed excessive revenues because a one cent per letter war tax had been added.

Actually, the watershed for present postal philosophy and the public-service concept may be dated from the Depression year of 1932, when (from the long view) the reform trend of the nineteenth century was reversed with the increase of first class postage rates from two to three cents per ounce. In many respects, but with less precision, the Great Depression marked the beginnings of a transitional period in postal transportation. First-class rail service had clearly lost a bit—a bit of spirit, a bit of mileage. The airplane and even the automobile seemed, as Wayne Fuller has suggested,[463] "the wave of the future," even as had the railroad some decades before.

Things seemed to move slowly. The R.M.S. did not die with one gasp. The airplane did not supplant the train with one mighty rush. The internal combustion engine mounted on a four-wheeled chassis did not haul mail between distant points, to a significant degree, until after World War II. But closed-pouch mail service, the form once associated with the stagecoaches and the Distributing Post Offices, cursed by Armstrong and others of his day, returned.

The airplane and automobile had changed the nature of the postal system for the second time within a century. The return of the closed-pouch system largely explains the concentration of efforts to improve the handling process within the walls of the post office.[464] Amazing conveyor belts and new containers appeared; the facer-canceler machines were true wonders to behold—the eye could not follow the flow of individual letters processed by the machines. Even the "fully automated" post office at Providence, Rhode Island, was celebrated on a postage stamp issued during ceremonies held on 20 October 1960.[465] Ultimately, the success of the new system seemed to depend on the use of the new ZIP Code. Did success rest largely on the shoulders of the users? An advertisement in a widely circulated magazine pointed out that "mail has to be sorted and re-sorted several times along its route. *A single unzipped letter can slow up the mail at 6 post offices.*"[466] The six-office trip was strongly reminiscent—if not a resurrection—of the old Distributing Post Office system.

The obvious improvements for distributing and transporting the mail were accompanied by a certain lack of vitality for the residential deliveries which, in 1950, had been reduced from two to one per day. Despite the contention that two deliveries per day were not really necessary for the householder, and that generally no additional burden was created at the local post office, the residents viewed the reduction for what it was—simply, a reduction of service. Patrons usually based opinions on how and what arrived at their doors. The problem of "junk mail," a nagging concern which has not been treated adequately in the text above, became more important in the post-World War II years. In fiscal year 1967 the Department had handled more than forty-two billion pieces of first class mail and more than twenty-one billion pieces of third class mail. First class mail brought in more than two and a half billion dollars of revenue, but the third class matter only accounted for some 725 million dollars of revenue, or about thirty percent of the first class revenue.[467] Increases in first class rates heightened public sensitivity to the junk mail problem.

Perhaps the brightest jewel in the crown of the postal system was the change in philosophy reflected by low rates which were introduced in the 1840s and which seemed to brighten with each rate reduction. Rowland Hill's reforms not only revolutionized the British system but that of virtually every nation in the world. The spirit of reform operated in domestic areas and, eventually, strongly influenced international rate structures. The people of the United States had benefitted from a standardized letter rate of three cents in 1863. Further reductions followed in the 1880s. And the rate remained at that level until 1932, with the brief exception of the war-tax rate during the First World War.

Postage rates increased more rapidly in response to prevailing economic conditions following World War II than during the period 1863-1932. If the period of low postage is enlarged to include the years between 1851 and 1958, when most of the letter mail was carried at either two or three cents, the problem of low rates and their relation to the general economy may be considered in a broader context. The problem is raised here because there is an unmistakable trend to rapidly increase rates—a trend wholly lacking for more than a century. Rate increases are easily justified if the cost of operating the postal system becomes a dominant concern. If public service is the chief consideration, low first class rates are seldom changed and rarely increased. The increase of first class rates from two to three cents in 1932 is a curious phenomenon, for it was used as a measure to balance a budget when the general economy was depressed. After World War II, the several first-class increases have been used to balance the postal budget during times of inflation.

If there has been a deterioration of the public-service philosophy within the postal organization, the reasons relate to conditions which have developed in arenas beyond the postal organization itself. A change in transportation patterns had an unsettling effect on the postal service. In addition, since World War II, the business community has increasingly turned to telephonic communications to conduct affairs of immediate and pressing importance. With this dependence on another communications system, the importance of the postal service certainly declined to a marked degree.

Other changes have occurred. The reason underlying the rate increases of 1932 and the postwar years is the desire to balance the postal budget. The Post Office Department is one of the few Federal agencies which bring in revenue. While the Departments of Defense, Labor, Agriculture, and others are not expected to return profits, the Post Office Department, in recent years, is expected to at least "break even." While many postal executives voiced the desire to balance the postal budget and perhaps return a profit to make up for the endless deficits, the desire remained somewhat of an ideal.

First class rates were never increased in a concerted effort to turn the ideal into reality until the Depression and post-World War II years.

The Post Office budget is but one part of the general Federal budget. During times of great national stress, one may expect the postal service to lose ground to more important Federal enterprises. In 1863, during the Civil War, the first class rates were standardized at three cents, an action which actually represented a reduction. Although postage rates were temporarily increased during World War I as a revenue measure, similar action was not taken during the Second World War. Nevertheless, the large and apparently permanent military establishment maintained in the 1950s and 1960s did pose new problems for those entrusted with public funds. In 1893, Marshall Cushing had entitled his book, *The Story of Our Post Office, the Greatest Government Department in all Its Phases.* Obviously, after World War II, the postal establishment could hardly be termed the "greatest" government department.

Under the conditions, it was easy for the public-service philosophy to lose ground. The political nature of the leadership in the Department and the inability of postal executives to make adjustments in many areas of operations without Congressional approval and legislation had always muddied postal waters. There were "bouts" of postal soul-searching after the Second World War, and suggestions to "professionalize" the service were not uncommon.[468] In 1967 Postmaster General Lawrence O'Brien suggested a drastic change in the organization of the Department, and methods were studied to remove "politics" from the establishment and perhaps create some sort of post office corporation. The President's Commission on Postal Organization explored the matter, and its objectives seemed equally divided between solving the problems of moving the mail and making the service pay its own way.[469]

Despite these problems, it must be emphasized that the United States Post Office has continued to function with remarkable success. The handling of more than 200 million pieces of mail per day represents an accomplishment of no small dimension. The telephone and other electronic communications systems have tended to detract from the importance of the postal system in recent years. Other Federal agencies enjoy larger budgets and perform tasks which are charged with great drama. Nevertheless, written communications remain a vital ingredient in our society, a fact fully recognized by The Post Office Department Advisory Board in 1963: "Because the mails are unquestionably our most important artery of commerce and communication, the service of America's postal employees forms an irreplaceable contribution to the Nation's economy and to the everyday life of our citizens."[470]

NOTES

Part III: Postal Service in the United States

[1]See Fitzpatrick, "Post Office of the Revolutionary War," pp. 575-576; Letter of the Salem Committee (of Safety) to the Boston Committee, 19 April 1774, in Pickering MSS Collection (Timothy Pickering); Rich, *History of U.S. Post Office*, pp. 46-49; Kantor, "William Giles Goddard," pp. 139-146.

[2]See A.D. Smith, *Rates of Postage*, p. 66, citing the Resolution of 30 September 1775, of the Continental Congress; Hecht, "Postal Relations," pp. 244-245; Sampson, *Colonial Postmark Catalog*, p. 5.

[3]See Sampson, *Colonial Postmark Catalog*, p. 5, for a list of rates; Fitzpatrick, "Post Office of the Revolutionary War," pp. 582-585.

[4]See Butler, *Doctor Franklin*, pp. 165-166; Kantor, "William Giles Goddard," p. 146.

[5]See Hecht, "Postal Relations," pp. 234-239; Butler, *Doctor Franklin*, pp. 167-172; Robinson, *British Mails Overseas*, pp. 50-59. See also, Postmaster General Timothy Pickering to Abraham G. Lansing, 11 January 1792, Letterbook A, 381-82, whereby special express riders were authorized to carry mails over the Albany-New York route when normal schedules prevented the arrival of mail in New York in time for the departure of the packet ships. This arrangement was continued by Pickering: Pickering to John Fay, 7 February 1794, Letterbook C, 120-121, in U.S. Postmasters General, Letterbooks.

[6]United States, *Ordinance, 1782*, partly reprinted in U.S.P.O.D., *U.S. Domestic Postage Rates*, pp. 49-50.

[7]United States, Papers of the Continental Congress, vol. 61, pp. 451, 445-447; Rich, *History of U.S. Post Office*, pp. 48-53, for detailed summary of developments for period 1775-1777.

[8]United States, *Ordinance, U.S., 1782*, passim; U.S.P.O.D., *Domestic Postage Rates*, pp. 49-50. See also, Rich, *History of U.S. Post Office*, pp. 56-59, 63.

[9]See Rich, *History of U.S. Post Office*, pp. 60-62. Despite the improved condition of the service, complaints remained numerous. It was difficult to enforce the monopoly and prevent coach drivers from carrying letters privately. See Postmaster General Samuel Osgood to Alexander Hamilton, Sec. of Treasury, 28 November 1789, Letterbook A, ms. p. 33; Osgood to John White, 9 January, 1790, Letterbook A, ms. p. 66, notes that the New York-Richmond mails had consumed six weeks in transit; in U.S. Postmasters General, Letterbooks.

[10]United States, Papers of the Continental Congress, vol. 61, pp. 331, 571, 572.

[11]See Rich, *History of U.S. Post Office*, p. 67, estimating about 2,400 miles of post roads, but cf. U.S.P.O.D., *U.S. Domestic Postage Rates*, p. 1, which estimates less than 2,000 miles of post roads.

[12]See U.S.P.O.D., *U.S. Domestic Postage Rates*, pp. 5, 21, 23 notes 3, 4. See also, Blake and Davis, *Postal Markings of Boston*, p. 82.

[13]U.S. Postmasters General, Letterbooks, Office of the Postmaster General to John White, 9 January 1790, Letterbook A, ms. p. 66. Pickering to von Beseler, Postmaster General of Hamburg, cited by Rich, *History of U.S. Post Office*, pp. 68-69.

[14]U.S. Postmasters General, Letterbooks, Pickering to John Hoomes, 26 April 1792, Letterbook A, ms. pp. 457, 458; Pickering to George Mancius, 9 June 1792, Letterbook A, ms. pp. 509, 510. For the development of the Ohio Valley mail route, see Pickering's "Communications to the Committee of Congress on Post Roads" and letters to Isaac Craig, Henry Lee, George Mitchell, Rufus Putnam, John Dodd, John McIntire, Abner Dunn, et al, May-August 1794, Letterbook C, 99, 277, 278-79, 286-87, 288, 298-99, 302-03, 316-17, 320-21, 356, 375, 377. The overland trail from Limestone touched the Ohio opposite Cincinnati, which was reached by ferry. See also, Cincinnati (Ohio) Post Office Account Book, September 1794-1795, entries for 16 August 1794; 25 August 1794; et passim, which take note of the departure of the post-rider. Lybarger, "Early Ohio Postal History," pp. 29-31. See also, Petri, *Postal History of Western New York*, pp. 9-10.

[15]Postmaster General Joseph Habersham to the Postmaster of Lexington, Ky., 10 January, 1799; ms, in Smithsonian Institution.

[16]William G. W. Lewis, quoted by Greve, *Centennial History of Cincinnati*, vol. 1, p. 458.

[17]See C. Corwith Wagner, "Postal Facilities and Postmarks." Lybarger, "Early Ohio Postal History," p. 31; Anonymous, "The Mail Comes to Cleveland," p. 2; Blinn, "Early Michigan Postal History," pp. 12-13; Rich, *History of U.S. Post Office*, pp. 76-83; Huber and Wagner, *The Great Mail*, pp. 6-34. By 1814 mail from Nashville reached New Orleans via Columbia, Natchez, and Baton Rouge.

[18]Postmaster General Gideon Granger to Postmasters of Albany, Buffalo, et al, 3 October 1812 and *Buffalo Gazette*, 30 March 1813, cited by Petri, "Express Mails of the War of 1812," pp. 63, 67. These were not the "first" expresses to expedite mail. See U.S. Postmasters General Letterbook A, ms. pp. 381, 382; Letterbook C, circular letter of 26 March 1794, ms. pp. 201-204, for Albany-New York City and general expresses to enforce the embargo of 26 March, 1794, against British shipping.

[19]U.S.P.M.G., Granger to Benjamin Hawkins, et al, 10 July-15 August 1806, Letterbook O, 54-55, 56, 86, 87; Granger to D. Darling, 16 February 1807, Letterbook O, 274-78. See also, Lybarger, "Early Ohio Postal History," pp. 36-37.

[20]W.P. Anderson to William Meridith, 17 April 1813; W. Humphreys to George W. Merriwether, 13 January 1815; mss in Smithsonian Institution.

[21]Elisha Dyer to William C. Potter, 6 February 1815, ms in Smithsonian Institution. Since express mails between Knoxville and northern cities presumably operated until 27 February 1815, the difficulty of maintaining rapid communication between various parts of the country becomes apparent. In this instance, allowing for a ten-day delay until the British forces withdrew completely, at least nineteen days were consumed in transit.

[22]See Rich, *History of U.S. Post Office*, p. 84.

[23]See *Ibid.*, pp. 83-84; Huber and Wagner, *The Great Mail*, pp. 50-54. Cf. *Ashbrook, U.S. One-Cent Stamp*, vol. 2, pp. 222-223. See U.S. Postmasters General, Letterbooks, Granger to John Hawkinson, 28 June 1813, Letterbook S, 178, for early steamboat mail service.

[24]See Huber and Wagner, *The Great Mail,* p. 35.

[25]See U.S. Statutes at Large, Act of 3 March 1823. The transportation of mail by steamboats is thoroughly reviewed by Meyer, "Markings on Steamboat Mail," pp. 23-28. See also, Johnstone, "Steamboat Mail Service, Lake Champlain," for early noncontract service and the contract service of 1837 on Lake Champlain. For canal boat mail, see Moore, "Early Mail Service on the Ohio and Erie Canal."

[26]See Rich, *History of U.S. Post Office,* pp. 87-88, 90. Florida remained without U.S. post offices until 1821. See Pickett, Rice, and Spelman, *Florida Postal History,* p. 70.

[27]Letter of Postmaster General Amos Kendall to J.S. Skinner, Postmaster at Baltimore, and William Jones, Postmaster at Washington, 16 September 1835, in U.S.P.O.D.R.M.S., *Railway Mail Service,* p. 19, for one of the earliest notices of officially sanctioned carriage of mail by a railroad.

[28]Postal markings indicating that letters entered the mails aboard trains as early as 1837 are discussed and illustrated by Remele in *U.S. Railroad Postmarks, 1837 to 1861,* pp. 135-136. See Huber and Wagner, *The Great Mail,* p. 54, for provisions of the early contract with Johnson and Strader for carrying mail by steamboat over Route No. 3,330 in 1837, requiring the contractor to furnish agents of the U.S. Post Office Department with "secure and convenient apartments."

[29]For detailed studies of the Eastern Pony Express service and routes, see Norona, "Express Mail"; Norona, "Express Mails of 1836 to 1839"; Norona, "Further Notes" Huber and Wagner, *The Great Mail,* pp. 37-45, which also discusses the competing private expresses of The (New Orleans) Picayune and the Government express of 1845.

[30]U.S.P.O.D., *Annual Report, 1956,* p. 124.

[31]Rich, *History of U.S. Post Office,* devotes Chapter 6 to the change in philosophy.

[32]U.S.P.M.G., 12 March, 1794, Letterbook C, 179.

[33]Pickering to Jonathan Palmer, Jr., 6 May 1794, Letterbook C, 265; bill for "postage due," Andalusia, Pa., Samuel Russell, Postmaster, to Samuel French, 1 October 1835, ms in Smithsonian Institution.

[34]U.S.P.M.G. Pickering to Uriah Tracy, Chairman of the Committee on the Post Office, 29 January 1794, Letterbook C, pp. 108-09. See also Pickering's "Observations of the Postmaster General relative to the Department of the Post Office presented to the Committee of Congress on the Post-Office," c. 6 January 1794, Letterbook C, p. 59.

[35]U.S.P.M.G., Pickering to Bulkley Emerson, 4 January 1792, Letterbook A, 367. Apparently the General Post Office provided stampers on request.

[36]See Bond, "First United States Standardized Postmarks were Distributed in 1799." See also, Norona, "Domestic Letter Postage Rates (1792 to 1932)," in Delf Norona, ed., vol. 1, p. 5.

[37]U.S.P.M.G., Pickering to William Wilkinson, 25 February 1794, Letterbook C, pp. 128-129.

[38]See U.S.P.M.G. An early use of the term "Department" appears in the title of Pickering's report to Uriah Tracy, 29 January 1794, Letterbook C, 108. For more detailed summaries of the Department's development, see Hecht, *Preliminary Inventory,* pp. 1-2; Hecht, Warriner, and Ashby, *Preliminary Inventory,* pp. 1-9; Rich, *History of U.S. Post Office,* Ch. 7; Roper, *The U.S. Post Office,* pp. 57-58, et passim.

39See Franklin W. Ball, "Just Express It," pp. 94-98.

40See Blake and Davis, *Postal Markings of Boston*, pp. 78-79.

41Cited by Remele, *Railroad Postmarks*, p. 156. See also Blake and Davis, *Postal Markings of Boston*, pp. 64-65.

42See Remele, *Railroad Postmarks*, pp. 156-157; Blake and Davis, *Postal Markings of Boston*, p. 72.

43Davis, *Postal Markings of Boston*, pp. 80-81.

44Perry and Hall, *100 Years Ago*, pp. 3-14. See also, Harmer and Costales, *Scott's Specialized Catalogue (1964)*, p. 486.

45Perry and Hall, *100 Years Ago*, pp. 18-40; U.S.P.O.D., *U.S. Domestic Postage Rates*, pp. 21, 53-54 (citing Act of 3 March, 1845, 5 Stat. 733, 737). The stipulation that "any packet weighing more than 3 pounds shall not be accepted for mailing" indicated that the Government was not interested in the business of carrying parcels. The carriage of newspapers presented too many problems as it was for post-riders, coach drivers, and route agents traveling aboard boats and trains.

46Announcement of Robert H. Morris, Postmaster of New York, 28 November, 1846, cited by Perry and Hall, *100 Years Ago*, p. 41.

47Harmer and Costales, *Scott's U.S. Specialized Catalogue* (1964), pp. 473-476, 507. See also, Perry and Hall, *The Chatham Square Post Office*, esp. pp. 11-13.

48See Harmer and Costales, *Scott's U.S. Specialized Catalogue* (1964), p. 299, for a more detailed summary of carrier service for the period 1851-1863, and pp. 300-304 for the "semi-official" stamps used for this service. Some of these stamps indicated the two-cent carrier fee, others the one-cent fee. The summary entitled "City Delivery Service" in U.S.P.O.D., *U.S. Domestic Postage Rates*, p. 5, is oversimplified and inaccurate. U.S.P.O.D., *Annual Report, 1855*, p. 118, clearly indicates that "the rates charged . . . in the several cities vary."

49U.S.P.O.D., *Annual Report, 1855*, p. 118.

50*U.S.P.O.D., U.S. Domestic Postage Rates*, p. 56.

51U.S.P.O.D., *Annual Report, 1863*, p. 8.

52The slight adjustment of 1825 had increased postage for the 151-400 mile zone from 18½ to 18¾ cents per single-sheet letter.

53See Robinson, "British Postal Reforms of 1840 and American Postal System", A.D. Smith, *Rates of Postage*, pp. 71-73.

54Act of 3 March, 1845 (5 Stat. 733, 737), abstracted in U.S.P.O.D., *U.S. Domestic Postage Rates*, pp. 53-54.

55Luff, *Stamps of U.S.* pp. 7-40; Harmer and Costales, *Scott's U.S. Specialized Catalogue*, (1964), pp. 23-26.

56See Luff, *Stamps of U.S.*, pp. 26, 41.

57The New York City Postmaster's Provisional Issue of 1845 had been prepared by Rawdon, Wright & Hatch.

58See Luff, *Stamps of U.S.*, pp. 42-47; Harmer and Costales, *Scott's U.S. Specialized Catalogue* (1964), pp. 29-30; C.C. Hart, "Five-Cent 1847 Issue"; "Unusual Demise of the 1847 Issue"; Brookman, *1847 Issue of United States Stamps*, passim; Brookman, *19th Century Postage Stamps, U.S.*, vol. 1, pp. 8-83.

[59]See A.D. Smith, *Rates of Postage*, pp. 74-75; U.S.P.O.D., *U.S. Domestic Postage Rates*, p. 54; Norona, "Domestic Letter Rates," in Norona, *Cyclopedia*, vol. 1, pp. 7-8, noting that the 12½ and 40-cent rates were to be applicable in the territories of Utah and New Mexico. The deficit of 1846 is obvious in published tables, e.g., U.S.P.O.D., *Annual Report, 1956*, p. 124.

[60]In A.D. Smith, *Rates of Postage*, p. 75.

[61]U.S.P.O.D., *U.S. Domestic Postage Rates*, p. 54.

[62]Brookman, *19th Century Stamps, U.S.*, vol. 1, pp. 90-126; Luff, *Stamps of U.S.*, pp. 48-57; Harmer and Costales, *Scott's U.S. Specialized Catalogue* (1964), pp. 31-34.

[63]See Harmer and Costales, *Scott's U.S. Specialized Catalogue* (1964), p. 36. Perforated stamps were originally introduced by Great Britain in 1854.

[64]See Norona, "Domestic Letter Rates," in Norona, *Cyclopedia*, vol. 1, pp. 10, 13. The provision for compulsory prepayment by postage stamps was a provision of the Act of 3 March 1855. Ignorance of the provision, however, was widespread.

[65]See Harmer and Costales, *Scott's U.S. Specialized Catalogue* (1964), pp. 313-17; Thorp, *Thorp-Bartels Catalogue*, pp. 17-27; T.D. Perry, *Guide* pp. 115-17, for a summary of early envelope manufacturing.

[66]See John N. Makris, *The Silent Investigators*, pp. 60-69; Bearslag, *Robbery By Mail*, pp. 293-324.

[67]See Mueller, "Registered" pp. 19-20; Mueller, "Registry Fees," p. 29; Norona, "Genesis."

[68]U.S.P.O.D., *Annual Report, 1855*, pp. 8-9.

[69]U.S.P.O.D., *U.S. Domestic Postage Rates*, pp. 13, 40-41, 56; Mueller, "Registered," pp. 20-24; Mueller, "Registry Fees."

[70]U.S.P.O.D., *Annual Reports*, for 1845, 1850, 1855, 1860; U.S.P.O.D.R.M.S., *Railway Mail Service*, p. 214.

[71]See Konwiser, *Texas Republic Postal System*; passim.

[72]U.S.P.O.D., *Annual Report*, 1846, pp. 684, 697.

[73]*Table of Post Offices in U.S., 1846*, pp. 356-357; *Table of Post Offices in U.S., 1851*, pp. 81-83.

[74]U.S.P.O.D., *Annual Report, 1861*, pp. 37, 54.

[75]See Hafen, *Overland Mail*, pp. 41, 53-57; U.S.P.O.D., *Annual Report*, 1847, p. 1328; Frickstad, *California Post Offices*, pp. 372-376, et passim.

[76]Hafen, *Overland Mail*, pp. 37-49; Ashbrook, *U.S. One-Cent Stamp*, vol. 2, pp. 240-274; Conkling and Conkling, *Butterfield Overland Mail*, vol. 1, pp. 55-78; U.S.P.O.D., *Annual Report, 1858*, pp. 6-10.

[77]Conkling and Conkling, *Butterfield Overland Mail*, vol. 1, pp. 85-100; Hafen, *Overland Mail*, pp. 56-75.

[78]*Table of Post Offices, 1851* . . ., pp. 135-136.

[79]Leach, *List of Post Offices, 1859* passim; U.S.P.O.D., *Annual Report, 1859*, pp. 54, 86-87.

[80]U.S.P.O.D., *Annual Report, 1858*, p. 10.

[81]U.S.P.O.D., *Annual Report, 1857*, pp. 26-33; Hafen, *Overland Mail*, pp. 79-94; Conkling and Conkling, *Butterfield Overland Mail*, vol. 1, pp. 124-133.

[82]U.S.P.O.D., *Annual Report, 1858*, pp. 6, 27-29; Hafen, *Overland Mail*, pp. 94-99; Ashbrook, *U.S. One-Cent Stamp, 1851-57*, vol. 2, pp. 275-278.

[83]U.S.P.O.D., *Annual Report, 1858*, pp. 33-51.

[84]See Hafen, *Overland Mail*, pp. 195-212, 223. The main-line route passed through Julesburg rather than Denver. Salt Lake City, however, was on the main line and received daily mails. See U.S.P.O.D., *Annual Report, 1861*, pp. 12-13.

[85]See Conkling and Conkling, *Butterfield Overland Mail*, vol. 2, pp. 335-344; Hafen, *Overland Mail*, pp. 218-223.

[86]See Ashbrook, *U.S. One-Cent Stamp, 1851-57*, vol. 2, pp. 262-265; Wiltsee, *Pioneer Miner and Pack Mule Express*, passim; Chapman, *The Pony Express*, pp. 32-39.

[87]Settle, *Pony Express*, pp. 103-108; Hafen, *Overland Mail*, pp. 145-69, 187-89. See also, Root and Hickman, "Pike's Peak Express Companies," vol. 13: no. 3, no. 4, no. 8; vol. 14, no. 1.

[88]See Hafen, *Overland Mail*, pp. 169-180; Bloss, *Pony Express*, pp. 27-41; Chapman, *Pony Express*, pp. 83-90.

[89]See Hafen, *Overland Mail*, pp. 170-174. Telegraphic dispatches from New York to San Francisco were picked up at the western end of the telegraph line and carried through in nine days; letters from New York could reach San Francisco in thirteen days. See Bloss, *Pony Express*, pp. 42-54; Chapman, *Pony Express*, pp. 91-148.

[90]See Settle, *Pony Express*, pp. 116-17; Hafen, *Overland Mail*, pp. 189-90; Nathan and Boggs, *The Pony Express*, pp. 5, 7, 19-20, 38, 45-46.

[91]Hafen, *Overland Mail*, pp. 180-181; Nathan and Boggs, *The Pony Express*, pp. 8-9, 15, 21, 32, 38, 46, 54-60.

[92]U.S.P.O.D., *Annual Report, 1861*, pp. 12-13; Hafen, *Overland Mail*, pp. 182-188. Horses and riders enroute on October 26, 1861, completed their trips in November. See Settle, *Pony Express*, pp. 120-121; Nathan and Boggs, *The Pony Express*, pp. 9, 10, 13-14, 19, 32, 53; Chapman, *Pony Express*, pp. 198-212, 280-309.

[93]See Settle, *Pony Express*, pp. 110-123; Hafen, *Overland Mail*, p. 189; Nathan and Boggs, *The Pony Express*, pp. 27-31, 35.

[94]Settle, *Pony Express*, pp. 123-125.

[95]U.S.P.O.D., *Annual Report, 1861*, pp. 20-21. For the year 1 July 1862-30 June 1863, the number of Confederate post offices reported was 8,287. See MacBride, et al., *Dietz Catalog*, pp. 252, 279; Dietz, *Postal Service, Confederate States*, pp. 1-19.

[96]See Ashbrook, *U.S. One-Cent Stamp, 1851-57*, vol. 2, pp. 28-35; Brookman, *19th Century Stamps, U.S.*, vol. 1, pp. 202-204; Thorp, "Star-Dies", York, "A Civil War Postal Measure."

[97]See MacBride, et al., *Dietz Confederate Catalog*, p. 199; Shenfield, *Confederate Special Routes*, pp. 51-61; Harmer and Costales, *Scott's U.S. Specialized Catalogue* (1964), p. 567.

[98]See Dietz, *Postal Service, Confederate States*, pp. 21-25, 393.

[99]*Ibid.*, pp. 26, 276; MacBride, et al, *Dietz Confederate Catalog*, pp. 9-154; Harmer and Costales, *Scott's U.S. Specialized Catalogue* (1964), pp. 543-566.

[100]MacBride, et al, *Dietz Confederate Catalog*, pp. 155-183; Antrim, *Prisons and Covers*, pp. 196-202; Dietz, *Postal Service, Confederate States*, pp. 277-86.

[101]Antrim, *Prisons and Covers*, pp. 18-32, et passim; Shenfield, *Confederate Special Routes*, pp. 12-15, 32-50; Dietz, *Postal Service, Confederate States*, pp. 329-45; Harmer and Costales, *Scott's U.S. Specialized Catalogue* (1964), p. 567; MacBride, et al, *Dietz Confederate Catalog*, pp. 184-91.

[102]See Shenfield, *Confederate Special Routes*, pp. 16-31; MacBride, et al, *Dietz Confederate Catalog*, pp. 192-97; Harmer and Costales, eds., *Scott's U.S. Specialized Catalogue* (1964), p. 566.

[103]MacBride, et al., "Fall of Cities, Military Occupations, Battles and Postal Data," in *Dietz Confederate Catalog*, p. 282.

[104]Shenfield, *Confederate Special Routes*, pp. 63-94; Dietz, *Postal Service of Confederate States*, pp. 287-94; MacBride, et al., *Dietz Confederate Catalog*, p. 202; Harmer and Costales, *Scott's U.S. Specialized Catalogue* (1964), p. 568.

[105]See MacBride, et al., eds., *Dietz Confederate Catalog*, pp. 204-18; Dietz, *Postal Service, Confederate States*, pp. 347-52.

[106]U.S.P.O.D., *Annual Report, 1861*, pp. 13, 19-20, 23-24.

[107]U.S.P.O.D., *Annual Report, 1862*, pp. 131-32.

[108]While admitting that losses suffered due to the cleaning of used stamps were negligible, the search for a stamp which could not be used again continued. See U.S.P.O.D., *Annual Report, 1863*, pp. 19-20. For postage currency, see Harmer and Costales, eds., *Scott's U.S. Specialized Catalogue* (1964), pp. 467-68.

[109]U.S.P.O.D., *Annual Report, 1862*, p. 136. In reviewing Dead Letter Office activities for this year, it is noted that 3,000 unpaid "valentines" were destroyed.

[110]U.S.P.O.D., *Annual Report, 1863*, p. 23.

[111]U.S.P.O.D., *Annual Reports* for 1865, pp. 9, 14; for 1866, p. 9; for 1867, pp. 23-24.

[112]U.S.P.O.D., *Annual Report, 1962*, table of audited statistics, p. 196.

[113]U.S.P.O.D., *Annual Report, 1862*, pp. 145-48; U.S.P.O.D., *U.S. Domestic Postage Rates*, pp. 22, 29, 33, 57-59. The four-pound limit did not apply to books published or circulated by order of Congress.

[114]U.S.P.O.D., *Annual Report, 1863*, p. 8.

[115]*Ibid.*, p. 28.

[116]U.S.P.O.D., *Annual Report, 1864*, pp. 21, 64-65.

[117]U.S.P.O.D., *Annual Report, 1865*, pp. 14, 60-61.

[118]U.S.P.O.D., *Annual Report, 1866*, p. 15.

[119]U.S.P.O.D., *Annual Report, 1867*, p. 24.

[120]U.S.P.O.D., *Annual Report, 1962*, pp. 200-01.

[121]U.S.P.O.D., *U.S. Domestic Postage Rates*, pp. 14, 43, 59; U.S.P.O.D., *Annual Report, 1864*, pp. 24-25.

[122]U.S.P.O.D., *Annual Report, 1962*, p. 197.

[123]See Stover, *American Railroads*, pp. 21-24, 26, 37-38, 41, 46-47, 51-52, 54; Bruce, *Steam Locomotive*, pp. 7-8, 24-26; Kennedy, "Train Wires to the Horizon," pp. 22-24.

[124]While termed "secondary," these really vital contract routes represented the greatest amount of mileage. The routes became known as "Star Routes" when clerks in the Contract Division began to place three stars in the record books to avoid writing the words "certainty, celerity, and security." See U.S.P.O.D., History of Star Routes, mimeographed copy of a letter of the Second Assistant Postmaster General, 6 January 1894, in Post Office Department Library.

[125]Reprinted in Long and Dennis, *Mail By Rail*, p. 98.

[126]*Ibid.*, pp. 99-102; U.S.P.O.D.R.M.S., *Railway Mail Service*, pp. 47-58.

[127]U.S.P.O.D., *Annual Report, 1861*, p. 13; Long and Dennis, *Mail By Rail*, pp. 108-09; U.S.P.O.D.R.M.S., *Railway Mail Service*, p. 58.

[128]U.S.P.O.D.R.M.S., *Railway Mail Service*, pp. 81-83; Long and Dennis, *Mail by Rail*, pp. 105-07.

[129]Long and Dennis, *Mail by Rail*, pp. 104-05, 108-11; Parson, *Railway Mail Service*, pp. 83-84.

[130]U.S.P.O.D., *Annual Report, 1865*, p. 9. See also, Long and Dennis, *Mail by Rail*, pp. 111-13.

[131]U.S.P.O.D., *Annual Report, 1867*, pp. 16-17; Long and Dennis, *Mail by Rail*, pp. 118-21.

[132]U.S.P.O.D., *Annual Report, 1869*, p. 5.

[133]*Ibid.*, pp. 5-6.

[134]*Ibid.*, pp. 8-9.

[135]*Ibid.*

[136]U.S.P.O.D., *Annual Reports*, for years listed.

[137]*Ibid.*

[138]U.S.P.O.D., *Annual Report, 1873*, pp. xxvi-xxvii; George M. Martin, *U.S. Postal Card Catalog*, p. iv; Fricke, "First Postal Card, 1873-75."

[139]Martin, *U.S. Postal Card Catalog*, p. iv; U.S.P.O.D., *U.S. Domestic Postage Rates*, pp. 5-6, 22-23, 60-61; Harmer and Costales, *Scott's U.S. Specialized Catalogue* (1964), pp. 355-363. Postal cards are issued by governments and bear imprinted postage stamps; post cards, originally termed Private Mailing Cards, are printed privately and require the user to affix an adhesive postage stamp before mailing.

[140]U.S.P.O.D., *Annual Report, 1872*, pp. 25-26.

[141]U.S.P.O.D., *Domestic Postage Rates*, p. 122; U.S.P.O.D., *Annual Report, 1873*, pp. xxvii-xxix; U.S.P.O.D., *Annual Report, 1874*, p. 5; Stern, *"Free Franking"* pp. 7-11; Harmer and Costales, *Scott's U.S. Specialized Catalogue* (1964), pp. 267-276, 349-354.

[142]U.S.P.O.D., *U.S. Domestic Postage Rates*, pp. 122-24; Harmer and Costales, *Scott's U.S. Specialized Catalogue*, p. 267.

[143]U.S.P.O.D., *Annual Report, 1873*, pp. xxxii-xliii.

[144]U.S.P.O.D., *Annual Report, 1874*, p. 28. See also Creswell's argument for Federal control of the telegraph system in U.S.P.O.D., *Annual Report, 1873*, pp. xliv-xlix.

[145]Cunard steamships, of course, were not the first steamships to cross the Atlantic. See Staff, *Transatlantic Mail*, pp. 59-95; U.S.P.O.D., *Annual Report, 1865*, p. 11.

[146]U.S.P.O.D., *Annual Report, 1895*, pp. 448-49; Codding, *Universal Postal Union*, pp. 16-17.

[147]U.S.P.O.D., *Annual Report, 1895*, p. 449.

[148]Codding, *Universal Postal Union*, pp. 18-24; Moroney, *Montgomery Blair*, pp. 27-30. See also, U.S.P.O.D., *Annual Report, 1863*, pp. 10-14, 109-64, for a complete report of the International Postal Conference at Paris, 1863.

[149]U.S.P.O.D., *Annual Report, 1875*, pp. xiv-xviii, 21-22, 144-202; Codding, *Universal Postal Union*, pp. 25-47.

[150]U.S.P.O.D., *Annual Report, 1876*, p. xii.

[151]See Staff, *Transatlantic Mail*, pp. 78, 83, 105.

[152]See the lengthy discussion of the Act of 3 March 1885 and the resulting difficulties in U.S.P.O.D., *Annual Report, 1885*, pp. 35-47, 99-150.

[153]U.S.P.O.D., *Annual Report, 1886*, pp. 29-30.

[154]U.S.P.O.D., *Annual Report, 1895*, p. 446.

[155]*Ibid.*, p. 447.

[156]See Long and Dennis, *Mail by Rail*, pp. 122-23.

[157]U.S.P.O.D., *Annual Report, 1875*, pp. xxvii-xxviii; U.S.P.O.D.R.M.S., *Railway Mail Service*, pp. 101-03; Long and Dennis, *Mail by Rail*, pp. 123-25; U.S.P.O.D., *Annual Report, 1876*, p. xxviii.

[158]U.S.P.O.D., *Annual Report, 1876*, pp. xxvii-xxviii.

[159]*Ibid.*, pp. xxviii-xxix.

[160]*Ibid.* See also, U.S.P.O.D.R.M.S., *Railway Mail Service*, pp. 103-107.

[161]U.S.P.O.D.R.M.S., *Railway Mail Service*, p. 108; Long and Dennis, *Mail by Rail*, pp. 125-27; U.S.P.O.D., *Annual Report, 1882*, pp. xviii-xix.

[162]U.S.P.O.D., *U.S. Domestic Postage Rates*, pp. 22-23, 64, 65.

[163]*Ibid.*, p. 14.

[164]See *Ibid.*, pp. 14, 43, 65; U.S.P.O.D., *Annual Report, 1885*, pp. 32-35; Harmer and Costales, *Scott's U.S. Specialized Catalogue* (1964), p. 257.

[165]See U.S.P.O.D., *U.S. Domestic Postage Rates* . . ., pp. 43, 65; U.S.P.O.D., *Annual Report, 1886*, pp. 18-19; Harmer and Costales, *Scott's U.S. Specialized Catalogue* (1964), p. 257.

[166]See Matejka, "Alaska," pp. 29-43.

[167]Report of N.A. Beddoe, 23 September, 1896, in U.S.P.O.D., *Annual Report, 1896*, pp. 202-203.

[168]U.S.P.O.D., *Annual Report, 1897*, pp. 170-171.

[169]U.S.P.O.D., *Annual Report, 1898*, pp. 14, 294-295, which reports the establishment of relay stations on the interior routes; U.S.P.O.D., *Annual Report, 1899*, pp. 22, 256; U.S.P.O.D., *Annual Report, 1900*, pp. 210-11.

[170]For the postal relations between Hawaii and the U.S., see Meyer, Harris, et al, *Hawaii*, passim.

[171]U.S.P.O.D., *Annual Report, 1898*, p. 9 (author's italics).

[172]See Meyer, Harris, et al., *Hawaii*, pp. 90-91.

[173]U.S.P.O.D., *Annual Report, 1898*, pp. 7-8.

[174]*Ibid.*, pp. 8-9.

[175]U.S.P.O.D., *Annual Report, 1899*, pp. 11-13.

[176]See Harmer and Costales, *Scott's U.S. Specialized Catalogue* (1964), pp. 595-600; U.S.P.O.D., *Annual Report, 1902*, p. 32.

[177]See Harmer and Costales, *Scott's U.S. Specialized Catalogue* (1964), pp. 637-39; U.S.P.O.D., *Annual Report, 1899*, p. 14; U.S.P.O.D., *Annual Report, 1900*, p. 109; U.S.P.O.D., *Annual Report, 1902*, p. 23.

[178]U.S.P.O.D., *Annual Report, 1899*, pp. 14-15. See also, U.S.P.O.D., *Annual Report, 1900*, pp. 35-48; Harmer and Costales, *Scott's U.S. Specialized Catalogue* (1964), pp. 613-16.

[179]U.S.P.O.D., *Annual Report, 1900*, p. 35.

[180]U.S.P.O.D., *Annual Report, 1901*, pp. 745, 899.

[181]Canal Zone Postal Service, *Canal Zone Stamps*, pp. 47-53.

[182]*Ibid.*, p. 53.

[183]McIlheny, *Canal Zone Post Offices*, 1954 reprint, pp. 1-2 Canal Zone Postal Service, *Canal Zone Stamps*, pp. 55-63, 71-74, 85-95, 159-88, 206-27; Harmer and Costales, *Scott's U.S. Specialized Catalogue* (1964) pp. 571-93.

[184]U.S.P.O.D., *Annual Report, 1917*, p. 67.

[185]U.S.P.O.D., *Annual Report, 1878*, pp. 31-34.

[186]U.S.P.O.D., *U.S. Domestic Postage Rates* . . ., pp. 10-11, 27-36.

[187]U.S.P.O.D., *Annual Reports*, for years listed.

[188]U.S.P.O.D., *Annual Report, 1878*, p. 34.

[189]See U.S.P.O.D., *Annual Report, 1894*, pp. 473-76; U.S.P.O.D., *Postage Stamps*, pp. 1, 24-25. New stamps produced at the Bureau did not appear until 1 July 1894. See

also, Smithsonian Institution Henry J. Holtzelaw to Francis J. McCall, 29 April 1960, ms attachment, "Rotary Intaglio Postage Stamp Printing Press," 3 pp.; Baxter, *Printing Postage Stamps,* pp. 134-39.

[190]U.S.P.O.D., *Annual Report, 1909,* pp. 81, 307; U.S.P.O.D., *Annual Report, 1910,* pp. 294-95; Martin, *U.S. Postal Card Catalog,* p. iv.

[191]U.S.P.O.D., *Annual Report, 1890,* p. 136.

[192]*Ibid.*

[193]*Ibid.,* p. 4.

[194]*Ibid., pp. 7-8.*

[195]See Fuller, *RFD,* pp. 1-16; Willey, "Rural Free Delivery Service," p. 56.

[196]See Fuller, *RFD,* pp. 18-21.

[197]U.S.P.O.D., *Annual Report, 1891,* pp. 82-86.

[198]U.S.P.O.D., *Annual Report, 1893,* p. ix; U.S.P.O.D., *Annual Report,* 1895, pp. 8-9; U.S.P.O.D., *Annual Report, 1896,* pp. 25, 129. See also, Fuller, *RFD,* pp. 27-35.

[199]Fuller, *RFD,* p. 36.

[200]U.S.P.O.D., *Annual Report, 1897,* pp. 12-13.

[201]*Ibid.,* p. 105.

[202]*Ibid.*

[203]See U.S.P.O.D., *Annual Report, 1898,* p. 155; Fuller, *RFD,* pp. 42-43.

[204]U.S.P.O.D., *Annual Report, 1899,* p. 17.

[205]See U.S.P.O.D., *Annual Report, 1897,* pp. 105-06; U.S.P.O.D., *Annual Report, 1898,* p. 163; U.S.P.O.D., *Annual Report, 1962,* pp. 196-98.

[206]U.S.P.O.D., *Rural Delivery,* p. 8.

[207]See Knight, "Rural Free Delivery", "Postal Markings", 20-32; U.S.P.O.D., *Annual Report, 1899,* 212-13; U.S.P.O.D., *Annual Report, 1900,* pp. 7-9.

[208]See U.S.P.O.D., *Annual Report, 1900,* pp. 183-184; Doane, "R.F.D." vol. 29: no. 29, no. 31, no. 35, no. 38.

[209]Fuller, *RFD,* p. 184.

[210]*Ibid.,* p. 144.

[211]U.S.P.O.D., *Rural Delivery,* p. 2.

[212]Unidentified carriage-maker's catalog page, Smithsonian Institution photograph no. 37940.

[213]See Fuller, *RFD,* pp. 142-76; U.S.P.O.D., *Annual Report, 1916,* pp. 203-07; U.S.P.O.D., *Annual Report, 1917,* pp. 41-45.

[214]See Smithsonian Institution, unpublished documents.

[215]U.S.P.O.D., *Annual Report, 1911,* pp. 11-12. A previous but unsuccessful Village Delivery Service had been terminated in 1895. See U.S.P.O.D., *Annual Report, 1896,* pp. 24-25.

[216]U.S.P.O.D., *Annual Report, 1912*, pp. 101-02. The service was inaugurated on 16 October 1912. See Roper, *U.S. Post Office*, p. 160.

[217]U.S.P.O.D., *Annual Report, 1915*, p. 284.

[218]*Ibid.*; Roper, *U.S. Post Office*, p. 160.

[219]Roper, *U.S. Post Office*, p. 160, U.S.P.O.D., *Annual Report, 1917*, p. 101.

[220]U.S.P.O.D.R.M.S., *Railway Mail Service*, p. 117.

[221]U.S.P.O.D., *Annual Report, 1897*, p. 506.

[222]U.S.P.O.D.R.M.S., *Railway Mail Service*, p. 118.

[223]See U.S.P.O.D., *Mobile Postal Transportation Clerks Instructions*, part 333.22.

[224]Statistics from U.S.P.O.D., *Annual Report, 1962*, pp. 196-199. Statistics are not available for the years 1914-1922. Figures for 1913 include parcel post mail matter, but in 1912 more than 17½ billion pieces were handled under the old 4-pound weight limit.

[225]Backstamping has been noted on letters dating from 1845 but was apparently first made a general requirement in the *Postal Laws and Regulations* of 3 March 1879, Sec. 379, p. 104. [See under U.S.P.O.D.] The Order of 8 May 1913 was confirmed by the *Postal Laws and Regulations* of 1 October 1913, Sec. 540 (2), p. 309. Some letters, e.g., those forwarded, missent, returned, etc., continued to receive backstamps, but the burdensome task of applying these markings to the bulk of letter mail was essentially eliminated in 1913. From 1879 to 1913, "backstamps" for postal cards were generally applied to the address-side to avoid obliteration of the message.

[226]U.S.P.O.D., *Annual Report, 1897*, p. 128. Heath's detailed discussion of the problem is found on pp. 128-134.

[227]Patents were issued to: J.C.W. Maas and Carl Fisher (Hamburg, Germany), U.S. Pat. No. 75,638; Charles E. Donnellan (Indianapolis, Ind.), U.S. Pat. No. 109, 882; Thomas C. Hargrave (Boston, Mass.), U.S. Pat. No. 121,099; Charles J. Goff and Elmer B. Hursy (Clarksburg, W.Va.), U.S. Pat. No. 147,630; Timothy G. Palmer (Schultzville, N.Y.), and Henry F. Clark (Poughkeepsie, N.Y.), U.S. Pat. No. 160, 947.

[228]U.S. Pat. No. 175,290.

[229]See Pike, "Cancelling Machines," pp. 99, 102, 104; Blake and Davis, *Postal Markings of Boston*, pp. 361-366. Only a relatively small number of markings from the early machines have been found.

[230]Pike, "Cancelling Machines," pp. 104-105.

[231]*Ibid.*, p. 99.

[232]*Ibid.*, p. 105, reproducing a brochure of the American Postal Machines Co. of c. 1890.

[233]Cushing, *Our Post Office*, pp. 189-191.

[234]U.S.P.O.D., *Annual Report, 1898*, p. 118.

[235]See Pike, "Cancelling Machines," pp. 104-109; U.S.P.O.D., *Annual Report, 1898*, p. 117; Cushing, *Our Post Office*, pp. 187, 189; Olson and Olson, *Rapid Cancelling Machines*, pp. 6-31.

[236]U.S.P.O.D., *Annual Report, 1910*, pp. 42, 104-105.

237U.S.P.O.D., *Annual Report, 1914*, p. 140; U.S.P.O.D., *Annual Report, 1920*, p. 118.

238Smithsonian Institution, Roy J. Joroleman collection.

239*Ibid.*

240*Ibid.*

241*Ibid.* See also, "Gehring," in photograph and pamphlet files in Post Office Department Library, Washington, D.C.

242Smithsonian Institution, Joroleman collection.

243Lyon, "Precancels"; U.S.P.O.D., Report for Calendar Year 1903; U.S.P.O.D., *Annual Report, 1913*, p. 18.

244Norona, "Bureau Precancels (1916-1934)," in Norona, *Cyclopedia*, vol. 2, pp. 1-2; Leavy, "Bureau Printed Pre-Cancelled Stamps."

245See U.S.P.M.G., orders, Postmaster General H.C. Payne, Order No. 1052, 20 September, 1904; U.S.P.O.D., *Supplement, 1907*, Section 483½, pp. 68-70; Swan, *Development of Postage Meter Machines* pp. 5-10; Overment, "Permit-Meter Systems," pp. 79-93.

246Cushing, *Our Post Office*, p. 181.

247*Ibid.*, pp. 183-84.

248U.S.P.O.D., *Annual Report, 1898*, p. 115. Ten-year leases were authorized in fiscal year 1898-1899.

249Van Norman, "The New York Post Office," pp. 580-581, 582, 584, 588.

250U.S.P.O.D., *Annual Report, 1910*, p. 105.

251*Ibid.*, p. 106. The court house-post office combination continued, however, in many cities.

252*Ibid.*, pp. 106-08; U.S.P.O.D., *Annual Report, 1911*, pp. 100-01; U.S.P.O.D., *Annual Report, 1912*, p. 102.

253U.S.P.O.D., *Annual Report, 1911*, pp. 88-89.

254U.S.P.O.D., *Annual Report, 1896*, p. 26.

255*Ibid.*, pp. 168-70.

256*Ibid.*, pp. 207-09.

257*Ibid.*, p. 209. See also U.S.P.O.D., *Annual Report, 1895*, pp. 159, 163.

258U.S.P.O.D., *Annual Report, 1895*, p. 159.

259U.S.P.O.D., *Annual Report, 1896*, p. 207.

260U.S.P.O.D., *Annual Report, 1895*, p. 160.

261*Philadelphia Inquirer*, 10 February 1956.

262See, e.g., U.S., Mail Messenger and Transfer Service, Post Office, Boston, Mass., *Time of Departure, Arrival and Transfer of Mails.*

[263]U.S.P.O.D., *Annual Report, 1895*, p. 162; U.S.P.O.D., *Annual Report, 1896*, pp. 33-34, 210-211. For the service in Buffalo, see Burr, "Wagon 'Collection & Distribution' Mail."

[264]See U.S.P.O.D., *Annual Report, 1891*, p. 82; Hutcheson, "Street Car Mail System," Moore, "The Street Car R.P.O. System," U.S.P.O.D., *Annual Report, 1895*, pp. 20, 383, 396-397. The earliest funds for streetcar mail service came from appropriations for both the Railway Mail Service and the Mail-Messenger Service.

[265]U.S.P.O.D., *Annual Report, 1895*, p. 397.

[266]U.S.P.O.D., *Annual Report, 1896*, pp. 33, 218-221.

[267]U.S.P.O.D., *Annual Reports* for years listed. See also Long and Dennis, *Mail by Rail*, pp. 236-246; Clover and Truax, "The Street R.P.O. System," vol. 48, no. 7; vol. 49, no. 10; vol. 50 no. 12; Clover, "Street Railway P.O. in Philadelphia;" Clover, "Street Railway Postal System of San Francisco"; Truax, "Cleveland Circuit R.P.O."; Clover and Truax, "A Check List of Street Railway Post Offices" [the list is incomplete]; Miller, "The Railway Post Offices of Baltimore," vol. 52: no. 4, no. 5, no. 6, no. 9..

[268]See U.S.P.O.D., *Annual Report, 1891*, pp. 70-74, 76-78, 82, 150-161; U.S.P.O.D., *Annual Report, 1895*, p. 162.

[269]Letter Carriers of Philadelphia, *Postal Guide*, pp. 37, 101; U.S. Post Office, Philadelphia, *Postal Guide, 1900* p. 65; Murray, *Pneumatic Tube History*, pp. 28-30; U.S.P.O.D., *Annual Report, 1896*, p. 212.

[270]*Ibid.*, pp. 34, 212-13.

[271]U.S.P.O., Philadelphia, *Postal Guide, 1900*, p. 65; U.S.P.O.D., *Annual Report, 1897*, pp. 15, 173-76; U.S.P.O.D., *Annual Report, 1898*, pp. 298-300.

[272]U.S.P.O.D., *Annual Report, 1897*, p. 174; U.S.P.O.D., *Annual Report, 1898*, pp. 298-300; U.S.P.O., Philadelphia, *Postal Guide, 1900*, p. 65. Some lines were ten inches in diameter. See U.S.P.O.D., *Annual Report, 1904*, p. 129.

[273]W.A.H. Bogardus, vice president and general manager, Tubular Dispatch Co. (N.Y.), to W.S. Shallenberger, 2nd Asst. Postmaster General, 18 October 1898, in Murray, *Pneumatic Tube History*, pp. 46-47.

[274]See U.S.P.O.D., *Annual Report, 1900*, p. 547; U.S.P.O.D., *Annual Report, 1901*, pp. 30, 322-325; U.S.P.O.D., *Annual Report, 1902*, p. 23. The Boston tubes were closed two years. See *The Boston Globe* (1 November, 1902), p. 4.

[275]U.S.P.O.D., *Annual Report, 1910*, p. 142; U.S.P.O.D., *Annual Report, 1915*, p. 161.

[276]U.S.P.O.D., *Annual Report, 1915*, pp. 22, 141; United States House of Representatives, "Pneumatic Tube Postal Commission," pp. 3-9.

[277]U.S.P.O.D., *Annual Report, 1917*, pp. 19-20.

[278]*Ibid.*, p. 21.

[279]*Ibid.*, pp. 20-21.

[280]See *Ibid.*, p. 22; U.S.P.O.D., *Annual Report, 1918*, pp. 13-14.

[281]For a long time after tube service was suspended, Philadelphians requested its restoration. See, e.g., *Philadelphia Bulletin* for 10 February 1917; 24 September 1917;

10 January 1920; 7 February 1924; 22 January 1925; and the *Philadelphia Record* for 3 October 1933, which indicated that the unused equipment was still in place.

[282]U.S.P.O.D., *Annual Report, 1926*, pp. 34-35.

[283]U.S.P.O.D., *Annual Report, 1927*, p. 40.

[284]*Ibid.*, pp. 40-41.

[285]Goldman, *New York, Post Office*, p. 339. See also, United Air Lines, "School and College Service: Picture Series," Photograph No. 13.

[286]Sidney Fields, "Underground Post Office," *New York Daily Mirror* (undated citation) in Goldman, *New York Post Office*, pp. 342-343.

[287]U.S.P.O.D., *Annual Report, 1950*, pp. 65-66.

[288]U.S.P.O.D., *Annual Report, 1951*, pp. 66-67.

[289]United States, House of Representatives, *Treasury-Post Office Department Appropriations for 1955*, p. 73. The actual suspension and start of the "pilot operation" began 1 December 1953, according to a formal report, *Ibid.*, p. 395. See also, United States Court of Claims, *Reports*, pp. 751-827.

[290]United States House of Representatives, *Treasury-Post Office Appropriations for 1955*, p. 395.

[291]Among the earliest references to automobiles are U.S.P.O.D., *Annual Report, 1895*, pp. 19, 160, 162; U.S.P.O.D., *Annual Report, 1896*, pp. 34, 211.

[292]See Acme Photograph dated 18 October 1937, in Free Library of Philadelphia, accession no. 77394. The service was carried out in cooperation with Pan American Airways.

[293]"Mail Collection," *The Horseless Age*, which includes a half-tone showing the truck on its route during the snow storm. See also, U.S.P.O.D., *Annual Report, 1899*, p. 148.

[294]U.S.P.O.D., *Annual Report, 1906*, p. 138.

[295]Ward, "U.S. Postal Authorities" See also, U.S.P.O.D., *Annual Report, 1909*, pp. 116-117; Ward, "Postal Collection by Machine", "Mail Collection by Motor Van." The first Washington experiment was conducted in 1907. Auto service in Detroit and Milwaukee began 1 July 1907. The 3-wheel motorcycle service was found unsatisfactory for heavy-mail districts by 1911 but was useful in residential and suburban areas. See U.S.P.O.D., *Annual Report, 1911*, p. 98; U.S.P.O.D., *Annual Report, 1912*, p. 101.

[296]Ward, "U.S. Postal Authorities", p. 286.

[297]U.S.P.O.D., *Annual Report, 1910*, pp. 100-101. Apparently, the first postal motor trucks were introduced in New York City in 1911. See U.S.P.O.D., *Annual Report, 1911*, p. 140.

[298]U.S.P.O.D., *Annual Report, 1914*, p. 106. See also U.S.P.O.D., *Annual Report, 1917*, p. 36.

[299]U.S.P.O.D., *Annual Report, 1915*, p. 140; U.S.P.O.D., *Annual Report, 1916*, pp. 88-89.

[300]E.g., see U.S.P.O.D., *Annual Report, 1917*, pp. 37-38.

[301] *Ibid.*, pp. 35-36; U.S.P.O.D., *Annual Report, 1918*, p. 27.

[302] U.S.P.O.D., *Annual Report, 1919*, pp. 42-44; U.S.P.O.D., *Annual Report, 1920*, pp. 53-55, 150-158.

[303] U.S.P.O.D., *Annual Report*, 1920, p. 56.

[304] See *Ibid.*, pp. 153-158.

[305] U.S.P.O.D., *Annual Report, 1921*, pp. 55-56. It is noted that 37 different types of postal trucks were operated in 1921.

[306] U.S.P.O.D., *Annual Reports* for years listed.

[307] U.S.P.O.D., *Annual Report, 1891*, p. 78; U.S.P.O.D., *Annual Report, 1892*, pp. 14-18; Cushing, *Our Post Office*, pp. 1001, 1005, 1012-1015. The collection trial was terminated in 1896. Apparently too many patrons were depositing letters in unauthorized boxes. See U.S.P.O.D., *Annual Report, 1896*, p. 25.

[308] U.S.P.O.D., *Annual Report, 1909*, p. 114.

[309] U.S.P.O.D., *Annual Report, 1912*, p. 100.

[310] U.S.P.O.D., *Annual Report, 1920*, pp. 51-52.

[311] U.S.P.O.D., *Regeneration*, pp. 6-7.

[312] U.S.P.O.D., *Annual Report, 1898*, p. 149; U.S.P.O.D., *Annual Report, 1899*, p. 148; Cushing, *Our Post Office*, pp. 238-39.

[313] U.S.P.O.D., *Annual Report, 1898*, p. 149. An ingenious package box had been developed by Postmaster Warfield of Baltimore about 1897 employing self-loading bags. See U.S.P.O.D., *Annual Report, 1897*, pp. 91-92.

[314] U.S.P.O.D., *Annual Report, 1912*, pp. 99-100.

[315] U.S.P.O.D., *Annual Report, 1905*, pp. 50-56, summarizes the development of mail chutes up to that time. The first chute was installed in 1883 in the Elwood Building, Rochester, N.Y. The device was patented by James G. Cutler (U.S. Pat. No. 284, 951).

[316] U.S.P.O.D., *Annual Report, 1899*, pp. 636-39; U.S.P.O.D., *Annual Report, 1900*, pp. 221, 586-87; United States Post Office, Chicago, *Postal Guide*, p. 9, which reproduces full text of a circular letter of 1 March, 1898. The scheme was primarily intended to facilitate separation of city mail aboard inbound trains. See, Scheele, "Zoned Addresses."

[317] Van Norman, "New York Post Office," 589.

[318] *Ibid.*, 584-585; U.S.P.O.D., *Annual Report, 1898*, p. 719.

[319] U.S.P.O.D., *Annual Report, 1915*, p. 150.

[320] Postmaster Enright of Detroit was also credited with implementing the service. See U.S.P.O.D., *Annual Report, 1897*, pp. 93-94. See also "Detroit's Marine Postal Service"; U.S.P.O.D., *Annual Report, 1900*, p. 112.

[321] U.S.P.O.D., *Annual Report, 1905*, pp. 191-192; U.S.P.O.D., *Annual Report, 1906*, pp. 166-67; U.S.P.O.D., *Annual Report, 1908*, pp. 161-62; U.S.P.O.D., *Annual Report, 1918*, p. 14. Chief Engineer Richardson, Chicago Post Office, Cross-Reference sheet, January 1935, in U.S.P.O.D., Chicago, Unpublished Records. The London tunnel was begun in 1914 but construction was delayed because of World War I.

322See Fuller, *RFD*, pp. 199-205.

323See Codding, *Universal Postal Union*, pp. 39-42; U.S.P.O.D., *Annual Report, 1888*, pp. 828-829; U.S.P.O.D., *Annual Report, 1899*, pp. 25-26, 713; U.S.P.O.D., *Annual Report, 1900*, p. 663; U.S.P.O.D., *Annual Report, 1910*, p. 268.

324See Fuller, *RFD*, pp. 205-10; U.S.P.O.D., *Annual Report, 1905*, pp. 674-675; Walker, "Postal Parcels Delivery."

325See Fuller, *RFD*, pp. 210-223.

326U.S.P.O.D., *Domestic Postage Rates . . .* , pp. 11-12, 16, 36-39, 44-45, 46, 68-70; U.S.P.O.D., *Annual Report, 1913*, pp. 9-12.

327See Wiley, *U.S. Parcel Post Stamps*, pp. 3-16; Melville, *U.S. Special Service Stamps*, pp. 36-42; Harmer and Costales, *Scott's U.S. Specialized Catalogue* (1964), pp. 291-293; Postmaster General Order No. 7241, 26 June, 1913, in U.S.P.O.D., *U.S. Domestic Postage Rates*, p. 70; U.S.P.O.D., *Annual Report, 1913*, pp. 10-11.

328Fuller, *RFD*, has a fascinating account of this experiment.

329See *Ibid.*, pp. 249-52.

330U.S.P.O.D., *Annual Report, 1920*, pp. 20-21. See also, Roper, *U.S. Post Office*, pp. 194-195.

331Roper, *U.S. Post Office*, pp. 199-200.

332U.S.P.O.D., *U.S. Domestic Postage Rates*, pp. 22, 30-31, 36-37, 72-74; U.S.P.O.D., *Annual Report, 1917*, pp. 60-66.

333U.S.P.O.D., *Annual Report, 1918*, pp. 48-49.

334*Ibid.*, p. 12.

335See the interesting and comprehensive account by Townsend, "The World War Mail."

336U.S.P.O.D., *Annual Report, 1918*, p. 11.

337*Ibid.*, pp. 22, 24, 30.

338U.S.P.O.D., *Annual Report, 1917*, pp. 10-11; Stover, *American Railroads*, pp. 181-188; U.S.P.O.D., *Annual Report, 1918*, p. 32.

339U.S.P.O.D., *Annual Report, 1918*, pp. 32-33.

340U.S.P.O.D., *Annual Report, 1919*, pp. 27-29.

341*Ibid.*, pp. 22-24; U.S.P.O.D., *Annual Report, 1920*, pp. 13-14, 129. The Federalization of the telegraph and telephone systems headed Burleson's list of recommendations to Congress. For President Wilson's Proclamation of 22 July 1918, see, U.S.P.O.D., *U.S. Official Postal Guide*, 3rd ser., vol. 11, no. 2 (August 1918), pp. 1-2.

342Wetherhill, "The First Official Air Mail"; Kessler, "A Major Philatelic Find"; Naves, "By Air Mail—London, 1784."

343See Gatchell, Angers, et al. *American Air Mail Catalogue*, vol. 2, pp. 856-862, 875-877. The balloons used at Metz were small, made of paper or silk, and inflated with ordinary illuminating gas. One carried 5,000 messages. For an accurate summary of the Paris flights, see Cohn, "The 1870 Flight."

[344]Gatchell, Angers, et al., *American Air Mail Catalogue,* vol. 1, pp. 78-79, 85 et passim; vol. 2, pp. 1068, 1091.

[345]See *Ibid.,* vol. 1, pp. 21-22; U.S.P.O.D., *Annual Report, 1917,* p. 40; U.S.P.O.D., *U.S. Domestic Postage Rates,* pp. 7, 25, 74.

[346]U.S.P.O.D., *Annual Report, 1918,* p. 16.

[347]See Shamburger, *Tracks Across the Sky,* pp. 11-24; *The Airmail,* pp. 1-23.

[348]U.S.P.O.D., *Annual Report, 1918,* pp. 16-17.

[349]*Ibid.,* p. 17. The six specially designed aircraft procured from Standard Aircraft Corporation were considered to be inadequate for the improved airmail service projected. See Lipsner, *The Airmail,* pp. 89-95.

[350]Gatchell, Angers, et al., *American Air Mail Catalogue,* vol. 1, pp. 110-111; U.S.P.O.D., *Annual Report, 1919,* p. 16.

[351]Gatchell, Angers, et al, *American Air Mail Catalogue,* vol. 1, pp. 114-115; U.S.P.O.D., *Annual Report, 1920,* pp. 57-59.

[352]Shamburger, *Tracks Across the Sky,* pp. 46-49; U.S.P.O.D., *Annual Report, 1921,* p. 47.

[353]Shamburger, *Tracks Across the Sky,* pp. 69-89; Lipsner, *The Airmail,* pp. 194-98.

[354]See Shamburger, *Tracks Across the Sky,* pp. 104-108; U.S.P.O.D., *Annual Report, 1924,* pp. 22-23; U.S.P.O.D., *Annual Report, 1925,* pp. 28-31; Gatchell, Angers, et al, *American Air Mail Catalogue,* vol. 1, pp. 118-119, 121; Van Zandt, "On the Trail of the Air Mail"; McConnell, "The Air Mail Pilot"; Nielson, *Saga,* passim; U.S.P.O.D., *A Brief History.*

[355]U.S.P.O.D., *Annual Report, 1926,* pp. 25-28; U.S.P.O.D., *Annual Report, 1927,* pp. 22-29. Each airmail route under the new system was designated as a Contract Air Mail Route (generally abbreviated as C.A.M.) and was assigned a number.

[356]U.S.P.O.D., *Annual Report, 1927,* p. 27.

[357]Gatchell, Angers, et al., *American Air Mail Catalogue,* vol. 1, pp. 162-163.

[358]U.S.P.O.D., *Annual Report, 1928,* p. 27.

[359]U.S.P.O.D., *Annual Report, 1933,* p. 23.

[360]*Ibid.*

[361]Lipsner, *The Airmail,* pp. 238-54; Shamburger, *Tracks Across the Sky,* pp. 152-66; U.S.P.O.D., *Annual Report, 1934,* pp. xi-xii, 24-25, which does not mention the tragedies associated with the Army service.

[362]Gatchell, Angers, et al., *American Air Mail Catalogue,* vol. 1, pp. 388-98; Shamburger, *Tracks Across the Sky,* pp. 167-177.

[363]U.S.P.O.D., *Annual Report, 1941,* pp. 22, 107.

[364]U.S.P.O.D., *U.S. Domestic Postage Rates,* pp. 7, 25.

365U.S.P.O.D., *A Brief History of Air Postal Transport,* p. 3; Gatchell, Angers, et al, *American Air Mail Catalogue,* vol. 2, pp. 632-34.

366U.S.P.O.D., *A Brief History of Air Postal Transport,* pp. 3-4; Gatchell, Angers, et al, *American Air Mail Catalogue,* vol. 2, pp. 636-39, 690-95, 707-10.

367Gatchell, Angers, et al., *American Air Mail Catalogue,* vol. 2, pp. 882-932; Toland, *Ships in the Sky,* passim.

368U.S. Pat. No. 20,306.

369*Ibid.*

370U.S. Pat. No. 165,520.

371U.S. Pat. No. 322,578. See Howard, *Stamp Machines and Coiled Stamps,* (1943) p. 3.

372See *Ibid.*; U.S. Pat. No. 337,450.

373See the interesting summary by Howard in *Stamp Machines,* pp. 3-5.

374*Ibid.,* pp. 5-7.

375*Ibid.,* pp. 7-31, et passim; Harmer and Costales, *Scott's U.S. Specialized Catalogue* (1964), pp. 79-80, 87, 225-231.

376Harmer and Costales, *Scott's U.S. Specialized Catalogue* (1964), p. 67; U.S.P.O.D., *Annual Report, 1928,* p. 6.

377Howard, *Stamp Machines,* pp. 37-59, 123.

378Swan, *Development of Postage Meter Machines,* p. 5; Thomas, *History of Metered Postage,* pp. 1-2. Heath, Acting Postmaster General, 3 October 1898, to C.N. Dull, Commissioner of Patents, Letterbook 46, p. 10, expressed interest in making a test of Wolff's machine.

379U.S. Pat. No. 710,997.

380Swan, *Development of Postage Meter Machines,* pp. 6-15; Thomas, *History of Metered Postage,* pp. 2-6. Overment, "Permit-Meter Systems."

381Swan, *Development of Postage Meter Machines,* pp. 17-18; Thomas, *History of Metered Postage,* pp. 7-9.

382Swan, *Development of Postage Meter Machines,* pp. 18-19; U.S.P.O.D., *Annual Report, 1920,* p. 28. First Class mailings without stamps affixed were authorized 24 April, 1920.

383Thomas, in the *History of Metered Postage,* pp. iv-v, 1-20, notes these features and describes the evolution of machine functions and safeguards.

384The Postage Meter Company, *Pitney-Bowes Postage Meter* passim; The Postage Meter Company, Research Dept., *Traffic in Stolen Stamps,* passim.

385Swan, *Meter Stamp Catalog,* p. vii; Thomas, *History of Metered Postage,* pp. 82-85. The N.R.A. "slogan" consisted of the blue eagle emblem identified with the National Recovery Administration.

386See Swan, *Meter Stamp Catalog,* pp. vi, 54-56; Thomas, History of Metered Postage, pp. 57-63.

387Thomas, *History of Metered Postage,* pp. 27, 43-44, 47, et passim.

388*Ibid.,* pp. 27-28. An experimental multirate meter machine was used in 1927. See also Swan, *Meter Stamp Catalog,* p. 67.

389Thomas, *History of Metered Postage,* pp. 64-69; Swan, *Meter Stamp Catalog,* pp. 74-75; Howard, *Stamp Machines,* pp. 12-13, citing U.S.P.O.D., *Annual Report, 1908.*

390Swan, *Meter Stamp Catalog,* pp. 57-63, 72-73; Thomas, *History of Metered Postage,* pp. 70-76.

391U.S.P.O.D., *Annual Report, 1957,* p. 94.

392Thomas, *History of Metered Postage,* p. iv.

393U.S.P.O.D., *Annual Report, 1962,* p. 198.

394*Ibid.*

395U.S.P.O.D., *U.S. Domestic Postage Rates,* pp. 4-44.

396U.S.P.O.D., *Annual Report, 1924,* p. 99.

397U.S.P.O.D., *Annual Report, 1925,* pp. 18, 33.

398Smithsonian Institution, Roy J. Joroleman collection.

399U.S.P.O.D., *Annual Report, 1925,* pp. 1-4.

400U.S.P.O.D., *Annual Report, 1962,* p. 198.

401Soule, *Economic Forces in American History,* p. 483.

402Shannon, *The Great Depression,* p. ix.

403See Stover, *American Railroads,* pp. 198-201, 210-211.

404U.S.P.O.D., *Annual Report, 1931,* p. 19.

405U.S.P.O.D., *Annual Report, 1932,* p. 16.

406U.S.P.O.D., *Annual Report, 1933,* p. 12.

407See especially *Ibid.,* pp. 12-13, noting a reduction in force of 1,363 Railway Mail Service employees.

408*Ibid.;* U.S.P.O.D., *Annual Report, 1929,* p. 30.

409U.S.P.O.D., *Annual Report, 1933,* p. vii. The unusual policy of raising rates during the Depression and, indeed, the entire fiscal policy of the Department during that period was typical of other fiscal policies pursued by private industry as well as Government. See, Arnold, "The Crash—And What It Meant," pp. 222-225.

410U.S.P.O.D., *Annual Report, 1933,* pp. viii, 46.

411*Ibid.,* p. 43.

412U.S.P.O.D., *Annual Report, 1934,* p. 47.

413See *Ibid.*

414U.S.P.O.D., *Annual Report, 1939,* p. xi.

415U.S.P.O.D., *U.S. Domestic Postage Rates,* p. 15.

[416]U.S.P.O.D., *Annual Report, 1909*, pp. 17-19.

[417]U.S.P.O.D., *Annual Report, 1962*, p. 202. See also, Summerfield, *U.S. Mail*, pp. 89-90.

[418]U.S.P.O.D., *Annual Report, 1941*, p. 20.

[419]*Ibid.*, p. 1.

[420]U.S.P.O.D., *Annual Report, 1942*, p. 1.

[421]*Ibid.*, pp. 1-2. Pay raises are enacted by Congress.

[422]*Ibid.*, p. 3.

[423]*Ibid.*, pp. 4-5.

[424]*Ibid.*, p. 6.

[425]*Ibid.*

[426]U.S.P.O.D., *Annual Report, 1944*, p. 31.

[427]*Ibid.*, p. 2.

[428]*Ibid.*, pp. 2-3.

[429]U.S.P.O.D., *Annual Report, 1943*, p. 12.

[430]U.S.P.O.D., *Annual Report, 1962*, p. 199.

[431]Goldman, *New York Post Office*, pp. 135-64.

[432]U.S.P.O.D., *Annual Report, 1951*, pp. 5-6.

[433]U.S.P.O.D., *Annual Report, 1959*, p. 29. See also, Summerfield, *U.S. Mail*, pp. 198-199; U.S.P.O.D., *Annual Report, 1951*, pp. 34-35.

[434]U.S.P.O.D., *Annual Report, 1954*, p. 19.

[435]U.S.P.O.D., *Annual Report, 1967*, pp. 38-39.

[436]E.g., see U.S.P.O.D., *Annual Report, 1960*, p. 40; U.S.P.O.D., *Annual Report, 1967*, p. 42.

[437]U.S.P.O.D., *Development of Postal Service* p. 94.

[438]U.S.P.O.D., *Annual Report, 1955*, p. 20.

[439]U.S.P.O.D., *Annual Report, 1957*, p. 41.

[440]*Ibid.*; U.S.P.O.D., *Development of Postal Service During Presidency of Truman . . .*, p. 25.

[441]U.S.P.O.D., *Annual Report, 1966*, pp. 89-90.

[442]U.S.P.O.D., *Development of Postal Service*, p. 95.

[443]U.S.P.O.D., *Annual Report, 1966*, p. 89.

[444]*Ibid.*

[445]U.S.P.O.D., *Annual Report, 1954*, pp. 20-21.

[446]U.S.P.O.D., *Annual Report, 1960*, p. 43. See also, U.S.P.O.D., *Anywhere U.S.A.*, passim.

[447]U.S.P.O.D., *Annual Report, 1966*, p. 62; U.S.P.O.D., *Annual Report, 1967*, pp. 39-40.

[448]U.S.P.O.D., *Anywhere U.S.A.*, passim: U.S.P.O.D., *1st Automated Post Office*, pp. 12, 14.

[449]U.S.P.O.D. Advisory Board, *Research, Development, and Mechanization*, p. 47.

[450]For an excellent survey, see U.S.P.O.D., *Annual Report, 1959*, pp. 13-28. For the early announcement of the programs, see U.S.P.O.D. *Annual Report, 1954*, p. 12.

[451]U.S.P.O.D., *Story of Detroit's New General Post Office*, p. 5. See also, U.S.P.O.D., *The World's Most Mechanized Post Office*, passim; U.S.P.O.D., *1st Automated Post Office*, passim.

[452]U.S.P.O.D., *Annual Report, 1965*, pp. 10-12.

[453]U.S.P.O.D., *Annual Report, 1966*, pp. 38-40.

[454]U.S.P.O.D., *Special Report, 1963*, p. 10. See also, U.S.P.O.D., *Annual Report, 1961*, pp. 9-12.

[455]See U.S.P.O.D., *Annual Report, 1962*, p. 10; U.S.P.O.D., *Annual Report, 1967*, pp. 24-26.

[456]U.S.P.O.D., *Annual Report, 1950*, p. 28.

[457]U.S.P.O.D., *Annual Report, 1953*, p. 19.

[458]U.S.P.O.D., *Annual Report, 1954*, p. 24.

[459]See U.S.P.O.D., *Report on Postal Progress*, back cover.

[460]U.S.P.O.D., *Annual Report, 1960*, p. 154.

[461]U.S.P.O.D., *Annual Report, 1967*, pp. 36-37.

[462]U.S.P.O.D., *Annual Report, 1960*, p. 35; U.S.P.O.D., *Annual Report, 1961*, p. 32.

[463]Fuller, unpublished "Comment" on paper by Carl H. Scheele.

[464]An observation made by Melvin Kranzberg of Case-Western Reserve University at the American Historical Association Meeting, Toronto, Canada, 30 December, 1967.

[465]See U.S.P.O.D., *1st Automated Post Office*, passim. Difficulties developed at the Providence Post Office, and the trouble received considerable publicity. For a sensible review of these problems, see U.S.P.O.D. Advisory Board, *Research, Development, and Mechanization*, pp. 51-52.

[466]U.S.P.O.D. and Advertising Council, Advertisement.

[467]See Worsnop, "Postal Problems," pp. 85, 93-94. See also Greenfield, "What's the Matter With the Mails?"

[468]E.g., see U.S.P.O.D., *Development of Postal Service*, pp. 21-33, 77-80, 83-84; Greenfield, "What's the Matter With the Mails?" pp. 23-25.

[469]President's Commission on Post Office Organization, Questionnaire. Postmaster General O'Brien announced the establishment of the President's Commission on Postal

Organization and commented on the nature of postal problems as conceived by the Administration in *Postal Bulletin,* vol. 88, no. 20584. (13 April 1967), p. 1. The ultimate findings and recommendations were published in the interesting document, *Towards Postal Excellence: The Report of the President's Commission on Postal Organization, June 1968* (Washington, D.C.: Government Printing Office, 1968), in which the Department is regarded as a "big business" venture.

470U.S.P.O.D. Advisory Board, *Research, Development, and Mechanization,* p. 49.

REFERENCES

Alling, Joseph T. *Paper: A brief account of how it is made.* Rochester, N.Y.: The Alling & Cory Co., 1929.

Alves, Gertrude. "Mail transportation of the Teutonic Knights." *Emco Journal* vol. 43, no. 439, (1963), p. 1.

American Association of State Highway Officials [A.A.S.H.O.]. *Historic American Highways.* N.p.: 1953.

Anonymous, "The mail comes to Cleveland," *The Historical Society News,* Western Reserve Historical Society, vol. 16, no. 6 (June 1962).

Antrim, Earl. *Civil War prisons and their covers.* New York: The Collectors Club, 1961.

Arnold, Thurmond. "The Crash—and what it meant." In Isabel Leighton, ed., *The Aspirin Age.* New York: Simon and Schuster, Inc., 1963, pp. 214-231.

Ascher. *Grosser ganzsachen-katalog, 1925, auf veranlassung des Berliner ganzsachen-Sammler-vereins zusammengestellt und Bearbeitet.* 2 vols. Leipzig: Robert Neske, 1925 and 1926.

Ashbrook, Stanley B. *The United States one-cent stamp of 1851-57.* 2 vols. New York: H. L. Lindquist, Publisher, 1938.

Baikie, James. *A history of Egypt from the earliest times to the end of the XVIIIth dynasty.* 2 vols. New York: The Macmillan Co., 1929.

Ball, Franklin W. "Just express it." *Railroad Magazine* vol. 47, no. 1 (October 1948) pp. 94-98.

Banci, Alfredo. *Catàlago prefilatelico e storia delle corriere e poste del Lombardo-Veneto.* Rome: Staderini Editore, n.d.

Barrow, R. H. *The Romans.* London: Penguin Books, 1949.

Baxter, James H. *Printing postage stamps by line engraving.* Fredericksburg, Md.: The American Philatelic Society, 1939.

Bayles, W. Harrison. "Postal service in the thirteen colonies." *The Journal of American History,* vol. 5, no. 3 (1911), pp. 429-458.

Bearslag, Karl. *Robbery by mail: The story of the U.S. Postal Inspectors.* New York: Farrar & Rinehart, Inc., 1938.

Beck, Guillaume. "Postal monopoly of the Tour-and-Taxis family in the Papal States (1522-23). *"Union Postale,* vol. 85, no. 5 (May 1960),pp. 76A-80A.

Belfiore, Anthony. "15th century Italian postmarks may be Europe's earliest types." *Covers,* vol. 11, no. 10 (October 1952), pp. 8-9.

Beverley, Robert. *The History and Present State of Virginia.* Louis B. Wright, ed. Chapel Hill, N.C.: The University of North Carolina Press, 1947; orig. ed. 1705; rev. ed. 1722.

Blake, Maurice C., and Davis, Wilbur W. *Postal markings of Boston, Massachusetts, to 1890.* Portland, Me.: Severn-Wylie-Jewett Co., 1949.

Blinn, Thomas W. "Early Michigan postal history." *Thirteenth American Philatelic Congress Book* (1947), pp. 5-24.

Bloss, Roy S. *Pony express—The great gamble.* Berkeley, Calif.: Howell-North, 1959.

Bond, Arthur H. "First United States standardized postmarks were distributed in 1799." *Postal History Journal,* vol. 6, no. 1 (June 1962), pp. 26-30.

Boston Globe, The. 1902.

Breasted, James Henry. *A history of Egypt, from the earliest times to the Persian conquest.* New York: 1st Scribner ed., 1905; Bantam Books ed., 1964.

Brookman, Lester G. *The 1847 issue of United States stamps.* Federalsburg, Md.: The American Philatelic Society, 1942.

———. *The 19th century postage stamps of the United States.* 2 vols. New York: H. L. Lindquist, 1947.

Bruce, Alfred W. *The steam locomotive in America: Its development in the twentieth century.* New York: Bonanza Books, 1952.

Burgess, Samuel M. "Early American postal history." *Record of the Columbia Historical Society of Washington, D.C., 1948-50,* vol. 50 (1952), pp. 245-263.

Burr, Gilbert M. "Wagon 'Collection & Distribution' mail." *Stamps* vol. 15, no. 2, (April 11, 1936), pp. 51, 54.

Butler, Ruth L. *Doctor Franklin, Postmaster General.* Garden City, N.Y.: Doubleday, Doran & Co., Inc., 1928.

Canal Zone Postal Service. *Canal Zone postage stamps.* Mount Hope, C.Z.: Canal Zone Government Printing Plant, 1961.

Cellini, Benvenuto. *The life of Benvenuto Cellini, by himself.* John Addington Symonds, trans. New York: published anonymously, 1930.

Chapman, Arthur. *The pony express, the record of a romantic adventure in business.* New York: G. P. Putnam's Sons, 1932.

Chiera, Edward. *They wrote on clay: The Babylonian tablets speak today.* George G. Cameron, ed. Chicago: The University of Chicago Press, 1938.

Childe, V. Gordon. *The prehistory of European society.* London: Penguin Books, Ltd., 1958.

China, The Directorate General of Posts. *Postage stamp catalogue of the Republic of China, 1878-1957.* Taipei, Taiwan: Directorate General of Posts, 1956.

China, Ministry of Communications, Directorate General of Posts. *Report on the Chinese post office for the tenth year of Chung-Hua Min-Kuo (1921) with which is incorporated an historical survey of the quarter-century (1896-1921),* II. Public series: no. 2, 18th issue. Shanghai: Supply Department, Directorate General of Posts, 1922.

Cincinnati (Ohio) Post Office Account Book, September 1794-1795. Ms copy in Cincinnati Historical and Philosophical Society of Ohio.

Clear, C. R. *Thomas Witherings and the birth of the postal service, together with a copy and a transcription of the proclamation of King Charles the First establishing the first state postal service for the conveyance of private letters in England and Scotland.* Post Office Green Papers, No. 15. London: General Post Office, 1935.

Cleator, P. E. *Lost languages.* New York: The New American Library, 1962 ed.

Clover, Richard S. "Street railway P.O. in Philadelphia." *The American Philatelist,* vol. 51, no. 3 (December 1937), pp. 276-277.

_____ . "Street railway postal system of San Francisco." *The American Philatelist,* vol. 51, no. 5 (February 1938), pp. 480-481.

_____ , and Truax, Robert A. "A check list of street railway post offices." *The American Philatelist,* vol. 51, no. 9 (June 1938), pp. 889-890.

_____ . "The street R.P.O. system." *The American Philatelist,* vol. 48, no. 7 (May 1935), pp. 431-433; vol. 49, no. 10 (July 1936), pp. 502-503; vol. 50, no. 12 (September 1937), pp. 701-02.

Codding, George A., Jr. *The Universal Postal Union, coordinator of the international mails.* New York: New York University Press, 1964.

Cohn, Ernst M. "The 1870 flight of the balloon La Ville de Paris." *Thirty-Second American Philatelic Congress Book* (1966), pp. 37-58.

Collections of the Massachusetts Historical Society. 3rd ser., vol. 7. Boston: Charles C. Little and James Brown, 1838.

Conkling, Roscoe P., and Conkling, Margaret B. *The Butterfield overland mail, 1857-1869.* 3 vols. Glendale, Calif.: Arthur H. Clark Co., 1947.

Connecticut. *The public records of the colony of Connecticut, from 1665 to 1678.* J. Hammond Trumbull, ed. Hartford: F. A. Brown, 1852.

_____ . *The public records of the colony of Connecticut, from August, 1689, to May, 1706.* 15 vols. Charles J. Hoadly, ed. Hartford, Conn.: Case, Lockwood, and Brainard, 1868.

Cushing, Marshall. *The story of our post office: The greatest Government department in all its phases.* Boston: A. M. Thayer & Co., 1893.

Dawson, Christopher. *The making of Europe: An introduction to the history of European unity.* New York: Meridian Books, 1956.

DeBurgh, W. G. *The legacy of the ancient world.* 2 vols. London: Penguin Books, Ltd., 1953.

"Detroit's marine postal service." *Harper's Weekly,* vol. 40 (February 15, 1896), p. 148.

Dietz, August. *The postal service of the Confederate States of America.* Richmond, Va.: The Dietz Printing Co., 1929.

Dill, Samuel. *Roman society, from Nero to Marcus Aurelius.* New York: Meridian Books, 1958; orig. ed., 1904.

Doane, Edith R. "Postal markings of 'Carroll County Plan' for Rural Free Delivery." *Bulletin of the Historical Society of Carroll County, Maryland,* vol. 3, no. 1 (November 1956), pp. 20-32.

_____ . "R.F.D. system postal markings, their evolution and classification." *Western Stamp Collector,* vol. 29, no. 29, (November 16, 1954), p. 9; no. 31 (November 23, 1954), p. 3; no. 35 (December 7, 1954), p. 3; no. 38 (December 18, 1954), p. 7.

Duke of Yorke's Book of Laws. Harrisburg, Pa.: 1879.

Evans, Major Edward B. *A description of the Mulready envelope and the various imitations and caricatures of its design.* London: Stanley Gibbons, Ltd., 1891.

Finlay, Hugh. Journal kept by Hugh Finlay, Surveyor of the Post Roads on the Continent of North America during his survey of the post offices between Falmouth in Casco Bay in the Province of Massachusetts and Savannah in Georgia; begun the 13th September 1773 & ended 26th June 1774. Transcript of the original, Division of Philately and Postal History, Smithsonian Institution.

Fisher, Edith M. "Postal history of Norway." *Covers,* vol. 12, no. 9 (September 1952), pp. 8-24.

Fitzpatrick, John C. "The post office of the Revolutionary War." *Daughters of the American Revolution Magazine,* vol. 56, no. 10 (October 1922), pp. 575-588.

Frankfort, Henri. *The birth of civilization in the Near East.* Garden City, N.Y.: Doubleday & Co., Inc., 1956.

Franklin, Benjamin. *The Papers of Benjamin Franklin.* Leonard W. Labaree and Whitfield J. Bell, Jr., eds. New Haven: Yale University Press, 1960, vols. 2 and 4.

Fricke, Charles A. "The first postal card, 1873-75." *Twenty-Seventh American Philatelic Congress Book* (1961), pp. 119-133.

Frickstead, Walter N. *A century of California post offices, 1848 to 1954.* Oakland, Calif.: Philatelic Research Society, 1955.

Fuller, Wayne E. *RFD: The changing face of rural America.* Bloomington, Ind.: Indiana University Press, 1964.

_____ . Unpublished "comment" on a paper by Carl H. Scheele, "The Post Office Department and urban congestion, 1893-1953," read at the Meeting of the American Historical Association, Toronto, Canada, 30 December 1967. Copy in files of Division of Philately and Postal History, Smithsonian Institution

Gatchell, L. B., Angers, George W.; et al., eds. *American air mail catalogue.* 2 vols. Albion, Pa.: The American Air Mail Society, 1947 and 1950.

Gibbon, Edward. *The history of the decline and fall of the Roman Empire.* 6 vols. Milman Guizot and William Smith, eds. New York: Harper & Bros. Co., n.d.; orig. prtg., 1776-1788.

Glanville, Stephen R. K., ed. *The legacy of Egypt.* Oxford: The Clarendon Press, 1942.

Goldman, Albert (Postmaster, N.Y., N.Y.). *The New York, N.Y., post office during the war years 1941-1945.* New York: Judicial Printing Co., 1949.

Grant, Michael. *The world of Rome.* New York: The New American Library, 1961.

Great Britain. Acts.

Great Britain, General Post Office. *Orders, 1737 to 1774.* 3 vols. Copy of orig. ms. in Division of Philately and Postal History, Smithsonian Institution.

Greenfield, Meg. "What's the matter with the mails?" *The Reporter* (February 11, 1965), pp. 21-25.

Greve, Charles T. *Centennial history of Cincinnati and representative citizens.* 2 vols. Chicago: Biographical Publishing Co., 1904.

Hafen, LeRoy R. *The overland mail, 1849-1869, promoter of settlement, precoursor of railroads.* Cleveland: Arthur H. Clark Co., 1926.

Harlow, Alvin F. *Old post bags: The story of the sending of a letter in ancient and modern times.* New York: D. Appleton & Co., 1928.

Harmer, Gordon R., and Costales, Eugene N., eds. *Scott's Specialized Catalogue of United States Stamps.* New York: Scott Publications, 1964 ed.

Hart, C. C. "Intriguing use of the five-cent 1847 issue of the United States." *Postal History Journal,* vol. 3, no. 1 (March 1959), pp. 62, 69.

Hecht, Arthur. "United States-Canadian postal relations of the eighteenth century. "*New York History,* vol. 38, no. 3 (July 1957), pp. 233-256.

_____ , comp. *Preliminary inventory of the records of the office of Postmaster General.* Record group 28. Preliminary inventory no. 99. Washington: The National Archives, 1957.

_____ ; Warriner, Fred W., Jr.; and Ashby, Charlotte M., comps. *Preliminary inventory of the records of the bureaus of the Third and Fourth Assistant Postmasters General, the Bureau of Accounts, and the Bureau of the Chief Inspector of the Post Office Department.* Record group 28. Preliminary inventory no. 144. Washington: The National Archives, 1959.

Hemmeon, J. C. *The history of the British post office*. London: Henry Frowde, Oxford University Press, 1912.

Henrioud, Marc. "The Franco-Swiss postal relations from the 13th century to the year 1815, *"Union Postale,* vol. 58, no. 6, (June 1933), pp. 196-201.

Herodotus. *The Persian Wars*. George Rawlinson, trans. New York: The Modern Library, 1942.

Hill, Rowland. *Post office reform: Its importance and practicability*. London: W. Cowles & Sons, 1837.

Holmes, Oliver W. *Stagecoach days in the District of Columbia*. Washington: Columbia Historical Society of Washington, D.C., 1948; reprinted in *Record of the Columbia Historical Society of Washington, D.C., 1948-50*, vol. 50 (1952), pp. 1-42.

Holy Bible, The. Authorized version.

Horseless Age, The "Mail Collection, Test with Winton Wagon," vol. 5 (20 December 1899), p. 14.

Howard, George P. *The stamp machines and coiled stamps*. New York: H. L. Lindquist Publications, 1943. Reprinted from *The Collectors Club Philatelist*, vol. 19, no. 1, (January 1940), pp. 1-31; vol. 19, no. 2, (April 1940), pp. 93-113; vol. 19, no. 3, (July 1940), pp. 177-193; vol. 19, no. 4, (October 1940), pp. 249-261; vol. 20, no. 1, (January 1941), pp. 35-49; vol. 20, no. 2, (April 1941), pp. 91-104; vol. 20, no. 3, (July 1941), pp. 190-203.

Huber, Leonard V., and Wagner, Clarence M. *The great mail: A postal history of New Orleans*. State College, Pa.: The American Philatelic Society, 1949.

Hubinont, Raoul. "Establishment of the first international European mails." Ernst M. Cohn, trans. *Postal History Journal,* vol. 7, no. 1 (June 1964), pp. 2-5.

Hunter, Dard. "Laid and Wove." In *Annual Report of the Board of Regents of the Smithsonian Institution, showing operations, expenditures, and condition of the Institution for the year ending June 30, 1921*. Washington: U.S. Government Printing Office, 1922, pp. 587-593.

Hurlimann, Werner. "The cursus publicus." *Union Postale,* vol. 86, no. 1, (January 1961), pp. 8A.-13A.

Hurt, E.F. "Pioneers of the posts: The earliest posts." *The American Philatelist,* vol. 65, no. 1 (October 1951), pp. 29-33.

_____ . "Pioneers of the posts: They made them princes." *The American Philatelist,* vol. 65, no. 2 (November 1951), pp. 141-147.

_____ . "Stepping stones of postal history." *The American Philatelist,* vol. 60, no. 2 (November 1946), pp. 154-157.

_____ , and Hollick, J. R. "Thurn & Taxis, founders of the posts of Europe; with a history of the family and their posts, the stamps and postal markings." In *Billig's Philatelic Handbook* vol. 8 (1948), pp. 88-212.

Hutcheson, Robert J. "The Saint Louis, Missouri, street car mail system." *Twenty-Ninth American Philatelic Congress Book* (1963), pp. 57-73.

Japan, Ministry of Postal Services. "History of Japanese mail service." In *Mail of Japan: Published in commemoration of [the] eightieth anniversary of Japanese postal service.* Tokyo: Postal Bureau, Ministry of Postal services, 1951, pp. 40-46.

Jastrow, Morris. *The civilization of Babylonia and Assyria: Its remains, language, history, religion, commerce, law, art, and literature.* Philadelphia and London: J. B. Lippincott Co., 1915.

Johnstone, Donald B. "The steamboat mail service of historic Lake Champlain." *Postal History Journal,* vol. 4, no. 1 (June 1960), pp. 11-24.

Jones, Stuart. *Companion to Roman history.* Oxford: The Clarendon Press, 1917.

Kantor, Alvin R. "William Giles Goddard: Early organizer of the United States postal system." *Thirty-First American Philatelic Congress Book* (1965), pp. 139-146.

Kay, George F. *Royal mail: The story of the posts in England from the time of Edward IVth to the present day.* London: Rockliff Publishing Corp., Ltd., 1951.

Kennedy, Ethne M. "Train wires to the horizon." *Railroad Magazine* vol. 42, no. 2, (March 1947), pp. 8-38.

Kessler, F. W. "A major philatelic find." *Stamps,* vol. 98, no. 7 (February 16, 1957), pp. 242-243.

Knight, Howard L. "Rural Free Delivery beginnings in Carroll County." *Bulletin of the Historical Society of Carroll County, Maryland,* vol. 3, no. 1 (November 1956), pp. 3-19.

Konwiser, Harry M. *Texas republic postal system: A brief story relating to the post office and postal markings of the Republic of Texas.* New York: Harry L. Lindquist, 1933.

Kramer, Samuel Noah. *History begins at Sumer.* Garden City, N.Y.: Doubleday & Co., Inc., 1959 ed.

Leach, D. D. T., comp. *List of post offices in the United States, with the names of postmasters, on the 13th of July, 1857. Also, the regulations and laws of the Post Office Department.* Washington: John C. Rives, 1857.

_____, comp. *List of Post Offices in the United States, with names of postmasters, on the 1st of April, 1859.* Washington: John C. Rives, 1859.

Leavy, Joseph B. "Bureau printed pre-cancelled stamps." *The American Philatelist* vol. 30, no. 11 (1 March 1917), pp. 134-135.

Letter Carriers of Philadelphia, Keystone Branch 157, National Association of Letter Carriers. *Postal guide and sketch of the Philadelphia post office and stations; souvenir of the sixth annual convention of the National Association of Letter Carriers, Philadelphia, September, 1895.* Philadelphia: Avil Publishing Co., 1895.

Lipsner, Benjamin B. *The airmail, Jennies to jets.* Chicago: Wilcox & Follet Co., 1951.

Lloyd, Seton. *Early Anatolia: The archaeology of Asia Minor before the Greeks.* London: Penguin Books, Ltd., 1956.

Long, Bryant Alden, and Dennis, William J. *Mail by rail: The story of the postal transportation service.* New York: Simmons-Boardman Publishing Co., 1951.

Lopez, Robert S. "The role of trade in the economic readjustment of Byzantium in the seventh century." In *Dumbarton Oaks Papers*. No. 13. Washington: The Dumbarton Oaks Research Library and Collection, 1959, pp. 67-85.

Luff, John N. *The postage stamps of the United States.* New York: The Scott Stamp & Coin Co., 1902.

Lybarger, Donald F. "Early Ohio postal history." *Eleventh American Philatelic Congress Book* (1945), pp. 28-38.

Lyon, Rolston. "Precancels and the Post Office Department." *The Bureau Specialist* vol. 32, no. 2 (February 1961), pp. 34-35.

MacBride, Van Dyke, et al., eds. *Dietz Confederate States catalog and handbook of the postage stamps and envelopes of the Confederate States of America.* Richmond, Va.: The Dietz Press, Inc., 1959, rev. ed.

"Mail collection by motor van." *The Commercial Vehicle* (July 1908), p. 148.

"Mail comes to Cleveland, The." *The Historical Society News.* (Western Reserve Historical Society), vol. 16, no. 6 (June 1962), p. 2.

Makris, John N. *The silent investigators: The great untold story of the United States Postal Inspection Service.* New York: E. P. Dutton & Co., Inc., 1959.

Marshall, C. F. Dendy. *The British post office, from its beginnings to the end of 1925.* London: Humphrey Milford, Oxford University Press, 1926.

Martin, George M., ed. *The United States postal card catalog.* Albany, Ore.: U. S. Postal Stationery Society, 1955.

Maryland. *Archives of Maryland, proceedings of the Council of Maryland, 1693-1696/97.* William Han Browne, ed. Baltimore: Maryland Historical Society, 1900.

Massachusetts. *Acts and resolves, public and private, of the Province of Massachusetts Bay.* 17 vols. Boston: 1869-1910.

Matejka, James J., Jr. "Alaska—the early years." *Twenty-Fifth American Philatelic Congrее Book* (1959), pp. 29-43.

Mattingly, Harold. *Roman imperial civilization.* Garden City, N.Y.: Doubleday & Co., Inc., 1959.

McConnell, Burt M. "The air mail pilot: Lindbergh was one, but there are others." *The American Review of Reviews,* vol. 76, no. 451 (August 1927), pp. 167-73.

McCusker, John J. "New York City and the Bristol Packet: A Chapter in Early Eighteenth Century Postal History," pp. 4-5. Unpublished ms in Division of Philately and Postal History, Smithsonian Institution.

McIlheny, Eleanor E. *Canal Zone post offices celebrate 50th anniversary.* Washington: Canal Zone Study Group, 1954, 6 pp. Reprinted from *The Bureau Specialist,* vol. 25, no. 11 (November 1954), pp. 268-275.

Melville, Fred J. *A penny all the way: The story of penny postage.* Boston: Warren H. Colson, 1908.

_____. *United States special service stamps.* London: Stanley Gibbons, Ltd., n.d.

Meroni, Charles F. *Evolution of world posts, with particular emphasis on postal markings and including catalogs of the sales of collections.* Chicago: privately printed, 1954.

Meyer, Henry A. "The significance of the markings on steamboat mail." *Eleventh American Philatelic Congress Book* (1945), pp. 106-129.

_____ ; Harris, Frederick R., et al. *Hawaii, its stamps and postal history.* New York: The Philatelic Foundation, 1948.

Miller, Michael. "The Railway Post Offices of Baltimore." *The American Philatelist,* vol. 52, no. 4 (January 1939), pp. 324-331; vol. 52, no. 5 (February 1939), pp. 418-425; vol. 52, no. 6 (March 1939), pp. 512-516; vol. 52, no. 9 (June 1939), pp. 790-793.

Moore, Earl D. "The street car R.P.O. system." *The Stamp Specialist, Chartreuse Book.* New York: H. L. Lindquist Publications, 1948, pp. 82-89.

Moore, Edward N. "Early mail service on the Ohio and Erie Canal." *Eleventh American Philatelic Congress Book* (1945), pp. 23-28.

Moroney, Rita Lloyd. *Montgomery Blair, Postmaster General.* Washington: U.S. Government Printing Office, 1963.

Mueller, Barbara. "Outline for postal history, I." *Covers,* vol. 13, no. 7 (July 1953), pp. 7-12.

_____ . "Registered: Covers and the system which produced tnem." *Postal History Journal* vol. 2, no. 1 (April 1958), pp. 19-24.

_____ . "U.S. registry fees, 1855-1955." *Twenty-first American Philatelic Congress Book* (1955), pp. 29-39.

Muller, Herbert J. *The loom of history.* New York: The New American Library, 1961 ed.

Murray, George J., comp. *Pneumatic tube history from reports of the Postmaster General, 1889-1910.* Boston: American Pneumatic Service Co., 1910.

Nathan, M. C., and Boggs, W. S. *The pony express.* New York: The Collectors Club, 1962.

Naumann, Joseph K. F. "Letters in the course of the ages." *Union Postale,* vol. 70, no. 1 (January 1945), pp. 9-21.

Naves, Glen W. "By air mail—London, 1784." *National Philatelic Museum* vol. 3, no. 7 (1950), pp. 898-899, 946.

New Hampshire. *Provincial documents and records relating to the Province of New Hampshire, from 1686 to 1783.* 8 vols. Nathaniel Bouton, ed. and comp. Manchester, N.H.: John F. Clark, 1867-1874.

New York. *Colonial Laws of New York from the year 1664 to the Revolution.* 5 vols. Albany: 1894.

_____ . *Documents relative to the colonial history of the state of New York; procured in Holland, England and France.* John R. Brodhead, ed. Albany: Weed, Parsons, and Co., 1853 14 vols.

Nielson, Dale, ed. *Saga of the U.S. air mail service, 1918-1927.* N.p.: Air Mail Pioneers, 1962.

Norona, Delf, ed. *Cyclopedia of United States postmarks and postal history.* 2 vols. Moundsville, W.Va.: published by the author under Handbook Committee of the American Philatelic Society, 1933.

———. "The express mail." *The American Philatelist* vol. 42, no. 11 (August 1929), pp. 721-724.

———. "The express mails of 1836 to 1839." *The American Philatelist,* vol. 56, no. 12 (September 1943), pp. 774-785.

———. "Further notes on the express mail of 1836-39." *The American Philatelist,* vol. 57, no. 1 (October 1943), pp. 33-35.

——. "Genesis of our registration system." *The American Philatelist,* vol. 47, no. 8 (May 1934), pp. 405-420.

Olson, K. F., and Olson, V. M. *Rapid cancelling machines, manufacturers, and impressions.* Handbook no. 1. Milwaukee: K. F. Olson, 1946.

Ostrogorsky, George. "The Byzantine empire in the world of the seventh century." In *Dumbarton Oaks Papers,* no. 13. Washington: The Dumbarton Oaks Research Library and Collection, 1959, pp. 1-21.

Overment, Alfred P. H. "United States permit-meter systems, 1898-1911: Early development and approbation." *"Twenty-Seventh American Philatelic Congress Book* (1961), pp. 79-93.

Palmerlee, Albert E. "The American posts, 1639-1692." *Weekly Philatelic Gossip,* vol. 65, no. 2 (September 7, 1957), pp. 53-55.

Pennsylvania. *Colonial records, 1683-1790.* 14 vols. Philadelphia: 1852-1853.

Perry, Elliott, and Hall, Arthur G. *The Chatham Square post office.* N.p.: American Philatelic Society, 1941.

———. *100 years ago, 1842-1942.* N.p.: Handbook Committee, American Philatelic Society, 1942.

Perry, Thomas Doane. *Guide to the stamped envelopes and wrappers of the United States.* Richmond, Va.: Dietz Press, 1940.

Petri, Pitt. "Express mails of the War of 1812; first pony express' in the U.S.A." *Postal History Journal,* vol. 3, no. 1 (March 1959), pp. 63-67.

———. *The postal history of western New York.* Buffalo, N.Y.: published by the author, 1960.

Philadelphia Bulletin. 1917, 1920, 1924, 1925.

Philadelphia Inquirer, February 10, 1956.

Philadelphia Record. 1933.

Phillips, Stanley. *Stamp collecting.* New York: Dodd, Mead & Co., n.d.

Pickering MSS collection (Timothy Pickering). In Massachusetts Historical Society. Boston, Massachusetts.

Pickett, Lee N.; Rice, Kenneth L.; and Spelman, Henry M., III. *Florida postal history and postal markings during the stampless period.* Palm Beach, Fla.: Palm Beach Stamp Club, 1957.

Pike, A. H. "History of rapid cancelling machines, with a classification of the postal markings." *Collectors' Digest* vol. 4, no. 6 (June-July 1922), pp. 99-109.

Pirenne, Henri. *A history of Europe.* 2 vols. Garden City, N.Y.: Doubleday & Co., Inc., 1958 ed.

_____ . *Economic and social history of Europe.* I. E. Clegg, trans. New York: Harcourt, Brace and Co., n.d.; orig. ed. 1933.

_____ . *Medieval cities, their origins and the revival of trade.* Garden City, N.Y.: Doubleday & Co., Inc., n.d.; orig. ed. 1925.

Polo, Marco. *The book of ser Marco Polo the Venetian concerning the kingdoms and marvels of the East.* Henry Yule, ed. 2 vols., 3rd ed., rev. London: John Murray, 1903.

Postage Meter Company, The. *The Pitney-Bowes postage meter.* New York: Wynkoop, Hallenbeck, Crawford Co., c. 1922.

Postage Meter Company, The, Research Dept. *The traffic in stolen stamps: Its extent, methods used, losses incurred by business firms.* Boston: Dickie-Raymond, 1934.

President's Commission on Postal Organization. Questionnaire. 1967. Copy in Smithsonian Institution, Division of Philately and Postal History.

Remele, C. W. *United States railroad postmarks, 1837 to 1861.* State College, Pa.: The U.S. 1851-1860 Unit of the American Philatelic Society, 1958.

Rich, Wesley Everett. *The history of the United States post office to the year 1829.* In *Harvard Economic Studies,* vol. 27. Cambridge: Harvard University Press, 1924.

Richmond, I. A. *Roman Britain.* Middlesex: Penguin Books, 1955.

Rider, John F. "Postal history of the Republic of Venice, 1436-1797." *The Collectors Club Philatelist,* vol. 36, no. 4 (July 1957), pp. 196-201.

_____ . "Several handstamp markings of the Republic of Venice." *Postal History Journal,* vol. 4, no. 1 (June 1960), pp. 2-10.

Robinson, Howard. "The British postal reforms of 1840 and the American postal system." *Twelfth American Philatelic Congress Book* (1946), pp. 43-46.

_____ . *Carrying British mails overseas.* Liverpool: New York University Press, 1964.

Rogers, Robert W. *A history of Babylonia and Assyria.* 2 vols., rev. ed. New York: The Abingdon Press, 1915.

Root, George A., and Hickman, Russell K. "Pike's Peak express companies." *The Kansas Historical Quarterly,* vol. 13, no. 3 (August 1944), pp. 163-195; vol. 13, no. 4 (November 1944), pp. 211-242; vol. 13, no. 8 (November 1945), pp. 485-526; vol. 14, no. 1 (February 1946), pp. 36-92.

Roper, Daniel C. *The United States post office: Its past record, present condition, and potential relation to the new world era.* New York: Funk & Wagnalls, Co., 1917.

Ruger, C.   "The development of the postal service in China." *Union Postale*, vol, 50, no. 5. (May 1925), p. 289.

Runciman, Steven.   *Byzantine civilization*. New York: Meridian Books, 1956; orig. ed. 1933.

Sampson, Edward N.   *American colonial postmark catalog, specialized*. N.p.: privately printed, 1953.

Scheele, Carl H.   "Zoned addresses: The early experiments." *Society of Philatelic Americans Journal*, vol. 29, no. 10 (June 1967), pp. 657-63.

Settle, Raymond W.   *Pony express: Heroic beginning, tragic end*. Reprinted from *Utah Historical Quarterly*, vol. 27 (April 1959), pp. 103-108.

Sewall, Samuel.   *Letterbook*. In *Collections of the Massachusetts Historical Society*, 6th ser., 2 vols. Boston: Massachusetts Historical Society, 1886 and 1888.

Seyffert, Oscar.   *A dictionary of classical antiquities*. Rev. and ed. by Henry Nettleship and J. E. Sandys. Cleveland: World Publishing Co., 1956; orig. ed. 1891.

Shamburger, Page.   *Tracks across the sky: The story of the pioneers of the U.S. air mail*. Philadelphia and New York: J. B. Lippincott Co., 1964.

Shannon, David A., ed.   *The great depression*. Englewood Cliffs, N.J.: Prentice Hall, Inc., 1960.

Shenfield, Lawrence L.   *Confederate States of America—The special postal routes*. New York: The Collectors Club, 1961.

Smith, A. D.   *The development of rates of postage: An historical and analytical study*. London: George Allen & Unwin, Ltd., 1917.

Smith, William.   "The colonial post-office." *American Historical Review*, vol. 21, no. 2 (January 1916), pp. 258-275.

—————— .   *The history of the post office in British North America, 1639-1870*. Cambridge, England: The University Press, 1920.

Smithsonian Institution, Division of Philately and Postal History. Collections, photographs, documents, and correspondence files.

Sokolow, N. J.   "Historical facts respecting the origin and growth of the Russian post." *Union Postale*, vol. 12, no. 11 (November 1896), pp. 173-179; vol. 12, no. 12 (December 1896), pp. 187-199.

Soule, George.   *Economic forces in American history*. New York: The Dryden Press, 1952.

Spotswood, Alexander.   *The official letters of Alexander Spotswood, Lieutenant-Governor of the colony of Virginia, 1710-1722. In the Collections of the Virginia Historical Society*. R. A. Brock, ed. New series, 2 vols. N.p.: 1885.

Staff, Frank.   *The transatlantic mail*. London: Adlard Coles, Ltd., 1956.

Steinberg, S. H.   *Five hundred years of printing*. Edinburgh: Penguin Books, Ltd., 1955.

Stern, Edward.   *History of "free franking" of mail in the United States*. New York: H. L. Lindquist, Publisher, 1936.

Stover, John F. *American railroads.* Chicago: The University of Chicago Press, 1961.

Suetonius. *The lives of the twelve Caesars.* New York: The Book League of America, Inc., 1937.

Summerfield, Arthur E. (as told to Charles Hurd). *U.S. mail: The story of the United States postal service.* New York: Holt, Rinehart and Winston, 1960.

Swain, Joseph Ward. *The ancient world.* 2 vols. New York: Harper & Bros., 1950.

Swan, Walter M. *The basic type meter stamp catalog.* 3rd ed. Corinth, N.Y.: J.A. Swan, 1958.

_____. *The development of the postage meter machines of the United States, 1898-1920.* Corinth, N.Y.: Walter M. Swan, 1952.

Sweden, Post Office. "The Swedish posts before 1636, I." *Union Postale,* vol. 33, no. 8 (August 1908), pp. 113-118.

Table of post offices in the United States on the first day of January, 1851, arranged in alphabetical order. Washington: W. & J. C. Greer, 1851.

Table of post offices in the United States on the first day of October, 1846, arranged in alphabetical order. Washington: John T. Towers, 1846.

Tacitus. *Annals.*

Thomas, William K. *History and evolution of metered postage.* State College, Pa.: The American Philatelic Society, 1962.

Thorp, Prescott Holden. "Star dies—demonitization, Confederate and pony express usage." *Covers,* vol. 21, no. 2 (February 1961), pp. 15-18.

_____, comp. and ed. *Thorp-Bartels catalogue of the stamped envelopes and wrappers of the United States.* Netcong, N.J.: Prescott H. Thorp, 1954.

Todd, T. *A history of British postage stamps.* London: Duckworth, 1941.

Toland, John. *Ships in the sky: The story of the great dirigibles.* New York: Henry Holt & Co., 1957.

Townsend, Captain A. C. "The World War mail." *Third American Philatelic Congress Book* (1937), pp. 81-84.

Truax, Robert A. "Cleveland Circuit R.P.O." *The American Philatelist,* vol. 51, no. 8 (May 1938), pp. 753, 787.

United Air Lines. "School and college service, picture series." (Published photographs, mail service.) c. 1948.

United States. *An ordinance for regulating the post-office of the United States of America, passed the 18th of October, 1782.* New York: Childs & Swaine, 1789.

_____. Papers of the Continental Congress.

United States, Court of Claims. *Court of Claims reports.* Washington: U.S. Government Printing Office, 1957, vol. 139.

United States, General Post-Office. *Post-office law, instructions and forms.* N.p.: 1810. Incomplete copy in Smithsonian Institution, Division of Philately and Postal History.

_____ . *Post-office law, instructions and forms, published for the regulation of the post-office.* Washington: Way & Gideon, 1825.

United States, House of Representatives. *Treasury-Post Office Department appropriations for 1955. Hearings before the subcommittee of the Committee on Appropriations, House of Representatives, 83rd Congress, 2nd Session.* Washington: U.S. Government Printing Office, 1954.

_____ . "Pneumatic Tube Postal Commission." *Report of the Pneumatic Tube Postal Commission; report of Victor Murdock, Representative from Kansas.* House Document no. 1629, 63rd Congress, 3rd Session. March 2, 1915.

United States, Mail Messenger and Transfer Service, Post Office, Boston, Mass. *Time of departure, arrival and transfer of mails.* Boston: Boston Post Office, 1896.

United States Patents.

United States Postmaster General. *Laws and regulations for the government of the Post Office Department, with an appendix.* Washington: John T. Towers, 1847.

United States Postmasters General. [U.S.P.M.G.] Letterbooks. Unpublished. In The National Archives and Records Service, Washington, D.C.

_____ . Orders. Unpublished. In Library of Post Office Department, Washington, D.C.

United States Post Office, Chicago. *Postal guide prepared by the Chicago post office (Bureau of Publications), containing revised and corrected postal information for the business public with time charts, scheme and schedules, showing arrival, departure, delivery and collection of mails.* Chicago: Post Office, 1898.

_____ . Unpublished records.

United States Post Office, Philadelphia. *Postal guide, Philadelphia post office, containing postal information revised and corrected to date July, 1900.* Philadelphia: Howard March, Printer, 1900.

United States Post Office Department [U.S.P.O.D.]. *A brief history of air postal transport.* Pamphlet. Washington: U.S. Government Printing Office, 1948.

_____ . *Annual Reports of the Postmasters General.* [The titles of the published annual reports change frequently.]

_____ . *Anywhere U.S.A., next day delivery.* Produced by ITT Intelex Systems, Inc. N.p.: International Telephone and Telegraph Co., c. 1960.

_____ . *Development of the postal service during the Presidency of Honorable Harry S. Truman.* Washington: U.S. Post Office Department, c. 1953.

_____ . *1st automated post office in the United States.* Washington: U.S. Government Printing Office, 1960.

_____ . History of Star Routes. Mimeographed copy of a letter of the Second Assistant Postmaster General, January 6, 1894. In Library of Post Office Department, Washington, D.C.

_____ . *Laws and regulations for the government of the Post Office Department.* Washington: C. Alexander, Printer, 1852.

_____ . *List of post offices in the United States, with the names of postmasters annexed, (except at suspended offices) with an appendix containing the names of post offices . . . embracing also certain important regulations, and other postal information . . . to July 1, 1862.* Washington: U.S. Government Printing Office, 1862.

_____ . *List of post offices and postmasters in the United States, with an appendix containing the names of post offices arranged by states and counties, and table of distances from Washington, D.C., to the county-seats of the several states and territories, etc . . . . revised and corrected by the Post Office Department to October 20, 1867.* Washington: U.S. Government *Printing Office, 1868.*

_____ . *Mobile postal transportation clerks instructions.* Washington: U.S. Post Office Department, 1958.

_____ . *Postage Stamps of the United States.* Washington: U.S. Government Printing Office, 1962.

_____ . *Postal Bulletin,* vol. 88, no. 20584 (13 April, 1967).

_____ . *The postal laws and regulations, published by authority of the Postmaster General.* Washington: U.S. Government Printing Office, under this or similar titles for the years 1866, 1873, 1879, 1887, 1893, 1902, 1913, 1924, 1932, 1941.

_____ . *The regeneration of the American postal system, biennial report, March 4, 1921, to March 4, 1923.* Washington: U.S. Post Office Department, 1923.

_____ . Report for calendar year 1903, Division of Classification. Abstract by Rolston Lyon; copy in Smithsonian Institution, Division of Philately and Postal History, Museum of History and Technology.

_____ . *A report on postal progress.* Washington: U.S. Government Printing Office, 1960.

_____ . *Research & Engineering: A rewarding career with the United States Post Office Department.* Publication 98. Washington: U.S. Government Printing Office, 1967.

_____ . Rural Delivery Service from its beginning. Publication IS-11. Washington: U.S. Government Printing Office, 1960.

_____ . *Special report, fiscal year 1963.* Washington: U.S. Government Printing Office, 1963.

_____ . *The story of Detroit's new general post office.* Washington: U.S. Government Printing Office, 1960.

_____ . *Supplement to the postal laws and regulations of the United States of America. Edition of 1902. In effect March 4, 1907.* Washington: U.S. Government Printing Office, 1907.

_____ . *United States domestic postage rates, 1789 to 1956.* Publication 15. Washington: U.S. Government Printing Office, 1956.

_____ . *United States official postal guide.* 2nd series (beginning September 1879); 3rd series (beginning July 1908); 4th series (beginning July 1921).

_____ . *The world's most mechanized post office: the story of the modernization of the Washington, D.C., post office. Washington: U.S. Government Printing Office, 1959.*

United States Post Office Department [U.S.P.O.D.] Advisory Board. *Research, development, and mechanization in the United States Post Office Department: an interim report to the Postmaster General.* Washington: U.S. Government Printing Office, 1963.

United States Post Office Department, Railway Mail Service. [U.S.P.O.-D.R.M.S.] *History of the Railway Mail Service; A chapter in the history of postal affairs in the United States.* Washington: U.S. Government Printing Office, 1885.

United States Post Office Department [U.S.P.O.D.] and Advertising Council. Advertisement. In *Life,* vol. 63, no. 19 (10 November, 1967), p. 59.

United States, President's Commission on Postal Organization. *Towards postal excellence: The report of the President's commission on postal organization, June 1968.* Washington: Government Printing Office, 1968.

United States Senate. *Rules and regulations governing the Post-Office Department in its various branches, furnished in response to a resolution adopted by the Senate of the United States February 1, 1907 . . . edition of 1902, in effect April 1, 1902; February 26, 1907.* Washington: U.S. Government Printing Office, 1907.

United States Statutes at Large.

Van Norman, Louis E. "The New York post office: Its achievements and its needs." *The American Monthly Review of Reviews,* vol. 33, no. 5 (May 1906), pp. 580-91.

Van Zandt, Lt. J. Parker. "On the trail of the air mail." *The National Geographic Magazine,* vol. 49, no. 1 (January 1926), pp. 1-61.

Vasiliev, A. A. *History of the Byzantine Empire.* S. Ragozin, trans. 2 vols. Madison, Wis.: University of Wisconsin, 1928.

Virginia. *Journals of the House of Burgesses of Virginia, 1659/60-1693.* H. R. McIlwaine, ed. Richmond, Va.: 1914.

Wagner, C. Corwith. "Postal facilities and postmarks, District of Louisiana, the Territory of Louisiana, and the Territory of Missouri, 1804-1821." *Twentieth American Philatelic Congress Book* (1954), pp. 1-16.

Walker, John B. "Postal parcels delivery at one cent a pound." *The Cosmopolitan,* vol. 36, no. 6 (April 1904), p. 635.

Ward, H. G. "Mail collection by motor van." *The Commercial Vehicle* (July 1908), p. 148.

————— . Postal collection by machine in Washington, D.C. *The Commercial Vehicle* (September 1908), p. 217.

————— . "U.S. postal authorities favor motor vehicles." *The Commercial Vehicle* (December 1908), pp. 285-286.

Watson, J. F. *Annals of Philadelphia and Pennsylvania.* 2 vols. Philadelphia: 1857.

Wetherhill, Richard B. "The first official air mail." *Indiana Magazine of History,* vol. 35, no. 4, (December 1939), pp. 390-99.

Wiley, H. L. *United States parcel post stamps, stamp booklets, postal savings stamps.* Boston: Mekeel-Severn-Wylie Co., c. 1914.

Willey, Day Allen. "The Rural Free Delivery service." *The American Monthly Review of Reviews,* vol. 27, no. 1 (January 1903), pp. 55-60.

Williams, L. N., and Williams, M. *The postage stamp: Its history and recognition.* London: Penguin Books, 1956.

Wiltsee, Ernest A. *The pioneer miner and pack mule express.* San Francisco: California Historical Society, 1931.

Woolley, Mary E. "Early History of the colonial post office." *Publications of the Rhode Island Historical Society,* vol. 1, no. 4 (January 1894), pp. 270-291.

Worsnop, Richard L. "Postal problems." *Editorial Research Reports,* vol. 1, no. 5, (1 February, 1967), pp. 83-99.

York, Norton D. "A Civil War postal measure: Aftermath of 1861 invalidation order." *The American Philatelist,* vol. 75, no. 10 (July 1962), pp. 757-762.

_____ . "The unusual demise of the 1847 issue." *Twenty-Eighth American Philatelic Congress Book* (1962), pp. 111-113.

INDEX

ABCD mail (Accelerated Business Collection Delivery), U.S., 181
Abingdon, Va., 67
Actuaria, 15
Adams Express Co., 83
Addresses: clay envelopes, 8; folded paper letters, 20. *See also* Dead Letter Office, General Delivery, House numbers, ZIP codes, Zone numbers
Address-reading machines, 181
Adhesive stamps. *See* Stamps, adhesive postage; Stamps, revenue
Adolphus, Gustavus, 29
Adrian, Mich., 117
Advertised letters, 76, 91
Advertising: meter slogans, 164-65
Affixing machines, stamp: 160-62
Ahasuerus. *See* Xerxes
Airmail: early European, 150; India, 151; United States: developed, 149-59; World War II, 173-74; (1945-65), 176; 1st Class mail, 178; growth, 178-79; by jets, 178-79. *See also* Balloons, Dirigibles, Pigeons, Zeppelins
Akers, Richard H., 157
Alaska, 107-08
Alaska Commercial Co., 107

Albany, N.Y.: colonial route, 54; Canadian-New York route, 64; express mails (1792), 189 *n.* 5; U.S. Express Mail, 72
Aleppo, 21
Alexander the Great, 10, 12, 13
Alexandria, La., 88
Alexandria, Va.: provisional stamp, 74
Alien registration, 172
Allahabad, India: first airplane mail, 151
All American Aviation, Inc., 157
Allen, Ralph, 32
Alphabet. *See* Writing
Amenhotep III, 11
American Bank Note Co., 112
American Expeditionary Forces: World War I mail, 146-49 *passim*
American Express Co., 83
American Postage Meter Co., 163
American Postal Machines Co., 121
Amsterdam, Netherlands: Swedish route, 29
Annapolis, Md.: colonial mail, 50; provisional stamp, 74
Antigonus, 10
Antioch, 10, 15
Appian Way (*Via Appia*), 13

230

Archer & Daley, 87

Archer, Henry, 35

Army, U.S.: mail service in West, 80; in Alaska, 107; Signal Corps and Cuban telegraphs, 109; and early airmail, 151-52; airmail (1934), 156-57. *See also* American Expeditionary Forces; Military mail

Armstrong, George B., 94-95, 103, 185

Articles of Confederation, postal service under, 64-66

Asia, province of ancient Rome, 14

Asshur-nasir-apal II, 36, *n.* 7

Assur, 8

Assyria, 8, 11

Astoria, Ore., 80

Athens, ancient Greece, 12

Augsberg: medieval Germany, 20; Thurn and Taxis posts, 23, 25

Augusta, Me., 139

Augustus, emperor of Rome, 13

Australia, 100, 110

Austria: postal cards, 97; and Prussia, 101

Austro-German Postal Union, 101

Autogiros, 157

Automobiles, U.S.: early references, 127, 136; for postal service, 128; development of service, 135-39; and pneumatic tubes, 133-35 *passim;* R.F.D., 117; highway truck, 177-78; buses, 178; during Depression, 170; in cities, 178; (1952-67), 182-83; 203 *n.* 295, *n.* 297; and mail distribution, 186; advantages of, 138, 139. *See also* Motorcycles

Babbitt, Almond W., 81

Babylonian Empire, 8, 11

Bache, Richard, 64

Backstamps. *See* Postal markings

Badges, postal: in China, 17; of Thurn and Taxis, 23

Badia, Italy, 21

Bags for mail. *See* Pouches, Saddle-bags

Bailey, Chester, 77

Bailey, G., 122

Balloons: European and U.S., 150; of Metz, France, 205 *n.* 343

Baltimore, Md.: letter carriers, 73; provisional stamps, 74; Streetcar R.P.O.s, 130; early mail trucks, 136; package boxes, 204 *n.* 313

Bangs, George S., 103

Barbados: packet mail, 50

Barnard's City Letter Express of Boston, 72

Barons, Benjamin, 52, 55

Basle, Swiss canton, stamp of, 35

Baton Rouge, La.: airmail, 151

Beddoe, N. A., 107

Bedford, Pa., 66

Bellefonte, Pa., 152

Belmont Park, N.Y., 152

Benger, Elliott, 49

Bergamo courier service, 21

Berlin, Germany, pneumatic tubes of, 131

Bermuda, U.S. airmail, 159

Biblical references to posts: 10, 14, 37 *n.* 30, 38 *n.* 39

Bicycles, U.S., 126; (1952-60), 182-83

Bissell, William, 114, 115

Bithynia, 14

Black, Camp, N.Y., 108

Black, Senator Hugo L., airmail investigation, 156-57

Blackmon, Fred L., 132

Blair, Montgomery, 86, 101

Blockade, Union, 87

Blood & Co., D. O., of Philadelphia, 72

Boats: for Continental Congress, 65; Ohio River, 67; Beddoe's Alaskan, 107; harbor mail transfer, 141-42; Great Lakes, 142; U.S. waterways (1945-65), 176. *See also* Canals; Packet ships and mail; Ship mail; Steamboats; Water routes

Bologna, Italy, 21

Bordeaux, France, U.S. postal agency in, 148

Boscowen, N.H., provisional stamp, 74

Boston, Mass.: first post office, 46; and New York route, 46; packet mail port, 54; ship mail, 56 *n.* 3; stagecoach, 55, private expresses, 71; U.S. Express Mail, 71; letter carriers, 66, 73; pneumatic tubes, 131-35 *passim,* 202 n. 274; mail trucks, 136; streetcar R.P.O.s, 129-30; precanceled stamps, 123; canceling machines, 120; sorting machine, 122; "Piggy-back" trucks, 177

Boston & Lowell Railroad, 71

Boten-Anstalten: medieval German postal service, 19

Bowes, Walter H., 163

"Bowes Mailing System," 163
Boyd, John T., 72
Boyle, George L., 152
Braddock's Defeat and packet line, 53
Brandon, Miss., 88
Brattleboro, Vt., provisional stamp, 74
Brazil: early stamp, 35; Zeppelin mail, 159
Bremen: and U.S. registered mail, 78; U.S. mail treaty with, 100
Brescia, Italy, 22
Bridger, Fort, 81
Bridges: Colonial Connecticut, 49; lack of, in interior U.S., 67; Brooklyn and pneumatic tubes, 131, 135
Bristol, England, mail packet port, 50
Brooklyn, N.Y.: Streetcar R.P.O.s, 130; pneumatic tubes, 131-35 *passim*
Brooks, N. M., 100-01
Brown, Aaron V., 81-82
Brundisium, ancient Rome, 13
Brush motor trucks, 136
Brussels, Belgium: Thurn and Taxis mails, 24, 25
Buffalo, N.Y.: private expresses, 71; Collection and Distribution Wagons, 128; early mail truck, 136, 137
Bulk mailings, U.S., 123
Bundsen, Victoria I. H., 160
Bureau of Engraving and Printing, U.S.: U.S. stamps, 112, 198 *n.* 189; Cuban stamps, 109; Canal Zone stamps, 111, precanceled stamps, 123; in World War I, 147
Burgos, Spain: Thurn and Taxis' Brussels route, 25
Burkert, Paul, 123
Burleson, A. S.: pneumatic tube service, 132, 133; on railway mail, 148; on telecommunications, 148, 205 *n.* 341; on automobiles, 133; on airmail, 151, 152
Buses. *See* Automobiles
Business mail. *See* ABCD mail; Commercial mail
Butte, Mont., 139
Butterfield, John, 82
Byzantine Empire, 20, 39 *n.* 56

Cabinet, U.S., Postmaster General in, 71
Cadillac automobiles, 136
Caesar, Julius, 13
Caesarius, Roman magistrate, 15

Cahokia, Ill., 67
Cairo, Ill.: Civil War mail congestion, 89, 94; Fast Mail train, 105 California: early mails to, 80, 81; R.F.D. in, 115
California, S.S., 80
Caligula, 13
Calpurnia, wife of Pliny, 14
Cambaluc (Peking), China, postal routes in, 16
Cambyses, 8, 10
Camden airport, 157
Camels: in ancient Persia, 10; in Egypt, 12
Campania, ancient Rome, 14
Campbell, James, 77-78
Canada: in British American system, 52, 53, 54; New York mails, 64, 142; postal reforms, 34; internal mails, 64
Canajoharie, N.Y., 67
Canals: in China, 17; in U.S., 68. *See also* Boats, Water routes
Canal Zone, 110-11, 159
Canceling devices: requested by U.S., 89; used on R.F.D. routes, 117
Canceling machines: U.S. developed, 120-22; Hoboken, World War I, 147; International Postal Supply, 122; Universal Stamping Machine, 163; with "DJS" facing table, 167-68; high-speed face-cancelers, 180-81; mentioned, 160
Cappadocia, 8, 9, 14
Capua, ancient Rome, 13
Carriers. *See* Letter carriers; Pneumatic tubes
Carroll County (Md.) Plan: R.F.D. distribution wagons, 116-17
Carson, "Kit," 80
Carson City, Nev., 85
Carson Valley, Nev., 81
Casca, 13
Casing of mail. *See* Distribution of mail; Sorting machines
Cellini, Benvenuto, 22-23
Cerigo and Venetian trade, 21
Censorship: by governments, 27; and monopoly, 40 *n.* 74; in France, 29, 30; in Great Britain, 31; Colonial American, 58 *n.* 41; American Revolution, 65; Articles of Confederation, 65; Civil War, 88; U.S., World

War I, 147; World War II, 172

Census, livestock, 172

Central America: U.S. airmail, 159

Central Overland, California & Pike's Express Co., 83, 86

Central Pacific Railroad, 95

Central Route, U.S., 82-86

Chamberstown, Pa., 65-66

Champagne, France, 19

Champlain, Lake: Colonial postal route, 54; R.F.D. for islands, 115

Charlemagne, 19

Charlestown, S.C.: Southern District, 52; mail packet port, 54, 64; overland service, 55; express post, 69

Charles Town, W. Va. and R.F.D., 115

Checkerboard Field, Chicago, 155

Cheyenne, Wyo.: railway mail, 96; airmail, 154

Chia Pu: Chinese postal administration, 16

Chilkoot Pass, Alaska, 107

Chillicothe, Ohio, 67

China: postal service, 16-18; paper, 20; U.S. mails to, 113

Chicago, Ill.: carrier service, 91; D.P.O., 94; express mails, 94; railway mail, 95, 96; Fast Mail trains, 103-05 *passim;* sorting machine, 122; conveyors, 125; streetcar R.P.O.s, 130; pneumatic tubes, 132-33; early "zone" experiment, 141; mail tunnel, 142-43; airmail, 152, 154, 155; meter machine tests, 162; parcel post highway trucks, 178; mentioned, 174

Chicago, Burlington & Quincy Railroad, Fast mail, 105

Chicago, Milwaukee & St. Paul Railroad, Fast Mail, 105

Chicago & North Western Railroad, first R.P.O. car, 95

Chou Dynasty, China, 16

Christmas rush mails, U.S.: and precanceled stamps, 123; World War I, 147-48

Churchill, Fort, Nev., and Pony Express, 85

Chutes for building mail, 141, 181-82, 204 *n.* 315

Cilicia, 9, 11

Cincinnati, Ohio: early mails, 67, 190 *n.* 14; streetcar R.P.O.s, 130; airmail, 157; parcel post highway trucks, 178

Circle City (Circle), Alaska, 107, 108

City Delivery: early U.S., 66; private expresses, 71, 72-73; New York City, 72; free U.S., 91; growth (1880-90), 92; (1890), 113; (1911), 118; (1925), 167; (1945-65), 176; Puerto Rico, 109; and rural mail, 114; mail for sorted on trains, 119-20; urban sprawl, 126; auto trucks, 136-39 *passim;* house boxes, 140; Detroit River, 142; high-rise structures, 182; reduced service, 182, 186. *See also* Automobiles; Bicycles; General Delivery; Letter carriers; Local posts; Private expresses; Village Delivery service; VIM

City Despatch Post, New York: issues first U.S. stamp, 35, 72; purchased by government, 72

City growth and congestion, U.S.: 71, 118, 126, 127-43 *passim,* 179-80; and parcel post, 146

Civic improvements and city delivery, 140

Civil Service Commission, 172

Civil War postal service, 86-90; reforms, 188; 72, 82, 93

Classes of mail, U.S., 91, 111

Claudius, 13

Clay tablets, 7, 8, 11

Cleopatra, 12

"Clerks of the fairs," 19

Clerks, postal: on trains, 94; sort city mail on trains, 119-20; work of, 120; working conditions, 124-25; hours and day off, 126; salaries (1925), 168; World War I, 148-49 *passim;* World War II, 174, 175

Cleveland, Ohio: served, 67; early registered mail, 77; Civil War mail congestion, 89; streetcar R.P.O.s, 130; early mail truck, 136; airmail, 152, 155; highway trucks, 178; curbside letter boxes, 182

Clinton, Ia., and R.P.O. cars, 95

Clovis, 18-19

Clunia, ancient Rome, 15

Coaches, *See* Stagecoaches

COD service, U.S., 145

Coffee houses, 45, 46

Coiled stamps: developed, 160-62 *passim;* Stickney machines for, 112

Collection and Distribution Wagons, 128

Cologne, medieval service in, 20

Colombia, Department of Panama stamps, 110

Colonial posts in America: early, 45-46; under Neale Patent, 47-49; under Parliament, 49-56; and Benjamin Franklin, 51-56; two districts for, 52

Colorado, early mails in, 83

Columbia motor trucks, 136

Columbia, S.C., Civil War, 87

Commerce, U.S. Department of, 155-56

Commercial Controls Corp., 165, 166

Commercial mail: importance of, 1; in Assyria, 8, 36 *n*, 7; Egypt, 11; China, 17; Milan, 28; and revival of European trade, 19; in Great Britain, 31; in American colonies, 54; early U.S., 68; and Express Posts (1836-39), 69; pneumatic tubes, 133; postal innovations, 141; and parcel post, 144-46 *passim;* mechanization of, 160-66; NIMS and ABCD, 181; new communications, 187, 188

Confederate States of America, 86-90 *passim;* 194 *n.* 95

Confucius, 16

Connecticut: Colonial posts, 46; service, 67

Constantinople, 15, 21

Constitution of U.S. and postal service, 64, 71

Continental Congress, posts, 63-64

Continental Postage Meter Corp., 165

Contract Air Mail Routes, U.S., 155, 206 *n.* 355

Conveyors, postal: early, 122; in city post offices, 125-26; during Depression, 170; improved, 180, 181; for high-rise structures, 182

Corbulo, Domitus, and Roman posts, 14

Corinth, ancient Rome, 14, 15

Cornbury, Lord, 49

Couriers, foot: in ancient times, 8; memorized messages, 36 *n.* 3; in Greece, 12; Roman, 13; Phebe, 14; and Paul's letters, 37 *n.* 30; in China, 17; European monastic, 19; for universities, 19; German *Metzger* system, 20; in Sweden, 29; Alaska, 107

Couriers mounted: ancient Persia, 9; Egypt, 11; Rome, 15; China, 16, 17; Japan, 18; medieval Germany, 19; Teutonic Order, 19, 20; "Clerks of

fairs," 19; lack in Europe, 19; in France, 29; Sweden, 29; Great Britain, 30, 31; Mexico, 79

Couriers, U.S.: New York-Boston route, 46; Portsmouth-Philadelphia, 48; 18th-century, 50; Savannah and St. Augustine, 54; negligent, 55; Philadelphia-Pittsburgh, 66; (1794-1810), 67; night service, 68; "Kit" Carson, 80; Pony Express, 84-85

Council Bluff, Ia.: served, 81; Fast Mail trains, 105

Covers: clay envelopes, 8; in China, 18; in France, 29; adopted with postal reform, 33-34; patriotic types, 88; Confederate home-made, 88; sealing machines for, 160-66 *passim. See also* Mailing machines; Stamped envelopes

Cowles, James I., 143, 144

Cracow, Poland, 28

Cranes, track-side mail, 95. *See also* "On-the-fly" mail exchanges

Crawfordsville, Ind., 150

Creswell, 98, 99

Crete, 21

Cristobal, C. Z., 159

Cuba: Spanish-American War mails, 108; posts under U.S., 109; Stickney printing presses in, 112; U.S. airmail, 159

Culling machines, 181

Culver, H. Paul, 152

Cumberland Gap, 67

Cunard steamships, 100, 102, 103, 197 *n.* 145

Cuneiform. *See* Writing

Cursus publicus. See Roman Empire, postal service

Curtiss JN4H aircraft, 151-52

Cutler, James G.: patents mail chute, 204 *n.* 315. *See also* Chutes for building mail

Cylinder seals, Xerxes, 10

Cyprus, 21

Cyrus the Great, 8

Czechoslovakia, Stickney printing presses in, 112

Dallas, Tex., 178

Dalmatia, 21

Damascus, 21

Danville, Ky., 67

Danzig, medieval, 20
Darius, 8, 9
Davis, Maj. Gen. George W., 110
Davis, William H., 94
Dawson City, Canada: on U.S.-Alaskan route, 107
Dead Letter Office, U.S.: established, 65; Civil War burden, 89; valuable mail, 92
Deficits, postal: absorbed by governments, 26; in France, 30; American under Neale Patent, 49; American Revolution, 65; and Public Service philosophy, 69; Postmaster General Key on, 111; of Depression, 169-71 *passim;* U.S. (1945-65), 176; mentioned, 185, 187, 188. *See also* Revenues, postal
De Havilland-4 (DH-4) aircraft, 151-55 *passim*
De Lancey, Peter, 52, 55
De La Rue & Co., Thomas, 87
Della Torre family, 23
Demotic. *See* Writing
Denmark, 28-29
Dennison, William, 95
Denver, Colo.: early mails, 82, 83, 194 *n.* 84; railway mail, 96
Department stamps, U.S.: *See* Official stamps
Depression, Great U.S.: and postal service, 169-71; and postal policy, 185-86; and pneumatic tubes, 134; airmail, 156; postage rates, 208 *n.* 409
Detroit, Mich.: served, 67; early registered mail, 77; mail trucks, 136, 137, 203 *n.* 295; airmail, 155; automated post office, 180-81; mentioned, 76
Detroit River: mail service on, 142
Dewey, Adm. George, 108
Dinsmore, William B., 85-86
Dioscurides carves Roman imperial seal, 13
Diplomata, Roman imperial post, 14
Diplomatic mails. *See* Official mail
Diptychs, 12
Dirigibles, 150, 159
Distributing Post Offices, U.S., 93-95, 186
Distribution of mail, U.S.: on trains, 94-97 *passim;* Fast Mail trains, 103-05 *passim;* city mails on R.P.O.s, 119-

20, 204 *n.* 316; on ocean vessels, 102, 124; in R.F.D. wagons, 116-17; and city growth, 126; in automobiles, 136, 137; harbor boats, 142; Highway Post Offices, 172; in-transit decline, 177; in stationary offices, 179-81; problems, 186. *See also* Clerks, postal; Post offices; Railway Mail Service; Sorting machines
"DJS" mail facing machine, U.S., 167-68
Dockwra's London Post, 41 *n.* 96
Dog sleds, Alaskan, 108
Dominion of New England and New York-Boston route, 46
Dongan, Gov. Thomas, 46
Downing, William, 105
Dromedaries in ancient Persia, 10
Drop letters, U.S.: 72, 73, 76
Dubuque, Ia., 68
Dummer, Edmund, 50
Dutch, in America, 46
Dyea, Alaska, 107

"Eastern Pony Express," U.S. (1836-39), 68-69
East Fortune, Great Britain: dirigible mail, 159
Edgerton, James C., 152
Edward IV of England, 30
Egypt, ancient: postal service, 10-12; supplies papyrus, 12
Embossed stamped stationery. *See* Stamped envelopes; Stamps, revenue
England. *See* Great Britain
Envelopes. *See* Covers; Postal stationery
Evasion of government postal monopoly. *See* "Out-of-the-mails"
Express posts: ancient Persia, 9; Roman Empire, 14; China, 16, 17-18; Japan, 18; British "stafetti," 31; Colonial Maryland and Virginia, 48; American Revolution, 65; U.S. (1792), 189 *n.* 5; (1794), 190 *n.* 18; War of 1812, 67, 70, 190 *n.* 21; U.S. Eastern (1836-39), 68-69; (1842), 71; U.S. Express Agents, 93, 94; Confederate, 88. *See also* Private expresses and mails; Pony Express; Special Delivery; Fast Mail trains

Facing machines: early, 122; "DJS" type, 167-68; high-speed, 180-81

Fairbanks, Richard, tavern, 46
Falmouth, England, mail packet port, 51, 53, 54
Farley, James A., 170
Farming of posts: for management, 27; in Poland, 28; Norway and Denmark, 28-29; France, 30; Great Britain, 31
Fast Mail trains, U.S., 103-05
"Feather Letters," in China, 16
Ferrara, Italy, 21
Ferry service: in China, 17; Connecticut, 48; Massachusetts, 48; Pennsylvania, 48; Ohio River, 190 *n.* 14
Finlay, Hugh, 54, 55, 64
"Flag of true" mail exchanges, Civil War, 88, 89
Flanders, 19
Florence, Italy, 21
Florida: added to British-American posts, 52; mail packets to, 54; U.S. route in Spanish, 67; U.S. mails to, 191 *n.* 26
Folsom, Calif., 81
Fords: Model T and R.F.D., 117; trucks, 139
Foreign mail in Great Britain, 31. *See also* International mail; Ship mail; Steamship mail; Transoceanic mail; Universal Postal Union
Forgeries, stamp, 164
Fort Worth, Tex., 178
Fourth Class mail, U.S., 111
Foxcroft, William, 51, 52, 64
France: Thurn and Taxis, 23, 25; posts in, 29-30; early prestamped stationery, 34; rate reforms, 34; and U.P.U., 102; U.S. postal agency in, 148; U.S. airmail, 159
Franco-Prussian War: international reform, 101; balloon mail, 150
Frankfort, medieval Germany, 20
Franking privilege: in Britain, 33; in U.S., 70; reformed, 97-99; in Texas Republic, 79; Postmaster General Key on, 111; U.S. forces in World Wars, 147, 173. *See also* Official mail
Franklin, Benjamin: Philadelphia postmaster, 50; Deputy Postmaster General for America, 49, 51; administration of, 51-56; inspects routes, 52; resides in England, 52; and

Northern District, 52; travels to Quebec, 54; dismissed by Crown, 51, 58 *n.* 41; Postmaster General under Continental Congress, 64; Commissioner to France, 64; arranges for French packet mails, 64; portrayed on U.S. stamps, 74, 76
Frederick III of Holy Roman Empire, 23, 27
Frederick Wilhelm I of Prussia, 29
Free mail. *See* Frankling privilege; Official mail
Freight: ancient Egyptian posts, 12; Roman posts, 14; Colonial American postmen, 55; U.S. railroad, 148
Friden Calculating Machine Co., postage meters of, 166
Friedrichshafen, Germany, 159

Galatia, ancient Rome, 14
Galba, 15
Galeazzo, Gian, 28
Galveston, Tex., 79
Galveston, S.S., 79, 80
Garden City, N.Y.: early airmail, 151
Gary, James A., 115
Gaul and papyrus, 20
Gehring Mail Distributing Machine tested, 122-23
General Delivery, early U.S., 66
General Postal Union, 101, 102. *See also* Universal Postal Union
General Post Office, U.S., 71
Geneva, Swiss canton, early stamp of, 34
Genoa, Republic of, 28
Georgia: served, 54, 55; R.F.D. in, 117
Germany: medieval posts, 20; U.S. parcel post, 144; Zeppelin mail, 159. *See also* pre-unification states
Ghent, Thurn and Taxis posts in, 23, 25
Glycias, 13
Goddard, William, 63, 64
Goldman, Albert, 135
Gold rushes and strikes: California, 80; Colorado, 83; Alaska, 107
Goths, 21
Government mail. *See* Official mail
Government-operated postal service: rise of, 1, 2; reasons for, 8, 40 *n.* 74, for Assyrian commercial mails, 8; Persian, 9; Egyptian, 11; advantages to Rome, 13-14; China, 16-18; medieval

Germany, 20; rise of European, 26-32; end of farms, 30, 31; British Crown controls American, 47, 63, 64; origins of U.S., 63-64. *See also* Monopoly; "Out-of-the-mails"; Private expresses and mail

Government Printing Office, U.S., 112

Graf Zeppelin, 159

Grand Central Station, N.Y., 125, 142

Granger, Gideon, 68

Great Britain: under ancient Rome, 14; postal treaty with Portugal, 28; posts in, 30-35; reforms, 34; first stamps, 34; and American posts, 49; postal savings, 99; dirigible mail, 159; U.S. airmail, 159; mail tunnels, 204 *n.* 321

Great Lakes: mail for boats, 142

"Great Mail, The," U.S. route, 68

Greece, 1, 12

Green River, Utah: Fast Mail train, 105

Greig, Alexander, 72

Grenada, Spain: Thurn and Taxis posts, 24

Guam: U.S. mails, 109-10, 159

Habersham, Joseph, 67

Hadrian, 14

Hale & Co., 71

Halifax, N.S.: as mail packet port, 54

Halltown, W. Va., and R.F.D., 115

Hamburg, medieval Germany, 20

Hamilton, Andrew, 47, 49

Hamilton, John, 49

Hammurabi, 36 *n.* 3

Handstamps. *See* Canceling devices; Postal markings

Han Dynasty, China, 16

Hannibal, Mo.: served, 68; and Civil War, 89

Hannibal & St. Joseph Railroad: mail sorted on, 94

Hanseatic League, 19

Harbor Mail Service, 141-42

Harlowe, J. B., and Streetcar mail, 128

Harndon, William F., 71

Harrisonburg, Va.: Highway Post Offices, 172

Hartford, Conn., 49

Harvard, S.S., 109

Havana, Cuba: U.S. airmail, 159

Hawaii: service, 108; airmail, 159

Hayward, E., 77

Hazard, Ebenezer, 64, 65

Heath, Perry S., on R.F.D., 115, 116; on canceling machines, 121

Hellenistic states, 10, 12

Henderson, N.Y., 150

Heralds. *See* Couriers, foot

Herba, Giovani del, of Genoa, 28

Herd, colonial postrider, 55

Herodotus: on Persian posts, 9-10; on writing materials, 12

Herrfeldt, J. von, 101

Hesse, Electoral, and Thurn and Taxis, 26

Hewitt Sealer & Stamper Co., 160-61

Hieratics. *See* Writing

Hieroglyphics. *See* Writing

Highway Post Offices, U.S.: developed, 172; (1945-65), 176; reduced, 177

Hill, Rowland, 33-34, 101, 187

Hindenburg, Zeppelin, 159

Hitchcock, Frank H., on Village Delivery, 118; on airmail, 151; on postal savings, 171

Hoboken, N.J.: Military post office, 147

Hockaday, John M., 83

Holliday, Benjamin, 86

Holy Roman Empire, 21, 23

Hong Kong: U.S. airmail, 159

Horses: Hyksos introduce, 11; in Persia, 9; Roman posts, 15; in China, 16, 17; at Siena, 22-23; Thurn and Taxis, 25; in Great Britain, 30; for Pony Express, 84. *See also* Couriers, mounted; Stagecoaches; Wagons

Household letter boxes. *See* Letter boxes, household

House numbers, U.S., 140

Houston, Tex., 182

Hubbard, Edward, 158

Hudson Terminal postal station, N.Y., 125

Huns, 21

Hunter, William, 49, 51

Huntington, W. Va., 157

Hyksos, 11

Icelus, Roman courier, 15

I chan. See China postal service

Illinois Central Railroad: Fast Mails, 105

Illinois Tunnel Co., Chicago, 142-43

Independence, Mo., 80, 81

India: first airplane mail, 151
Indianapolis, Ind., 136
Indian motorcycle, 136
Indians, 85, 115
Inns. *See* Taverns
Innsbruck, Holy Roman Empire, 24, 25
Inspection Service, postal, U.S., 77
Inspectors, in China, 17
Intercolonial posts: New York-Boston, 46
International and Colonial Postage Association, 101
International Aviation Tournament, 151
International mail: regulation in Britain, 31; Franco-Swiss, 40 *n.* 82; Penny Postage movement, 40 *n.* 96; U.S. contracts, 102; discussed, 99-103; airmail, 158-59. *See also* Foreign mail, Ship mail, Steamships; Transoceanic mail; Universal Postal Union
International Postal Supply Co.: canceling machines, 122, 147; meter machines, 165
International Telegraph Union, 101
Ionian Islands, 21
Istria, 21
Italy and use of papyrus, 20; posts before unification, 28; dirigibles, 159

Jackson, Pres. Andrew, 71
Jacksonville, Fla., 178
Japan: posts, 18; U.S. mails to, 113; Zeppelin mail, 159
Jamaica: ship mail, 54; U.S. parcel post, 143
Jamestown, N.Y., 157
Jams: early Russian post offices, 40 *n.* 79
Jewell, Marshall, 99
Jerome, Idaho, 157
Job, on speed of posts, 38 *n.* 39
Johnson, Cave, 73
Jones, John S., 83
Jones, Rice, 79
Jonges: couriers of Teutonic Order, 19, 20
Joroleman, Roy J., 118, 122
Julesburg, Colo., 194 *n.* 84
Juneau, Alaska, 107
"Junk" mail, U.S., 186-87
Jupiter balloon, 150

Kairwan and Venetian trade, 21
Kanesh, Cappadocia, 8, 20

Kansas, early, 81
Kearny, Fort, 85
Kendall, Amos, 73
Kentucky, 67
Key, D. McK., on deficits, 111
Key West, Fla., 159
Kinkead, John H., 107
Knight, James H. "Jack," 154-55
Knoxville, Tenn., 67
Kublai Khan, 16-17, 18

"Lady McLeod" stamp, Trinidad, 35
Lafayette, Ind., 150
Lake Carriers' Association, 142
Lakehurst, N.J.: dirigible mail, 159
Lake Shore & Michigan Southern Railroad: Fast Mails, 103-05 *passim*
Laramie, Fort, Wyo., 81
Leather: writing on, 37 *n.* 22
Leavenworth & Pike's Peak Express Co., 83
Leavitt, Thomas and Martin, 120-21
Legislation, postal: French reform, 30; British Act of 1711, 31-32; British reform, 32, 33, 34; first in America, 46; U.S. Ordinance of 1782, 64, 65; U.S. reforms (1845-55), 73-77; transcontinental mail route, 82; building mail chutes, 141; U.S. War Revenue Act (1917), 147
Letter-bags. *See* Pouches
Letter boxes, household: experimental collection and delivery, 140, 204 *n.* 307; required, 140; R.F.D.: introduced, 115; Joroleman's standard, 118; street: in U.S., 72, 91; and streetcar R.P.O.s, 128-30 *passim;* auto truck collections, 136-39 *passim;* improved, 140-41; curbside, 182; for packages, 204 *n.* 313. *See also* Chutes for building mail; Mailomats
Letter carriers: New York City, 72; in U.S. cities, 73; U.S. (1863), 91; in villages, 118; and letter boxes, 140-41; World War I, 148; and high rise structures, 182; salaries (1925), 168. *See also* City delivery; Rural Free Delivery; Village delivery
Letters: paper, 20. *See also* Clay tablets; Covers; Cylinder seals; Papyrus;

Parchment; Scribes; Stylus; Wax-coated tablets
Letter-sheets, prepaid: Hill suggests, 33; Great Britain, 34; U.S. V-mail, 173
Lewis, Samuel, 67
Lexington, Ky., 67
Liege, Belgium: Thurn and Taxis, 25
Liliuokalani, Queen of Hawaii, 108
Limestone, Ky., 67, 190 n. 14
Lincoln, Abraham, 84
Lindbergh, Charles A., 156, 159
Lisbon, Portugal: Thurn and Taxis, 25
Literacy: growth of, 2; European decline, 19; in America, 54
Little Rock, Ark., 68, 82
Lloyd, John, 49
Local Carrier stamps, 73
Local posts: Venice, 21; Great Britain, 30; early U.S., 66. See also City delivery; Letter carriers; Private expresses and mails; Village delivery
Lockport, N.Y.: provisional stamp, 74
Lombards, 21
London, England: Confederate stamps from, 87; mail tunnels, 204 n. 321
Long Beach, Calif., 151
Los Angeles, Calif., airmail, 152, 159, 179
Lothair, Franco-Germanic king, 21
Louis XIV of France, 29
Louisville, Ky.: steamboat service, 68; Civil War, 88; city delivery, 91; railway mail, 96
Lovelace, Gov. Francis, 46
Lucania, S.S., 103
Luneville, Peace of, 25
Lydia, ancient Persia, 9
Lynch, Head, 49
LZ-130, Zeppelin, 159

Machen, August W., 115-16
Maejima, Hisoka, 18
Magni Nuncii, 19
Mail boxes. See Letter boxes
"Mail-Flo" systems, 180-81
Mailing machines, 160-66 passim
Mailmen. See Letter carriers
Mail-messenger service, U.S., 127
Mailomats, 165
Mailometer Co.: affixing and mailing machines, 162; meter machines, 165
Mail order business, 145

Maine, 115
Manchu Dynasty, China, 18
Manila, P. I., 159
Mantova, Italy, 21
Marathon, Battle of, 12
Marco Polo, 16-17, 18
Margaret, Queen of Norway and Denmark, 28
Marienburg, East Prussia, 19
Markings, postal. See Postal markings
Marseilles, France (and Gaul), 19
Maryland, 46, 48, 50
Massachusetts: Colonial legislation, 46; Neale Patent, 48; R.F.D. in, 115
Mauritius, early stamps, 35
Mechanical Efficiency Co.: sorting machine, 122-23
Medieval European postal systems, 18-20
Mediterranean Sea, 15, 19
Meiji, Emperor of Japan, 18
Memorized messages. See Couriers, foot
Memphis, Egypt, 8
Memphis, Tenn.: western mails, 82; carrier service, 91; highway trucks, 178
Merchandise. See COD service; Freight; Parcel post; Private expresses and mail; Rural Free Delivery
Merchants, mail of. See Commercial mail
Meridian, Miss., 88
Mesopotamia, 7, 10, 11
Messengers. See Couriers
Messina, Straits of, 15
Mestach, George, 151
Meter machines and mail: U.S. tests, 123; development, 162-66
Metz, France: balloon mail, 150, 205 n. 343
Metzger: medieval German couriers, 20
Mexico, 78, 79, 147
Mexico, Gulf of, 79
Miami, Fla., 136
Microfilm: for French balloons, 150; U.S. V-mail, 173
Migratory Bird Hunting Stamps, 172
Mikhaylovich, Alexis, Czar of Russia, 28
Milan, Italy, 28
Millbury, Mass.: provisional stamp, 74
Military mail: Spanish-American War, 108-09; U.S., World War I, 146-49 passim; U.S. World War II, 172-75 passim
Milwaukee, Wisc., mail trucks, 136, 137, 203 n. 295

Min-chii: Chinese private expresses, 17-18

Mineola, N.Y., 151

Ming Dynasty, China, 17

Minnesota, 81

Mississippi River: 68, 80, 82, 88

Missouri, 117

Missouri River, 83, 85

Mitanni, 11

Mobile, Ala.: steamboat mail, 68; express post, 69; early registered mail, 77

Mochilla: Pony Express saddle-bags, 84-85

Monasteries, 19

Money: in Assyrian mails, 8; in Chinese posts, 17; by posts of University of Paris, 19; by private posts in Colonies, 55; U.S. Express Mail, 72; in U.S. mail, 70, 77; and postal notes, 106. *See also* Money Orders

Money Orders, U.S.: inaugurated, 92; improved, 106; in Cuba, 109; extent of service, 113; no monopoly, 146; as savings accounts, 171

Monopoly, postal: in Venice, 21; in Holy Roman Empire, 23; asserted against Thurn and Taxis, 25; in Europe, 26-27; in Spain, 28; Portugal, 28; France, 30; British foreign letters, 31; British domestic, 31; and revenues and censorship, 40 *n.* 74; granted by colonies, 47-48; flouted in America, 55; under Articles of Confederation, 65; in U.S., 71; U.S. limited 146; on U.S. telecommunications, 149; enforcement problems, 189 *n.* 9

Monroe, James, 71

Montelupi, Sebastian, 28

Montgomery Ward, 145

Montreal, Canadia, 54

Moors, 20

Mordecai, 10

Moreland motor trucks, 139

Mormons, 80

Morris, Meriweather, 69

Moscow, Russia, 28

Motorcycles, 136, 138-39, 203 *n.* 295

Motor Vehicle Tax stamps, 172

Mules, 10, 15

Mulready, William, 34

Multipost Co.: meter machines, 165

Murdock, Victor, 132

Naini, India: first airplane mail, 151

Naples, Italy, 25

Nashville, Tenn.: (1814), 109 *n.* 17; route to Knoxville, 67; Civil War mails, 88; carrier service, 91

Natchez, Miss., served, 67; steamboats, 68

National Bank Note Co., 89

National Cash Register Co.: meter machines, 165, 166

National Express Co., 83

National Grange: supports R.F.D., 114; on parcel post, 144

National Mailing Machine, 162

National Postal Meter Co., 165

National Recovery Administration (N.R.A.) and meter slogan, 165, 207 *n.* 385

National Tribune: and meter machine tests, 162

Navy Department, U.S.: and Guam, 109

Neale Patent, 47-49

Neale, Thomas, 47

Nebraska, 81

Nebuchadnezzar, 8

Nero, 14

Nesbitt, George F., 76

New, Harry S., 134

New Amsterdam, 46

New Hampshire, 48

New Haven, Conn.: provisional stamp, 74

New Jersey, 49

New Mexico: early, 81; postage rates, 193 *n.* 59

New Netherlands, 46

New Orleans, La.: served, 67; Nashville mails (1814), 190 *n.* 17; steamboat terminal, 68; express post, 69; letter carriers, 73; early registered mail, 77; Texas mail, 79; San Francisco mail, 80; railway mail, 96; airmail, 151, 158-59

New Orleans (La.), Battle of, 68

Newspapers and news slips: in British mails, 33; Colonial American mails, 52; under Articles of Confederation, 65; and express posts (1836-39), 69; by letter carriers, 73; in Texas, 79; by Pony Express, 85; U.S. rates (1863), 91; on Fast Mail trains, 103; by R.F.D., 115; in U.S. mail, 192 *n.* 45

New York, colonial, 46, 47. *See also* New Netherlands

New York, N.Y. (city of): Colonial posts, 46; General Letter Office, 47; as mail packet port, 50, 51, 53; early express mails, 189 *n.* 5; mail to South (1790), 189 *n.* 9; and Express Post (1836-39), 69; U.S. Express Mail, 71; private expresses in, 72; letter carriers, 73; provisional stamp, 74, 192 *n.* 57; Western Pony Express, 194 *n.* 89; San Francisco mails, 80; Civil War mails, 89; carrier service, 91; railway mail, 96; and transcontinental mails, 102, 103; Fast Mail trains, 103-05 *passim;* mails sorted on trains, 119; post office congestion, 124-25; new post office (1912), 126; mail-messengers, 127; Collection and Distribution Wagons, 128; streetcar R.P.O.s, 129; pneumatic tubes, 131-35 *passim;* building mail chutes, 141; "mail early" campaign, 141; postal harbor boats, 141-42; airmail, 151-59 *passim;* "Piggy-back" mail trucks, 177; jet airmail, 179; Mailomats, 165; mail trucks, 203 *n.* 297; mentioned, 150. *See also* New Amsterdam

New York, S.S., 79, 80, 109

New York Central & Hudson River Railroad: Fast Mails, 103-05 *passim*

Nicaragua, Isthmus of, 80, 83

Night mails: in Persia, 9; Rome, 15; China, 17; Franklin. and Foxcroft, 54; during Revolution, 65; early U.S. coach, 67; mounted couriers, 68; by rail, 92; Boston-New York-Washington, 94; airmail, 154-56 *passim,* 160

Nile River, 11, 37 *n.* 17; papyrus plant, 11

NIMS (Nationwide Improved Mail Service), 141, 181

Ninevah, 8

Ningpo, China, 17

North Carolina, 48, 55

Northern Express Co., 107

North Jersey Truck Terminal, 178

North Platte, Neb., 154

Norway, 28-29

N.R.A. *See* National Recovery Administration

Nuncii: couriers, 30. *See also Magni Nuncii; Parvi Nuncii*

O'Brien, Lawrence, 188

Oceanic Steamship Co., 110

"Ocean Penny Postage," 40 *n.* 96

"Ocean Route" to California, 80

Official mail: in ancient Assyria, 8; Persia, 9; Egypt, 11; Rome, 13-14; China, 16-17, 18; Japan, 18; of Teutonic Order, 20; Thurn and Taxis, 23; in Milan, 28; Great Britain, 30, 31; Swedish diplomatic, 40 *n.* 80; France, 29; under Neale Patent, 48; carried by warships, 45, 50; in Virginia, 46; Boston-New York route, 46; in Connecticut, 46; Massachusetts, 56 *n.* 4; Confederate states, 88; U.S. reform, 97-99; meter machine tests, 162; and private and government-operated posts, 26. *See also* Franking privilege

Official stamps, U.S., 98-99. *See also* Franking privilege

Ogden, Utah: Fast Mail train, 105

Ohio, 67

Ohio River, 67

Oldenburg, 26

Omaha, Neb.: Fast Mail trains, 105; streetcar R.P.O.s, 130; airmail, 154-55

Onesimus, 37 *n.* 30

"On-the-fly" mail exchanges: on railroads, 93, 95, 96; on Detroit River, 142; by airplane, 157

Oregon, 80, 81

Oregon City, Ore., 80

Oregon, S.S., 80

Osgood, Samuel, 66

Ostia, ancient Rome, 15

"Out-of-the-mails" carriage of letters: in France, 30; in Britain, 32-33; Colonial America, 55, 56; during Revolution, 65; U.S. (1789), 189 *n.* 9; in early U.S., 70, 71; and parcels, 143; rural carriers, 144

Overland auto truck, 139

Overland Mail Co., 82, 85-86. *See also* Transcontinental U.S. mails

Overseas mail. *See* Airmail; International

mail; Ship mail; Steamship mail; Transoceanic mail; Universal Postal Union
Ovington, Earl, 151

Pacific Express Co., 107
Pacific Mail Steamship Co., 80, 82
Pack animals and U.S. mails, 81
Packet ships and mail: Dummer's and Warren's 50; rates (1711), 51; Bristol-New York, 51; Falmouth-New York, 51, 53-54; British and French during Revolution, 64; and U.S. express riders, 189 *n.* 5; replaced, 100
Pago Pago, Samoa, 110
Palermo, 21
Palestine, 11
Palmer, John, 31
Panama: U.S. mails to West via, 80; postage stamps, 110; and Canal Zone mails, 110, 111
Panama City, Panama, 80
Panama Railroad, 80
Pan American Airways, 203 *n.* 292
Panic of 1873: and postal savings, 99
Panic of 1893, 114
Paper and papermaking: China, 20; Persia, 20; Europe, 20; ideal for letters, 20
Papyrus: in ancient Egypt, 11; in Rome, 12, 13; late use, 20
Parcel post: in Egypt, 12; Prussia, 29; Colonial private, 143; U.S. mails, 71; by U.S. Express Mails, 72; U.S. general development, 143-46; U.S.-foreign, 143-44; and letter boxes, 140; World War I tax on, 147; intercity trucks, 178; and mail volume, 200 *n.* 224. *See also* Freight; Private expresses and mail
Parcel sorting machines, 180-81
Parchment, 12-13, 20
Paris, France: Thurn and Taxis route, 23, 24; Brussels route, 25; route to Sweden, 29; pre-stamped stationery, 34; international conference, 101; pneumatic tubes, 131; balloon mail, 150; dirigible mail, 150; Lindbergh flight, 156
Paris, S.S., 109

Paris, University of, 19
Parker, James, 52
Parliament, British, 49
Parvi Nuncii: foot couriers, 19. *See also* Nuncii
Passengers carried by post, 14, 30
Paul, the Apostle, 14
PAX, dirigible, 150
Peking, China, and postal routes in, 16
Penalty clause and envelopes, U.S., 98-99. *See also* Official mail
Pennsylvania: Colonial posts, 46, 47, 49; R.F.D. in, 117; airmail, 157
Pennsylvania Railroad: Fast Mail train, 104, 105; mentioned, 142
Penny postage: proposed, 33; adopted, 34; movement, 40 *n.* 96
Penny Posts: Dockwra's and international, 41 *n.* 96; U.S., 72-73
Pensacola, Fla.: Colonial packet service, 54
Perfins, 164
Perforations, stamp: in Britain, 35; U.S., 76; Stickney equipment for, 112; and coiled stamps, 160-62 *passim*
Perkins, Bacon, and Petch, 34
Permit mail, U.S., 123
Pergamum: ancient state, 10, 13
Persia, 8-10, 12
Peter, the Apostle, 14
Peter the Great, 28
Phebe, 14
Philadelphia, Pa.: Colonial, 46; as packet port, 64; Express route (1836-39), 69; letter carriers, 73; early registry service, 77; carrier service, 91; express mails, 94; late use of wagons, 127; streetcar R.P.O.s, 130; pneumatic tubes, 131-33 *passim;* airmail, 151-59 *passim;* mentioned, 150
Philippines: in Spanish-American War, 108-09; under U.S., 110; airmail, 159
Phrygia, 9
Pickering, Timothy: on service, 66; on public service philosophy, 69; on franking privilege, 70; on money in mail, 70
Pigeons: in China, 16; in Franco-Prussian War, 150
"Piggy-back" truck service, U.S., 177, 178
Pilottown, La., 158-59

Pitney, Arthur H., 162 163
Pitney-Bowes: postage meters, 163, 165, 166
Pittsburgh, Pa.: served, 65; streetcar R.P.O.s, 130; airmail, 157; highway trucks, 178; mentioned, 66
Placerville, Calif., 81
Pliny, 14
Plitt, George, 73
Pneumatic tubes: intra-office system, St. Louis, 125; U.S. development, 131-35; popularity of, 202 n. 281; mentioned, 166
Poland, 28
Pontus, ancient Rome, 14
Pony express, eastern U.S., 68-69
Pony Express, Western U.S.: 82-86, 115. See also Express mails; Private expresses and mails
Population: effect of 2; and postage, 71
Portmanteaus, U.S. mail, 70
Portsmouth, England: as packet port, 50
Portsmouth, N.H., 55
Port Townsend, Wash., 107
Portugal, 28; U.S. airmail, 159
Post, origin of word, 30
Postage, monthly accounts in U.S., 70. See also Rates of Postage
Postage currency, 89
Postage meter machines. See Meter machines and mail
Postage stamps. See Stamps, adhesive; Stamped envelopes
Postalia meter machines, 166
Postal cards: defined, 196 n. 139; introduced, 97; U.S., 105; U.S. produces Cuban, 109; produced by Government Printing Office, 112; and canceling machines, 121
Postal inspectors. See Inspection Service, postal
Postal Marine Service, 142
Postal markings: of Augustus, 13; Colonial Massachusetts, 48; early U.S. devices for, 70; handstamped rate marks, 74; early registry markings, 77; applied in trains, 93; in R.F.D. wagons, 116-17; aboard ocean vessels, 102; of Collection and Distribution Wagons, 128; streetcar R.P.Os, 128; clarity of, 120; U.S. backstamps, 120, 200 n. 225; World

War I, 147; and meter impressions, 164; mentioned, 68, 160. See also Canceling devices; Canceling machines; Meter machines and mail; Precanceled stamps
Postal Notes, U.S., 106
Postal Progress League, 144
Postal reforms. See Reforms, postal
Postal Savings System: U.S. requested, 99; in Great Britain, 99; U.S. development, 171; no monopoly, 146
"Postboys." See Couriers, mounted
Post cards: defined, 196 n. 139; introduced, 97
Post-chaises, 13
Postmarks. See Postal markings
Postmaster General, U.S., office of, 71
Postmaster General, S.S., 142
Postmasters: in China, 17; Teutonic Order, 19; murdered by Cellini, 22-23; various U.S. issue stamps, 35; U.S. salaries (1925), 168
Postmasters' provisional stamps and stationery, U.S., 35, 74
Post Office Department, U.S.: administrative development, 71; diminished importance, 188
Post Office Department Advisory Board, 188
Post offices: Boston, 46; early U.S., 66; U.S. (1845), 69; U.S. (1845-60), 78; Texas, 80; West Coast, 80; Western, 81; Confederate States, 86, 194 n. 95; Civil War congestion in, 89; Southern, 90; U.S. (1860-67), 90; (1889), 113; (1895), 114; Military, World War I, 146-49 passim; and court houses, 201 n. 251; in country stores, 114; and R.F.D., 116; U.S. village, 118; stations and substations, 124-25 passim, 126; during Depression, 170; congestion, U.S. cities, 119-26 passim, 146, 179-82 passim; meter machines in, 165-66; landing pads on, 157; truck facilities, 178; for high-rise structures, 181-82.
Post-riders. See Couriers, mounted
Post roads: early U.S., 66, 189 n. 11; New Orleans, 67; steamboat lines become, 68; railroads, 68; U.S. growth, 113
Pouches, mail: ancient Rome, 15; Teu-

tonic Order, 20; in taverns, 45; and coach drivers, 68; Pony Express, 84-85; in Confederate hands, 89; and route agents, 93; exchanged in transit, 93, 95, 96, 142, 157; U.S., 180; sorting machines, 180-81. *See also* Portmanteaus; Saddle-bags

Precanceled stamps, U.S., 123

Prepayment of postage: suggested, 33; in U.S., 73, 76; by stamps, 76, 193 *n.* 64

President's Commission on Postal Organization, 188

Prestamped stationery. *See* Letter sheets; Postal cards; Stamps, revenue: Stamped envelopes

Preston, 82

Priests, 36 *n.* 4

Printing presses, 112

Prisoner-of-war mail, Civil War, 88

Private correspondence: in Egypt, 11; Rome, 13, 14; by Thurn and Taxis, 23; by government post, 27; Milan, 28; China, 17; Japan, 18; Norway and Denmark, 28; Poland, 28; Portugal, 28; Prussia, 29; France, 29; Sweden, 29; Great Britain, 30-31; on Hamburg-Markyard route, 40 *n.* 80; early American, 45, 46; and Revolution, 65; Civil War exchanges, 86, 88. *See also* Commercial mail; Government-operated postal service; Private expresses and mail

Private expresses and mail: in Egypt, 11; Rome, 14; China, 17-18; Japan, 18; and official correspondence, 26; competition with governments, 27; France, 30; Great Britain, 31; and Neale Patent, 47; in American colonies, 49, 55; U.S., 71-73; (1845), 191 *n.* 29; intercity mail, 71-72; 80; Western, 80, 83-86; Civil War, 88; Alaska, 107; parcel carriage, 143-46 *passim;* and Post Office Department, 188

Private mailing cards, defined, 196 *n.* 139. *See also* Post cards

Profits: postal, 1, 2; U.S., 187. *See also* Revenue, postal

Providence, R.I.: provisional stamp, 74; automated post office, 210 *n.* 465

Provisional stamps: in Confederate states,

87. *See also* Postmasters' provisional stamps

Prussia: under Teutonic Order, 19; postal service, 29; purchases Thurn and Taxis system, 26; and U.S. registered mail, 78; mails to Austria, 101

Ptolemies, 10, 12

Public service philosophy: U.S., 69, 76; Postmaster General Key on, 112; deterioration of, 185-88 *passim*

Puerto Rico: in Spanish-American War, 108; under U.S., 109

Pulcher, Claudius, 13

Putoli, ancient Rome, 15

Quebec, Canada, 54

R-34, dirigible, 159

Radios: airmail service, 153, 155; mail trucks, 182

Railroads: declared post roads, 68; and express post (1836-39), 69; mail service, 78; in Texas, 80; Far West, 81; transcontinental proposed, 82; "on-the-fly" mail exchanges, 93; 95, 96; night service, 94; mail sorted on, 94-97 *passim;* mail on (1860-74), 97; technological improvement of, 92-93, 105; terminals and city congestion, 126; Chicago mail tunnel, 142-43; express service, 143; and early airmail, 154; mail volume, 167; in World War I, 148-49; World War II, 173-74; decline of first class, 169-70 *passim,* 177. *See also* Railway Mail Service; Railway Post Offices; Streetcars; Streetcar R.P.O.s; Tunnels

Railroads' War Board, 148

Railway Mail Service, U.S.: development, 92-97; trackside cranes, 95; transcontinental service, 95-96; New Orleans, 96; Fast Mail trains, 103-05; (1875-95), 112; and Spanish-American War, 108-09; city mails distributed, 119-20, 141; streetcar, 128-30; city "zone" trials, 141; World War I, 148-49 *passim;* World War II, 173-74; operates Highway Post Offices, 172; decline of, 169-70 *passim,* 175-77; importance of, 185-86; mentioned, 179. *See also* City growth and congestion; Collection and Distribution Wagons; Highway Post Offices; Post offices, congestion; Railroads; Railway Post Offices; Streetcar R.P.O.s

Railway Post Offices, U.S.: introduced, 95; "full-length," 95; reduced, 170; World War I, 148-49 *passim;* mentioned, 113. *See also* Railway Mail Service; Streetcar R.P.O.s

Randall, Alexander W., 91-92

Rates of postage: China, 17; Venice, 22; Thurn and Taxis, 24; France, 29, 30; collected from addressees, 32; distance zones, 33; based on weight, proposed, 33; Great Britain, 31, 32; British reform of, 34; Penny Postage movement, 40 *n.* 96; Colonial Massachusetts, 46; under Neale Patent, 47-48, 49; Act of Queen Anne (1710), 50-51; for newspapers, 52; Act of 1765, 53; Continental Congress, 63-64; as taxes, 29, 32, 55-56, 66, 147; U.S. (1825), 192 *n.* 52; (1812-45), 66; (1851), 72; marked on mail before stamps, 70, 74; for Utah and New Mexico, 193 *n.* 59; U.S. express posts (1836-39), 69; U.S. based on weight, 73; high early U.S., 70, 71; U.S. (1845), 72; (1845-51), 74-75, 76; drop letters, 72, 73, 76; Republic of Texas, 79; Pony Express, 85; Confederate, 87, 88; U.S. (1863), 91; postal cards, 97; U.S.-international, 99-103 *passim,* 105; Universal Postal Union, 101-02, 103; U.S. (1883, 1885), 105-06; U.S. in ex-Spanish colonies, 110; Canal Zone, 110; Wanamaker on, 113; U.S. World War I, 147; U.S. airmail, 151, 158; U.S. (1919-28), 167; Great Depression, 208 *n.* 409, 170; World War II, 184; and deficits, 187-88 *passim*

Rathbone, Maj. E.G., 109

Rawdon, Wright & Hatch, 192 *n.* 57

Rawdon, Wright, Hatch & Edson, 74

Reagon, John H., 86

Reforms, postal: China, 18; Japan, 18; French, 29, 30, 34; British, 32-35; Canada, 34; British influence on U.S., 34, 73-74; U.S. (1845), 73-76;

(1851), 76; Civil War, 90-95 *passim;* U.S. Railway Mail, 94-95; international, 101-03 *passim;* proposed by Creswell, 97-99; by Wanamaker, 113-14; importance of, 32, 187, 188

Registered mail: U.S., 77-78; U.S.-foreign, 78; in Cuba, 109. *See also* Money; Robbery

Regulation wagons, U.S., 127. *See also* Screen wagons; Wagons

Rehack, James, 122

Relay stations: Persia, 9; Egypt, 11; Rome, 13, 14-15; China, 16, 17; Japan, 18; Teutonic Order, 19-20; medieval Germany, 20; Thurn and Taxis, 23; France, 29; England, 30; U.S. Pony Express, 85

Reliability of mails. *See* Safety and Reliability of mails

Reno, Nev., 154

Research and Engineering Laboratory, U.S. postal, 180

Revenues, postal: of Thurn and Taxis, 23, 26; governments desire, 27; France, 30; Great Britain, 33, 34; under Neale Patent, 47, 49; as tax in Virginia, 50; under Franklin, 54; early U.S., 69; (1845-60), 79; of Pony Express, 86; from ex-Spanish colonies, 110; (1875-95), 112; U.S. World War I, 147; (1919), 166; (1920-30), 167; (1930-36), 169-71 *passim;* (1945-65), 176; and "junk" mail, 186-87; and monopoly, 40 *n.* 74. *See also* Deficits; Profits

Revenue stamps. *See* Stamps, revenue

Revolutionary War, American, 63-65

R.F.D. *See* Rural Free Delivery

Rheims, ancient Rome, 15

Rhode Island, 48

Rhone River, 19

Richardson, "Billy," 85

Richelieu, Cardinal, 29

Richmond, Va., 189 *n.* 9

Riga, Latvia, 28

Riker auto trucks, 139

River boats. *See* Boats; Steamboats

Roads: and Persian posts, 9; in Greece, 11; Roman, 13, 14; Chinese, 16, 17; Roman after fall of Empire, 19; Byzantine Empire, 20, 39 *n.* 56; under Neale Patent, 48; Colonial Connecticut, 49; to Annapolis, 50; N.H.-Ga. route (1786), 65; early U.S., 67; Zane's Trace, 67; and R.F.D., 115, 116, 117. *See also* Post Roads

Robbery, 70, 77, 92, 164

Rochester, N.Y.: Streetcar R.P.O.s, 130; chutes for building mail, 141, 204 *n.* 315

Rocket and missile mail, 183-84

Rock Island, Ill., 68

Rock Springs, Wyo., 155

Rogers, Galbraith P., 150-51

Rolled letters, 37 *n.* 20

Roman Empire, posts, 1, 9, 12-15, 17, 18, 27

Rome, ancient Republic of, 37 *n.* 25

Rome, city of, 13, 15, 19, 21, 25, 28

Roosevelt Field, N.Y., 159

Roper, Daniel C., 146

Roupell, George, 52

Route Agents, U.S.: steamboats, 68, 191 *n.* 28; railroads, 68, 93, 94, 95; and Railway Mail Service, 95

Rovigo, Italy, 22

Royal Anne, brig, 50

Runners. *See* Couriers, foot

Rural Free Delivery, U.S.: development, 114-18; and Parcel Post, 144-45; (1925), 167; (1945-65), 176; carriers' salaries, 168

Russel, Majors & Waddell, 83-86

Russel, William H., 83-86 *passim*

Russia, posts in, 28; *jams,* 40 *n.* 79; and Alaska, 107; mail to U.S. forces in, 148

Sacramento, Calif., 85

Saddle-bags, 70, 84-85

Safety and reliability of mails: in Kanesh, 8; Rome, 13-14, 15; China, 16-17; medieval Europe, 20; on Adriatic, 21; of Venetian, 21; to Paris, 23; 16th-century Italy, 23; of government posts, 26-27; early U.S., 70; Wanamaker on, 113; metered mail, 164. *See also* Government-operated mail service; Inspection Service; Inspectors; Money; Money Orders; Night mails; Postal Notes; Robbery; Sanctity of mails; Speed of mails

St. Augustine, Fla., 54

St. John, N.B., Canada, 54

St. Joseph, Mo., western mails, 81; Pony Express, 85; Civil War, 89; sorting on trains, 94

St. Louis, Mo.: provisional stamp, 74; served, 67; steamboat service, 68; express post, 69; western mails, 82; railway mail, 96; Fast Mail trains, 104, 105; post office, 125; streetcar R.P.O.s, 128; pneumatic tubes, 132-33; balloon flight, 150; airmail, 156

St. Louis, S.S., 109

St. Michaels, Alaska, 108

St. Paul, S.S., 109

St. Petersburg, Russia, 28

Salamis, Battle of, 9

Salaries, pay, and allowances, U.S. postal: comment, 69; city carriers, 73, 91, 126; R.F.D. carriers, 115, 117; village carriers, 118; clerks' 8-hr. day, 126; general increases, 168, 175; World War II, 172, 174-75

Salt Lake City, Utah, served, 80, 81; western mails, 83, 194 *n.* 84; Pony Express, 85, 86; curb-side mail boxes, 182

Samoa, U.S., 110

San Antonio, Tex., 79, 81

Sanctity of mails: government posts, 27. *See also* Censorship; Safety and reliability of mails

San Francisco, Calif.: served, 80, 82; Pony Express, 85, 194 *n.* 89; railway mail, 96; Fast Mail trains, 105; Alaskan mail, 107; Spanish-American War service, 109; Samoan and Australian mails, 110; Streetcar R.P.O.s, 130; harbor mail service, 142; airmail, 152-55 *passim,* 159; jet airmail, 179

Santa Fe, N.M., 79, 81

Santa Rosa, Calif., 139

Saone River, 19

Sardinia, early stamped stationery, 34

Sardis, 9

Savannah, Ga., 54

Schenectady, N.Y., 67

Schermack, Joseph J., 161-62

Schermack Mailing Machine Co., 161

Schwarzburg - Rudolstadt, Thurn and Taxis, 26

Screen wagons, U.S., 127. *See also* Wagons

Scribes: Babylonian and Assyrian, 36 *n.* 4; Egyptian, 11-12

Seals, 13. *See also* Cylinder seals; Signet rings

Sea Post Offices, 102, 124

Sears Roebuck & Co., 145

Seattle Wash.: Streetcar R.P.O.s, 130; airmail, 158

Sectionalism, 82, 84

Sehested, Hannibal, 28-29

Selden motor trucks, 139

Seleucis, 10

Servants, 30. *See also* Slaves

Seven Years' War, 29

Severo, Augusto, 150

Severus, Septimius, 14

Seville, Spain, 25

Sforza, Francesco, 28

Shaw, John L., 160

Sheepshead Bay, N.Y., 150

Sherman, Tex., 127

Ship mail: Nile, 37 *n.* 17; Rome, 15; Byzantine, 20, 39 *n.* 56; Republic of Venice, 21; American Colonial, 45, 46, 56 *n.* 3; Neale Patent, 47; (1711), 51; Act of 1765, 53; Congressional "advice boats," 65; discussed, 100; and airmail, 158-59. *See also* Boats; Canal boats; Foreign mail; International mail; Packet ships and mail; Steamships; Transoceanic mail; Universal Postal Union

Shorter, Captain, 50

Shreveport, La., 88

Shriver, Edwin W., 116

Siberia: U.S. forces in, 148

Sidney, Australia, U.S. mail to, 110

Sidon, 8

Sienna, Italy, 22-23

Sigismund, King of Poland, 28

Signal Corps, U.S.: and Cuban telegraphs, 109

Signet rings, 10

Singapore: U.S. airmail to, 159

Sitka, Alaska, 107

Skagway, Alaska, 108

Slavery, 82

Slaves: Egypt, 11; Rome, 13

Smith, Charles E., 108, 144

Smoky Hill Route, 96

Snow, George K., 160

South America: U.S. airmail to, 159

South Carolina, 48

"Southern Route,": transcontinental U.S., 82

Southhampton, England, U.S. airmail to, 159

Sorting machines, mail: early U.S., 122; Bailey's, 122; Gehring's, 122-23; Burkert's pneumatic, 123; high-speed, 180-81

Sorting of mail. *See* Distribution of mail

Spain, 28

Spanish-American War, 108-09

Special Delivery, U.S.: development of, 106; and pneumatic tubes, 132

"Speed Mail," U.S., 184

Speed of mails: in ancient world, 38 *n.* 39; in Persia, 9; Rome, 15; China, 16, 17; Republic of Venice, 21, 22; and Thurn and Taxis, 23, 24, 25; in American Colonies, 50, 52, 54, 55; and U.S. postage rates, 185; (1790), 189 *n.* 9; (1815), 190 *n.* 21; early Kentucky and Ohio, 67; improved, 68; express posts (1836-39), 69, 71-72; U.S. Express Mails, 94; Far West, 80, 81, 82; Pony Express, 85, 194 *n.* 89; transatlantic, 102-03; by rail, 96; Fast Mail trains, 103-05 *passim;* Wanamaker on, 113; pneumatic tubes, 132-35 *passim;* automobile, 136-39 *passim;* city carriers, 140; city wagons, 136; airmail, 152-59 *passim;* jet, 179; comment, 2

Spire, 25

Spotswood, Alexander, 49

Springfield, Ill., 156

"Stafetti" mail, 31

Stagecoaches: Great Britain, 31; Colonial American, 55; U.S., 65; west of Alleghanies, 67; mail service, 78; in West, 81, 82; inferior to railroads, 68, 93; parcel service, 143; mentioned, 69

Stages of postal routes. *See* Relay stations

Stamford, Conn., 163

Stamped envelopes: suggested, 33; Great Britain, 34; U.S., 76, 79; U.S. prepares Cuban, 109; Puerto Rican, 109; made by private firms, 112

Stamps, adhesive postage: proposed, 33-34; issued, 34; perforated, 35; and

U.S. reform, 34, 72, 73-74; for carriers, 72-73, 192 *n.* 48; local U.S. postmasters', 74, 192 *n.* 57; U.S. general issue, 34, 74; (1851), 76; (1850-60), 79; compulsory use, 193 *n.* 64; Confederate States, 86, 87; U.S. demonitized, 86; Civil War, 89; for money, 89; non-reusable, 195 *n.* 108; U.S. Department issues, 98-99; special delivery, 106; Hawaiian, 108; U.S. prepares Cuban, 109; Puerto Rico, 109; Guam, 110; Canal Zone, 110-11; U.S. Bureau of Engraving and Printing, 112, 198 *n.* 189; sold by carriers, 140; World War I, 147; *Vin Fiz Flyer,* 151; U.S. airmail error, 151; meter impressions, 164, 166; "perfins," 164; and "Mr. ZIP," 181; rocket mail, 184. *See also* Affixing machines; Coiled stamps; Meter impressions and machines; Permit mail; Precanceled stamps; Postmasters' Provisional stamps; Provisional stamps

Stamps, revenue: Greece, 34; British embossed, 34; U.S. Migratory Bird Hunting Stamps, 172; Motor Vehicle Tax, 172; for U.S. parcels, 147

Standard Aircraft Corp., 206 *n.* 349

Star Routes: origin of name, 196 *n.* 124; and stagecoaches, 93; and R.F.D., 116; funds for wagons, 127; and railway mail, 169; (1945-65), 176

Steamboats: early U.S., 68; become post roads, 68; Great Mail route, 68; Express route (1836-39), 69; service, 78; Texas, 80; West, 81; inferior to rail, 96, 97

Steamships: New Orleans-Galveston, 79; California, 80; international, 100-03 *passim;* speed of, 102-03; Alaskan, 107; Fast Mail, 109; transatlantic, 197 *n.* 145

Stephan, Heinrich von, 101

Stettin: medieval Germany, 20

Stickney, Benjamin R., 112

Streetcar Railway Post Offices: in cities, 128-30; and trucks, 138; appropriations for, 202 *n.* 264

Streetcars: letter drops, 140; mentioned, 126, 127

Stuyvesant, Peter, 46

Stylus, writing, 7, 12, 13

Suetonius, 13

Sui Dynasty, China, 16

Sumeria, 7

Summerfield, Arthur, 135

Susa, Assyria, 8, 9, 10

Swabia: late use of wax tablets, 37 *n.* 21

Swart's City Dispatch Post of N.Y., 72

Sweden, 29, 112

Switzerland, 28, 35

Syria, 10

Tablets. *See* Clay tablets; Wax-coated tablets

Tacitus, 14, 15

Taft Agreement, 111

Tahuantepec, Isthmus of, 80

T'ang Dynasty, China, 16

Tarraco, ancient Rome, 15

Tarsus, Assyria, 8

Tasso, Amadeo, 21

Tasso family, 23

Taverns, as Colonial post offices, 45, 46, 48

Tax. *See* Rates of postage; Revenues, postal

Taxis, Franz von, 23, 24

Taxis, Johann Baptista von, 25

Taxis, Lamoral von, 24-25

Taxis, Leonard I von, 25

Taxis, Roger I von, 23, 27

Telegraph: transcontinental U.S., 83; and Pony Express, 85, 194 *n.* 89, *n.* 92; and railroads, 93; and postal monopoly, 99; international reform, 101; in Cuba, 109; Wanamaker on, 113, 114; under U.S. Post Office Dept., 149; facsimile transmission, 184; and government control, 185; and commercial mail, 188

Telephones: Wanamaker on, 114; under U.S. Post Office Dept., 149; and government control, 185; and commercial mail, 187, 188

Teutonic Order (Teutonic Knights of St. Mary's Hospital at Jerusalem), 19-20

Texas: under Mexico, 78-79; Republic of, 79; U.S. posts, 79-80; mails interrupted, 83

Theodosius, 14, 15

Thirty Years' War, 25, 29

Thomas, Eddy Taylor, 160
Thomas, Henry T., 72
Three Rivers, Canada, 54
Thurn and Taxis, 23-26, 29-30
Tiberius, Roman emperor, 13, 14
Tientsin Treaty, 18
"Tobacco Post," 46
Tokyo, Japan, Zeppelin mail, 159
Toler, Daniel J., 79-80
Toppan, Carpenter, Casilear & Co., 76
Trajan, 14
Transcontinental U.S. posts: "Kit" Carson, 80; attempted, 80; established, 80-86; Butterfield route, 82-83; Civil War, 83; and railroads, 80, 95-96, 105; airmail, 152-57 *passim*, 179; mentioned, 113
Transoceanic mails: and American Colonies, 45, 46, 47, 48, 50, 51, 53, 54; under Continental Congress, 64; U.S., 99-103 *passim*; Confederate States, 87; transpacific, 100, 110; steamships, 197 *n*. 145; and Lindbergh's flight, 156; airmail, 158-59
Transportation: effect of low-cost, 2; of persons and goods, 14; improved rail, 92-93; steam on high seas, 103; World War I crisis, 148; aircraft, 149-59 *passim*; and U.S. mails, 185
Travelers: in Rome, 14; Great Britain, 32-34; medieval Europe, 20. *See also* Passengers
Treaties, postal: Venetian, 21; Thurn and Taxis, France, and Spain, 23; Portugal-Great Britain, 28; Confederacy, 87; U.S. international, 100-01; U.S.-Hawaiian, 108. *See also* Universal Postal Union
Treves, 25
Treviso, Italy, 22
Trinidad, "Lady McLeod" stamp, 35
Trucks, auto. *See* Automobiles
Tryon, Gov. of North Carolina, 55
Tunnels, mail: St. Louis, 125; Chicago, 142-43; London, 204 *n*. 321
Tutuila, Samoa, 110
Tychicus, 37 *n*. 30
Tyner, James N., on General Postal Union, 102; on Fast Mail trains, 104-05

Union Pacific Railroad, 95-96
United States Express Mail, 71-72

United Store Service Co. facing machine, 122
Universal Postal Union: founded, 27, 101; China, 18; Japan, 18; Hawaii, 108; and Canal Zone, 110; parcel post, 143; mentioned, 113. *See also* General Postal Union
Universal Stamping Machine Co., 163
Universities, 19, 20, 30
Utah: served, 80, 81; early rates, 193 *n*. 59

Uvilla, W. Va., 115

Vaille, F. W., 110
Vanderbilt, Cornelius, 80
Vending machines, stamp: development, 161, 180; metered mail, 165
Venetian Couriers, Company of, 21
Venice, Italy, 19, 21
Venice, Republic of, 21-23, 28
Ventilating systems: Chicago post office, 125
Vermont, 67
Verona, Italy, 22, 25
Victor Emmanual, 28
Victoria, B.C.: U.S. airmail, 158
Victoria, Queen, 34
Vienna, in medieval period, 19; Holy Roman Empire and Thurn and Taxis, 25; Swedish route, 29
Village Delivery Service: experimental, 199 *n*. 215; developed, 118, 167
VIM program (Virtical Improved Mail service), 181-82
Vincennes, Ind., 67
Vin Fiz Flyer, 150-51
Virginia, 46, 48, 49, 50
Virgin Islands, 111
V-mail, U.S., 173-174
Volume of mail: Great Britain, 34; Butterfield line, 82; Pony Express, 85; Alaska, 107; U.S. growth, 70, 113, 114, 120, 167, 175, 176, 180, 188; U.S. and world, 166; U.S. cities, 73, 91, 124-26 *passim*; Pneumatic tube, 131-35 *passim*; parcel post, 146; U.S. World War I, 147-48; U.S. airmail, 152, 155-57 *passim*; meter machines, 166; U.S. World War II, 172, 174; V-mail, 173

Wagons: in Rome, 15; celerity, 82; R.F.D., 116-117; U.S. cities, 127-28, 129-37 *passim*, 146; and Chicago tunnels, 142-43. *See also* Collection and Distribution Wagons; Post-chaises

Wake Island, 159

Wanamaker, John, on progress and public service, 113-14; tries R.F.D., 114; and house letter boxes, 140; on parcel post, 143; mentioned, 119, 185

Warfield, Postmaster of Baltimore, 204 *n.* 313

War of 1812, 66, 67

Warren, William, 50

War Savings Bonds and Stamps, 172

Washington, 81

Washington, D.C.: stagecoaches, 67; private expresses in,71; Civil War, 86; railway mail, 96; mechanical facing table, 122; post offices, 125, 126; Collection and Distribution Wagons, 128; streetcar R.P.O.s, 130; mail trucks, 136, 137, 203 *n.* 295; airmail, 151-52; meter machines, 162; Mailomats, 165; Highway Post Offices, 172; Research and Engineering Laboratory, 180

Washington, George, 74, 76

Washington, Ky., 67

Water routes: China, 16; Texas mail, 79; California, 80; U.S. (1860-90), 96. *See also* Boats; International mail; Ship mail; Steamboats; Steamships

Wax-coated tablets: in Greece and Rome, 12; late use of, 37 *n.* 21

Weather: effect on Persian system, 9; in Rome, 15; and western U.S. mails, 81; and Pony Express, 81; Puerto Rico, 109; R.F.D. service, 115, 117; city mails, 131-35 *passim;* mail trucks, 136; balloon mail, 150; Franco-Prussian War pigeons, 150; airmail reports, 153, 155; effect on airmail, 154-55

Webb, Torrey, 152

Weber Canyon, Utah, 157

Weight: U.S. letter mail, 73; 3-lb. limit, 192 *n.* 45; 4-lb. limit, 91, 111, 195 *n.* 113, 200 *n.* 224; parcel post, 144-45; World War I limit, 148

Wells Fargo and Co.: in West, 83, 95-96; in Alaska, 107; and parcel post, 144

West, Robert, 47

West Indies: mail packets, 54

West Virginia: and R.F.D., 115

Wheeling, Va., 67

White, James E., 141

Whitlock Metered Mail Co. machines, 165

Wickliffe, Charles A., 73

Wilson, William L., 115

Wilson, Woodrow, 152

William III of England, 47

Willcox, William R., 141

Winton motor truck, 136

Wise, John, 150

Witherings, Thomas, 31

Wolff, Elmer E.: postage meter machine, 162, 207 *n.* 278

World War I: U.S. rates, 106, 188; and pneumatic tubes, 133; postal trucks, 138-39; parcel post, 145; postal service, 146-49; airmail, 151-52; U.S. military mail, 174; and London mail tunnels, 204 *n.* 321; mentioned, 66

World War II: U.S. postal service, 171-75; U.S. postage rates, 188; mentioned, 134

Writing: ancient cuneiform, 7, 8, 11; by scribes, 11; demotic, hieratics, hieroglyphics, 11; Chinese, 16; on leather, 37 *n.* 22

Wurttemburg, 25

Wythings: postmasters of Teutonic Order, 19

Xerxes, 9, 10

Yale, S.S., 109

Yamb: Chinese relay stations, 16

Yu. See China, postal service

Yuma, Fort, 82

Yung Lo, emperor of China, 17

Youth's Companion and precanceled stamps, 123

Zane's Trace, Ohio, 67

Zeppelins, 159

Zevely, A. N., and Railway Mail Service, 94; sorts city mail on trains, 119

ZIP Code, U.S.: and large mailings, 178; developed, 181; and distribution, 186; mentioned, 174

Zone numbers, address: early experiments, 141; introduced, 174

Zone systems of postal rates. *See* Rates of postage

Zurich, Swiss canton: early stamp, 34

"Although there have been many books written about the postal service, there is no single up-to-date volume in the United States which provides an Old World background and which presents a continuous survey of American posts from Colonial times to the present. During the past fifty years, philatelists have examined certain phases of postal history in great detail. Their work, however, tends to be centered around physical evidence in the nature of postage stamps, markings, and covers. Therefore, certain aspects of the postal service—the use of automobiles, for example—are generally neglected. This, then, is an attempt to at least touch upon all important material aspects of postal history in one outline history."

—AUTHOR'S INTRODUCTION

The first postal legislation in America, designating Richard Fairbanks' tavern in Boston as the servicing center for overseas mail, was passed in Massachusetts in September 1639. This fact-filled book follows the course of mail service in America from such makeshift beginnings through three centuries of development to the ZIP-code world of today. The author also provides brief background information on the methods devised by various Old World civilizations, some as early as that of Mesopotamia, for transporting written messages from one point to another.

The author discusses a wide range of subjects such as Benjamin Franklin's administration of Colonial posts, the growth of private express companies, the institution of the Western Pony Express, the railway post office system, international postal reform, rural free delivery, and the rapid postwar innovations for handling what currently amounts to over seventy billion pieces of mail annually. (A complete list of topics is given on the back cover.) Scheele not only